Christopher Dawson

Nothing is more difficult for the natural man than to understand a culture or social tradition different from his own, for it involves an almost superhuman detachment from inherited ways of thought and education and the unconscious influence of his social environment. Indeed the more highly educated he is in his own tradition the less will he be able to appreciate all that diverges from it. It is the old contrast between Hellene and Barbarian, Jew and Gentile which reappears today in the mutual incomprehension of American and European, or Latin and Teuton, or Occidental and Oriental. We cannot bridge the gulf by a purely scientific study of social facts, by the statistical and documentary methods that have been so much used by modern sociologists, for these can never grasp the essential difference of quality that makes a culture what it is. No amount of detailed and accurate external knowledge will compensate for the lack of that immediate vision which springs from the comprehension of a social tradition as a living unity, a vision which is the natural birthright of those who share in the common experience of the society, but which members of other cultures can only obtain by an immense effort of sympathetic imagination.

CHRISTOPHER DAWSON, *The Dynamics of World History*

THE CENTRE FOR FAITH & CULTURE

Opened at the end of 1994, the Centre exists as a partnership between T&T Clark Ltd and Westminster College in Oxford (founded by the Methodist Church in 1851). It is one of a network of research centres at Westminster College representing different religious traditions and areas of interest.

The purpose of the Centre for Faith & Culture is to promote greater understanding of the Roman Catholic tradition in the light of the Second Vatican Council, and to encourage the continued development of Catholic theology, particularly as it applies to contemporary cultural, social and ethical issues.

It aims to do this through research, lectures, seminars and annual conferences at Westminster College (sometimes in collaboration with other institutions and societies), as well as by the publication of books and journals.

ETERNITY IN TIME

ETERNITY IN TIME

*Christopher Dawson and the
Catholic Idea of History*

Edited by
STRATFORD CALDECOTT
and
JOHN MORRILL

A PUBLICATION OF
THE CENTRE FOR FAITH & CULTURE
WESTMINSTER COLLEGE, OXFORD

T&T CLARK
EDINBURGH

T&T CLARK LTD
59 GEORGE STREET
EDINBURGH EH2 2LQ
SCOTLAND

First published 1997

ISBN 0 567 08548 1

British Library Cataloguing-in-Publication Data
A catalogue record for this book is available from the British Library

Typeset by Waverley Typesetters, Galashiels
Printed and bound in Great Britain by Bookcraft Ltd, Avon

Contents

Introduction

JOHN MORRILL

I

This book celebrates the life and work of Christopher Dawson (1889–1970). Dawson was much loved but rather less effectively honoured, holding no full-time post until the age of sixty-eight when he became Professor of Roman Catholic studies at Harvard. Dawson always wrote on unfashionably large subjects – *The Making of Europe, Religion and the Rise of Christian Culture, Medieval Religion, The Problem of Metahistory* – and he called not for the professionalization of increasingly hermetically-sealed disciplines but for their reintegration. As *Litterae Humaniores* crumbled as the blue-riband discipline (one year in the late 1920s the civil service refused to believe that a student of the Honours School of Modern History could out-perform the best of the classicists in '*Lit. Hum.*' and preferred to believe in the fallacy of their own examinations!), so Dawson campaigned for a modern equivalent, a training of the mind in *Christian* philosophy, history, literature and art.

The silver jubilee of his death seems an appropriate time to review his work and to examine his prophetic message in the light of the future he sought to shape. This book is the product of a conference held at Westminster College, Oxford, in September 1995. Like the conference, the book falls fairly naturally into two parts: meditations on Dawson's writings, and especially on their hermeneutic; and discussions by a group of Catholic historians and educationalists of what a *Catholic* engagement with the discipline might entail in the 1990s. The

1

conference resulted in an interchange of rare quality and excitement. The papers served their essential purpose – to stimulate some outstanding discussions and to facilitate a truly multi-disciplinary meeting of minds. It can only be hoped that this collection of papers, to which one by Fr Aidan Nichols OP has been added, will prove similarly exhilarating wherever they are read or discussed.

II

Dawson was first and foremost a man for whom the heroic enterprise of recreating the mental world of actors in the past required a willingness to engage not only with the written texts but with art and artefacts. He was a scholar who worked in an age which privileged certain kinds of evidence as 'historical' and downgraded, even refused to deal with, 'literary' texts and cultural artefacts and images as other than adornments to the product of rigorous historical analysis and exegesis. In the buildings erected by historians, poems and paintings could never be used as load-bearing walls. This more than anything else has kept him out of the pantheon of great historians in the eyes of the 'profession' – at least in the United Kingdom. It is striking that his work is discussed in *The Concise Cambridge History of English Literature* (as 'among the ranks of distinguished historians who are also men of letters') but not in several recent biographical dictionaries of history and historians. Dawson was in a sense an archaeologist of text and image.

Here at least, his witness has not been in vain. No longer do the disciplines of history and literature reach unspoken agreements about text which are denied to the other. Let me just draw a couple of examples from my own area of specialism. Books are now written by historians from (as well as about) the work of Jacobean playwrights, or from (as well as about) Milton's epics; texts which were hitherto in no-man's land (the sermons of John Donne – too theological to be in the literary canon; too much the work of a writer in the literary canon to be read by historians) are now read by both. My own university of Cambridge now offers a course to first-year historians entitled 'The Image as Historical Evidence'. Many other universities have similar courses and there is a corresponding boom in historical writing sensitive to the interpretation of the art-work and artefact.

I am not saying – however much I would like to be able to do so – that this development can be credited to Dawson; simply that historians have now reached the position he was always in. Nor is this the only way in which he can now be seen demonstrably to have been ahead of his time.

III

Christopher Dawson wrote in an age when the history of ideas was bedevilled by two intellectually deadening givens. The first was a vulgar Marxist notion: the ideas that persons or groups espoused were a more or less sophisticated (and 'subjective') extrapolation from the underlying ('objective') economic and political realities in which they found themselves. The task of the historian was to identify those realities and to demonstrate how far the ideas were rooted in a 'true' understanding or 'false' understanding ('mystification') of those uttering them. The second given was that a literary work was complete of itself, and capable of explication without anything other than the attentive eye and keen mind of the historian. Dawson was entirely innocent of the first fault, but perhaps not of the second. He knew that social and economic experience conditioned what one came to believe and how one came to act; but it never occurred to him that such experiences *determined* belief. Yet if he did not – in the modern way[1] – meticulously correlate the language of core texts with comparable (or contrasting) usages in contemporary ('circumjacent') texts, the sheer breadth, attentiveness and retentiveness of his reading means that his own writings achieve much the same effect unselfconsciously.

In exactly the same way, his plea that the historian enter into the minds and sensibilities of his subject (witness his tribute to Gibbon: 'he felt as a Roman; he thought as a Roman; he wrote as a Roman')[2] anticipated, in an unargued way, the influential injunctions of R. G. Collingwood in his *Practice of History*, that the task of the historian is to enter into the mind of actors in the past.

In all these ways, Dawson's books have become *more* not less books that catch the mood of the present day. Unlike many scholars more fashionable at the time, his method and his palette have a strong contemporary feel to them.

IV

On the other hand his passionate commitment to metahistory and his proclamation of the deeply moral purpose of the historian have become ever more out of favour with historians. The rise of revisionism in the 1970s as a reaction against Marxist and Marx-tainted historiographies with their strong teleologies has led to an ever-greater *pointillisme* and (more respectably) to a concern less with the vertical dimension of historical study (how the past came to inform the present) than with the horizontal dimension of the past (why the past was as it was).

This is how I elsewhere explained the difference between vertical and horizontal history:

> 'Vertical' history is that which discards the dross of the particular and the contingent – the prejudices, blindnesses and contentions of an age – in order to extract the residual gold, the truth and insight of enduring value. In intellectual history this is the history of an idea . . . in ecclesiastical history it is the search for the core of a denominational testimony, in political history the birth of a party or a similar exercise in scholarly embryology. 'Horizontal' history resolutely sets out to place each event, idea, institution in its contemporary contexts. It seeks out not the enduring, the survival of the fittest idea, but rather the contingent and the ordinary in the context of the time. The vertical approach emphasises the continuity of past and present; the horizontal approach, as William Lamont has it, 'can serve best by restoring a sense of inaccessibility'.[3]

Does such an approach preclude a properly 'Catholic' history? As several essays in this collection make clear, the answer is that it does not preclude it. There is no doubt that Catholic history as denominational history always has been, and would probably necessarily have to be, vertical history. But the kind of Catholic history that Christopher Dawson stood up for was not denominational history. He deplored those Catholic historians who tended to 'make history a department of apologetics and to idealize medieval culture in order to exalt their own ideals'. Both of these things are critical to our understanding of his vision.

Let us look first at the rejection of an exclusivist historiography. Rereading Dawson's writings of the first forty years of the twentieth century constantly brought to my mind the ecumenicism of the last forty years of the century. A Catholic history is one informed by a Catholic understanding of the Incarnation, of a world suffused with the presence of its Creator and Redeemer; but it is a history open to honouring the witness and sanctity of those outside the Catholic tradition. The preface to *The Making of Europe* (1932) shares the mental world of the Council Decree on Ecumenism, *Unitatis Redintegratio* (1965):

> The separated churches and communities . . . have been by no means deprived of significance and importance in the mystery of salvation. For the Spirit of Christ has not refrained from using them as means of salvation which derive their efficacy from the very fullness of grace and truth entrusted to the Catholic Church.[4]

Dawson was not advocating a Christian history that justified the present, but a Christian history that helped towards an informed faith in the future. And that is something which cannot be written off as a wrongheaded teleology.

There is a second obvious point here. Although it is true that historians – especially historians writing about all the centuries before this one – are reluctant to make connections between past and present, and prefer to see the past as a foreign country where they did things differently, they need not be particularly hostile to Dawson's meta-vision. Above all, although they have *legitimate* complaints about the high teleology of the Marxists and the Whig historians, they should have fewer historiographical complaints about what (as a compliment) I will call the weak teleology of Dawson, so that the kind of Catholic history he advocated remains a worthwhile (I will suggest necessary) enterprise.

Here we are helped by the recent work of Glenn Burgess in examining what was inadequate about the old Whig and Marxist histories of the English Revolution. He distinguishes between a 'weak teleology', which is a history written as an account of how particular stories in the past came to a particular resolution, and a 'strong' teleology which seeks either to explain how the present is a particular outcome of the past or – *more particularly* – to give an account of the past which uses present-day categories to organize our accounts of the past, i.e. a deliberate resort to structuring our accounts in anachronism. A meta-history rooted in teleology is a completely different matter from a metahistory rooted in anachronism, and here Dawson's history lays claim to the first – and necessary – process and pleads not guilty of the second. It raises him above most of the metahistorians of the century.[5]

V

Vertical history seeks to explain how the past informs the present; horizontal history seeks to explain why the past was how it was. The best history integrates the two approaches. It is what I have elsewhere called *solera* history. A solera madeira is a fortified wine kept in a vat begun in a certain year. Every year thereafter some of the wine is drawn off and young wine added. And so as it constantly evolves, it is constantly changing and yet it is also cumulatively reminiscent of its own past. Its maturity and richness of texture is its glory; and the molecules from years of particular character will always linger in it and will be recognizable within it.

It is this which gives every small community its unique character. It is this which explains why, for example, every parish and every school is so unique. It is not their present which determines their uniqueness, but the culmination of their past experiences. And so it is with national institutions, with nations, with a Church or faith. The University of Cambridge can be explained only by reference to its history – by reference to its origins as a guild of scholars each taking apprentices in learning, just as a baker took apprentices in baking or a fuller apprentices in dressing cloth; and by reference to the later development of the collegiate and tutorial systems. There is no rationality to the structures of University of Cambridge except for a historical rationality. Similarly, to understand the British Parliament, one needs to understand how two aspects of its origins still act as fundamentals of its character. The first is that it originated both as an enhanced meeting of the King's council and as a High Court of Justice. The presence of the executive in the legislature remains perhaps its distinctive feature. But this needs to be combined with the fortuitous circumstance that the original meeting place of the Commons was a chapel with antiphonal seating, producing the eyeball-to-eyeball confrontations of 'parties' with results so different from that produced in the hemispherical assembly rooms of most modern states. The presence of the executive in the legislature in far from euphonious antiphonal exchanges across the chamber is a – the? – determining characteristic of it as an institution. It is thirteenth-century accident with twentieth-century consequences. In both these examples, an understanding of the particularity of the past and the development to the present are equally important.

If such an approach can help towards a recovery of the historical processes that shape the present and indicate possibilities for the future, then this is particularly helpful in creating a non-confessional Catholic history. As Francesca Murphy demonstrates in chapter 7, much 'Catholic history' escapes the crude anachronisms of denominational history but remains embedded in a more sophisticated anachronism that is secularist in its attribution of motivation and action. It never ceases to amaze me that so many good historians – many confessing Christians – can develop sophisticated hermeneutics with respect to canonical historical texts such as the *Ecclesiastical History* of the Venerable Bede, but hermeneutics which simply pass over as unhistorical his accounts of miracles which he had witnessed. It is bad history to accept his accounts uncritically, but surely the worst kind of anachronism to see them as the white noise of medieval historical writing and to filter them out with the equivalent of a historiographical Dolby system.

As I turn to my own period of specialization – the long centuries of Reformation – two things seem obvious. First, it is very easy to see how Reformation historiography has been vitiated by a strong teleology plus anachronism. For example, an unthinking logocentrism assumes that a religion of the Word will triumph in a world of the printed book and mass illiteracy. The corrective comes from a more sophisticated Catholic hermeneutic. For example, Eamon Duffy's *The Stripping of the Altars* examines a system of belief and practice which functioned as well as man-made structures ever function and demonstrates how that system could be wilfully ripped away from a people unprepared for something so much less universal in appeal. If at times Duffy's book reads uncomfortably like a lament for a liturgical vandalism visited in modern times upon the English-speaking world by ICEL, it nonetheless tells a teleological story in a way deeply empathetic with the mental world of the fifteenth and sixteenth centuries.

The second aspect of this problem needs to be treated more autobiographically. For many years I have written, with, I think, a fair degree of empathy and understanding, about English Protestants and English Puritans in particular. I have written about the mind of Oliver Cromwell, about the religious passions of John Pym and William Brereton, about what turned William Dowsing, an obscure farmer on the Essex/Suffolk border, into perhaps the most formidable iconoclast in English history.[6] I have been interested – as a commentator put it to me once after a paper in Toronto – more in the political and religious *psychology* of the people I have studied than in their political and religious thought.[7] I put aside a natural intellectual repugnance for their stark and judgemental Calvinism and admire the courage and determination with which they sought to live out a life in obedience to what they understood to be the will of God for them. It was only at the Dawson conference in Oxford that I came to realize that the reason why I always write about Puritans and never write about Catholics is that I leave no space for the action of the Holy Spirit in the lives of the men and women I write about. I accept the action of the Holy Spirit in myself and those I know, and cannot then deny Him a role in relation to men and women in the past. It is simply a frailty in me that while I have not been able to write about Catholics in the early modern period because of an unrecognized unwillingness to attempt to integrate the action of the Spirit in my account of them, I have felt able to write about those Puritans whose understanding of the gospel seems to me at once disastrously skewed and yet deeply honourable, and to write about them in a way that is intellectually empathetic and spiritually secularized.

The conference therefore issued a new challenge, the need in myself to transcend my own unrecognized ducking of issues, my own inability to relate the past to the present through a recognition of the action of the Holy Spirit in the world of the past. The challenge of a Catholic history is then to integrate not only – as Christopher Dawson taught us – the insights that as Catholics we have about Christian philosophy, history, literature and art, but also to integrate into it a Catholic understanding of the human person and the personal encounter of men and women with their God.

What inspired me to write the above was hearing – and subsequently reading – the essay with which Stratford Caldecott ended the conference and this book. Everything that Christopher Dawson stood for, everything that the conference and hopefully this volume achieves, has its *telos* in that essay and in Pope John Paul's Apostolic Letter *Tertio Millennio Adveniente*.

Read on. I am sure every reader will make her or his own connections. This is an important book that challenges us to a new openness of mind and method, a new agenda and new commitment.

NOTES

1 See D. LaCapra, 'Rethinking Intellectual History and Reading Texts', *History and Theory*, xix (1980), pp. 245–76; P. L. Janssen, 'Political Thought as Traditionary Action', *History and Theory*, xxiv (1985), pp. 115–46.

2 C. Dawson, Introduction to Edward Gibbon, *Decline and Fall of the Roman Empire*, Everyman edn, 6 vols (1954), vol. 1, p. xi.

3 J. Morrill in *The History Debate*, ed. J. Gardiner (1990), pp. 93–4; cf. J. Morrill, 'The Historian and the "Historical Filter"', in P. Geach et al., *The Past and the Present: Problems of Understanding* (Oxford, 1993), pp. 93–100. For the short final quote and stimulus for the foregoing, see W. Lamont, *Richard Baxter and the Millennium* (1981), pp. 22–4. And see now P. Collinson, 'The Vertical and the Horizontal', in A. Ford and J. McGuire (eds), *As by Law Established* (Cambridge, 1995).

4 A. Flannery OP (ed.), *Vatican Council II. The Conciliar and Post Conciliar Documents* (1992 edn), I, p. 456.

5 G. Burgess, 'On Revisionism: An Analysis of Early Stuart Historiography in the 1970s and 1980s', *Historical Journal*, 33 no. 3 (1990), pp. 609–28, esp. at pp. 614–16.

6 See J. S. Morrill, *The Nature of the English Revolution* (London, 1993), chs 3, 4, 6; 'William Brereton and England's "Wars of Religion"', *J. British Studies* (1985); 'The Unweariableness of Mr Pym', in S. Amussen and M. Kishlansky (eds), *Political Culture and the Culture of Politics in Early Modern England* (Manchester, 1995); 'William Dowsing: The Bureaucratic Puritan', in J. S. Morrill et al. (eds), *Public Men and Private Conscience in Seventeenth-Century England* (Oxford, 1992).

7 The commentator was Barbara Shapiro and I owe much to our discussion on that day in October 1984.

1

The vision and legacy of Christopher Dawson

CHRISTINA SCOTT

I

On 12 October 1969, when Christopher Dawson celebrated his eightieth birthday, he received a telegram from his publishers, Frank and Maisie Sheed of Sheed & Ward. It contained two words written in Latin: '*Exegisti monumentum*'. The word 'monument' immediately conjures up something static, solid and unchangeable such as the pyramids of Egypt or the ruins of ancient Rome, but as classical scholars will recognize, the two words are a gloss on a quotation from Horace – 'I have made a monument more durable than bronze'.[1] Christopher Dawson's monument is the great edifice of his writings built on the structure of a vast accumulation of learning from which flowed some very powerful ideas.

Chief among these ideas and one which could be said to be the mainspring of all his thought was a conviction which had dominated his mind ever since he had begun to write. This was the belief that 'the society or culture which has lost its spiritual roots is a dying culture, however prosperous it may appear externally'.[2] This was his theme from which he never wavered and never looked back: it is the cornerstone of the monument he built and consequently of the legacy about which my paper is concerned.

II

I am not going to dwell too much on the circumstances of my father's life because I have already written about this in my biography of him, and although my book has not sold a million copies or anything like, most people seem fairly well acquainted with the facts.

From an early age, Christopher Dawson had a clear idea of his vocation as a historian. The two great interests of his life – history and religion – were acquired not from school or university but from his home life and his childhood impressions. As he wrote in his autobiographical memoir:

> [I]t was then I acquired my love of history, my interest in the differences of cultures and my sense of the importance of religion in human life, as a massive unquestioned power that entered into everything and impressed its mark on the external as well as the internal world.[3]

He had read Gibbon's *The Decline and Fall of the Roman Empire* as well as St Augustine's *City of God* before he went up to Oxford and the influence of these two great works – the one so different from the other – has a significant bearing upon the kind of historian he became. Gibbon and Augustine were his early heroes: when he first visited Rome at the age of nineteen he retraced Gibbon's pilgrimage to the steps of the Capitol where he had been inspired to write the *Decline and Fall*. In this same place, Christopher Dawson conceived the idea of writing a history of culture, that is to say a history of the life of civilizations from prehistoric times to the modern age, which he envisaged over a span of five volumes.

His enthusiasm for Gibbon at this stage knew no bounds and it was only matched by his admiration for St Augustine and the *City of God*. Later when he came to analyse Gibbon's work as a historian, first in a lecture he gave before the British Academy in 1934[4] and later in an introduction to the Everyman edition of the *Decline and Fall*,[5] his enthusiasm had been tempered by a more critical attitude. He admired Gibbon because as one of the last of the humanist historians he achieved 'a complete fusion between history and literature and for the mastery of his style which only reflected a no less perfect mastery over his material'.[6] The humanist and literary ideal was also Christopher Dawson's own aim in his treatment of history, and his name has been recorded in *The Concise Cambridge History of English Literature* (1970) as 'among the ranks of distinguished historians who are also men of letters'.[7]

Furthermore, Dawson reckoned that history must be treated with imagination and vision: in an article in *History Today* replying to the present Lord Bullock, who had attacked the work of metahistorians such as Spengler and Toynbee from the point of view of an academic historian, he pointed out that

> the mastery of the techniques of historical criticism and research although important will not produce great history, any more than a mastery of metrical technique will produce great poetry. For this something more is necessary – intuitive understanding, creative imagination and finally a universal vision transcending the relative limitation of the particular field of historical study.[8]

Where Gibbon failed in Dawson's view was in his failure to understand the Christian past. To Gibbon the history of the Christian Empire was an illusion and he only succeeded in explaining it away. As Dawson wrote:

> The world had conceived emptiness and brought forth wind. There was nothing left to write about but the battles of kites and crows and the aimless procession of phantom emperors. There remained only the shadow of the great name of Rome like the shadow of a great rock in an empty land.[9]

But in spite of this judgement and in spite of the fact that Dawson considered him unjust to Christianity, the Catholic Church, and the Byzantine Empire, he believed that his great strength and the reason why he would retain his position as the classical historian of the decline of the Roman Empire was his unique gift of identifying himself with his subject – 'He felt as a Roman; he thought as a Roman; he wrote as a Roman.'[10]

A few years earlier (in 1930) Dawson had written two major essays on St Augustine – 'The Dying World' and 'The City of God'[11] – and it is here that we can see how the thought of St Augustine with its message of hope in another kingdom became in Dawson's view the antidote to Gibbon's pessimism. It was also the inspiration for his own serene vision of the unity of history when he was writing during the Second World War and the years of confusion which followed. Of Augustine he wrote: 'To him the ruin of civilization and the destruction of the Empire were not very important things' for 'he looked beyond the aimless and bloody chaos of history to the world of eternal realities';[12] he had faith in another city – the City of God – 'a transcendent and timeless reality which was nothing less than the spiritual unity of the whole universe'.[13]

Dawson was always the first to appreciate genius wherever he found it and however opposing the view to his own. There is his generous treatment of H. G. Wells, for instance, when in his review of *The Outline of History*[14] he remarked that Wells had a real gift of historical vision and a power of synthesis that many historians have lacked. Likewise, although he did not share Arnold Toynbee's views on the syncretism of the world religions, in a review of *The Study of History* he wrote that any historian would gain new insights from 'this scholar of immense learning and universal cultural interests'.[15]

Dawson's first book, *The Age of the Gods*, was published in 1928 by John Murray, when the author was thirty-nine. It was the fruit of fourteen years of independent and intensive study into the civilizations of the ancient world and it has been generally acknowledged to be his greatest single achievement. It certainly shows the extraordinary extent and depth of his scholarship. The bibliographies alone (organized for each chapter) are a witness to his extensive reading. There is here a mind-boggling array of books on the archaeology and anthropology of the Ancient East as well as corresponding chronological tables for the different cultures. Yet he carried his learning lightly: Professor Gordon Childe, one of the first authorities of that time on archaeology, wrote, in a review of the book, that he had always hoped that someone with more ample leisure and a wider vision would reassemble the dry bones served up by himself and others. He found *The Age of the Gods* the most successful effort in that direction that he had come across.[16]

This work was the first volume in the projected history of culture. Two more followed – *Progress and Religion* in 1929, which was planned as the introduction to the whole scheme, and *The Making of Europe* (1932) which covered the period hitherto known as the Dark Ages. It has often been said, with some justification, that on these three books, Dawson's reputation as a historian and philosopher of history rests. They demonstrate above all the unity of his thought: he was inspired by a single idea, namely, that religion is the soul of a culture, or to put it simply, faith and culture are one. Out of this rose his vision of European unity when, from his study of the origins of Europe, he saw how Western civilization was born from a complete fusion of the Christian faith and a Christian way of life, which came to be called Christendom. The possible disintegration of that civilization was the major concern of all his subsequent writing and thought.

This history of culture was never completed in its original five-volume form, partly because in the political chaos of the pre-war years and then the crisis of the Second World War itself, he gave his mind to analysing and – as one commentator put it – 'calmly disentangling the sociological threads in Europe'.[17] Nevertheless, in his subsequent writings – his articles in *The Dublin Review* and other journals and in his Gifford and Harvard Lectures particularly – he did in the end cover the whole field which he had set out to encompass.

Dawson has often been compared to Acton for the broadness of his vision as a historian but there is also a parallel in the destinies of the two men, as the late James Oliver once pointed out. 'For while Acton's fame as a historian', Oliver wrote, 'rests upon a history of freedom which he never wrote and the idea of a *Cambridge Modern History* which was the work of others, so Dawson's reputation was bound up with a history of culture which he never finished in its original form while his destiny led him to write so much more in other fields.'[18]

III

You will be hearing about *The Making of Europe* in the chapter by Dr Fernando Cervantes, and I will not trespass on his territory. But there is one point I wish to make. In the introduction to this book Dawson also outlined his approach to the writing of

Catholic history, deploring the propagandist attitude of many Catholic historians of the Middle Ages and their tendency to 'make history a department of apologetics and to idealise mediaeval culture in order to exalt their ideals'.[19] While Dawson wrote as a Catholic historian, he did so with scrupulous fairness and an openness of mind quite contrary to their own. The Dark Ages to him were indeed ages of barbarism, cruelty and suffering but they were also the ages of dawn and of a spiritual awakening to a new Christian civilization. It was for this reason that his works appealed not only to Catholic readers but to Christians of other denominations such as Dean Inge, who once said that Christopher Dawson was the only Roman Catholic who didn't annoy him. Even the agnostic, Aldous Huxley, wrote in a review of *The Making of Europe*: 'The Dark Ages lose their darkness, and take on form and significance. Thanks to the author's erudition and marshalling of facts, we begin to have a notion of what it is all about.'[20]

This was his great strength as a Catholic historian and he stood apart, as Professor Cameron noted in his Robert Lowell Lecture at Boston College,[21] from 'the militant fighters for an integralist Catholicism' such as Belloc and Arnold Lunn. Never a dogmatist nor a polemicist, Dawson was above all a defender of the truth wherever he found it. Consequently, his writings should never be used as a handle in current theological issues, as has happened in America during the last two decades. It may be added that one can understand his mild fury when a Marxist professor (Christopher Hill) once referred to him as 'A Roman Catholic publicist'[22] nor incidentally did he like the epithet 'Roman' as applied to Catholic which he considered a contradiction in terms.

In his own time he was never part of a clique of Catholic writers but he was foremost in the Catholic intellectual revival of the 1930s which attempted to bring English Catholicism out of the sacristy and into line with the new movements on the Continent. A series of booklets was produced under the general title of *Essays in Order* edited by Christopher Dawson and Tom Burns and published by Sheed & Ward. Subjects ranged from theology, philosophy and politics to psychology and literature and writers included names such as Claudel, Maritain, Mauriac and Gilson from France, others from Germany and Central Europe, and E. I. Watkin, Herbert Read and Christopher Dawson himself in England, to cite only a few. The cover of these books was embellished with a woodcut of a unicorn by David Jones and published at the very modest price of 2/6, i.e. about 20 pence today.

IV

From 1939 onwards, with the publication of his book, *Beyond Politics*, Dawson, the historian, became more than ever a 'meta-historian' – a historian with a message. Many of his writings now seem prophetic.

The outbreak of war brought new challenges and the following year Dawson rose to a great opportunity when Cardinal Hinsley invited him to become Vice-President of The Sword of the Spirit, an organization formed to crusade against totalitarianism. Almost simultaneously, the Cardinal offered him the editorship of *The Dublin Review* in succession to Algar Thorold, its editor for many years, who had recently died.

Cardinal Heenan, in an account of the Sword of the Spirit movement which he wrote after Hinsley's death in 1943, paid tribute to Dawson's part in it and described him as 'the ablest defender of Christian values among English writers'.[23] Nowhere have the basic aims of the movement been put more explicitly than in Dawson's own words which were also a tribute to Cardinal Hinsley. He spoke first of the Cardinal as a man of great spiritual power and wide human sympathies. He had understood that Catholicism is not a religion of the sacristy but the heart of human life and he wished to bring the deepest spiritual forces to bear on the most vital practical issues. The aims of the movement were, Dawson explained, first and fore-most that it should be a spiritual one, a return to the founda-tions on which Western civilization and our own national life were built and therefore opposed alike to the deliberate apostasy of the totalitarian state and the superficial materialism of our own secularized culture. In the second place, he went on, it was to be a movement for unity – to provide a platform on which Catholics of all classes and all parties could unite.

Thirdly – and this is perhaps even more relevant today than it was then – it aimed not only at unity among Catholics but at co-operation between all Christians who have the same cause at heart. Finally, the Cardinal had wished The Sword of the Spirit to stand for the cause of international unity, and to work for the restoration of Christendom and Christian civilization in accordance with the movement's primary aims.[24]

The Sword of the Spirit was indeed an international movement: London was offering shelter to a growing number of exiled European governments, whose ministers would eventually be shaping the political order in Europe after the hoped-for victory. There was also the vast number of refugees from every part of Europe – Poles, French, Belgians, Dutch and Czechs – to whom England had given a home, and Oxford, where Dawson was living at the time, had its fair share of them. The Sword of the Spirit enabled such people to meet together on common spiritual ground.

Unfortunately, Hinsley's efforts towards Christian co-operation were doomed and Dawson and his fellow workers in the movement found themselves constantly under attack. Their opponents were not non-Catholics – on the contrary they had firm allies among Anglicans, such as Bishop Bell of Chichester – the hostility came from the Catholic hierarchy itself and most notably from two theologians (Drs Smith and Mahoney) who rigorously opposed the idea of reciting the Lord's Prayer at joint meetings with members of other denominations.

In a letter to the Cardinal on the subject Dawson wrote of his dismay at the intransigent attitude of these theologians, who seemed oblivious to the scandal that could arise as a result. 'If' he wrote,

> the Anglicans get the impression that we do not regard them as Christians and that we are only prepared to collaborate with them to the same extent that we co-operate with heathens, it will be most disastrous . . . Surely we must believe that we have something in common with the Christians who are our separated brethren which we have not got with the worshippers of Mumbo-Jumbo. And this something must be religious even though it is difficult to give it a clear theological definition.[25]

Fortunately these dogmatists were overruled by a Jesuit theologian from Heythrop College and the Lord's Prayer was said by all denominations at a mass meeting at the Stoll Theatre in London in 1941.

Under Dawson's editorship, *The Dublin Review* also developed an international character. Articles were published by eminent Germans in exile along with Polish and Spanish writers. A brilliant stroke of Dawson's was to cable to the French writer, George Bernanos, then living in Brazil, to ask him for his views on 'St Louis and the honour of France'. At the height of war – this was in 1940 after the fall of France – and in the middle of a tropical rainstorm, the cable duly arrived and the reply came back in the form of an extract from the famous *Lettre aux Anglais* and was published in *The Dublin Review* in 1941.[26]

But with Cardinal Hinsley's death in 1943 The Sword of the Spirit lost both its leader and its ecumenical character, and Dawson resigned his position in 1944. He was also removed from the editorship of *The Dublin Review* by a surreptitious move on the part of Douglas Jerrold, who as chairman of Burns & Oates controlled publication of the *Review*. His objection to Dawson's editorship was that he had published articles by Maritain and Bernanos, both of whom had supported the Republicans in the Spanish Civil War. Jerrold had been, and remained, an ardent supporter of General Franco.[27]

All through the Second World War, Dawson had written on the pressing need for European unity, particularly when it came to the remaking of Europe which must follow victory. When in September 1944 Pope Pius XII broadcast a message to the world, expressing the hope that the statesmen and military authorities would pursue peace in a spirit of charity, Dawson deplored the fact that 'the Pope's noble words should be greeted (as they were) with derision and scorn' but concluded that this was inevitable in a secularized society. He remembered the mistakes of the Treaty of Versailles and others further back still, which far from putting an end to war had engendered conflicts even more bloody and disastrous.[28]

After the war, Dawson's concern was more than ever to convince his fellow-Catholics that European unity was their special responsibility and in an article which appeared in the

Catholic Herald in 1947 he made the point that 'if Catholics could mobilise the latent Christian resources of our culture – if they could act as spokesmen and leaders to the scattered and inarticulate mass of Christians and even semi-Christians, they would alter the whole balance of power in this country, and through this country in Europe, and through Europe in the world.' But, as he commented, they could not do this if they continued to adopt the narrow sectarian attitude to non-Catholics which was prevalent at the time. 'Some Catholics', he wrote, 'treat the possession of supernatural truth as a dog treats a bone'. The Church had to show its strength as united against the forces of Antichrist, and this might do more to convince our separated brethren of the necessity of Catholic unity than any argument against the validity of Anglican orders.[29]

V

In post-war Europe, disintegrated and divided, many Europeans began to lose faith in their cultural future. Dawson never lost hope in the restoration of Western civilization but he had little respect for the 'activities of the modern planners and international reformers' who, he wrote, 'bear the same relation to the world crisis as the activities of a mining engineer or even a plumber to a volcanic eruption'.[30]

It was, however, in America in the late 1950s that Dawson entered into the most active period of his life, when he was appointed the first Professor of Roman Catholic Studies at Harvard University. He saw it as a 'call' and a great opportunity to promote his idea for a new educational venture. This was a course for the study of Christian culture in American universities. Inspired by Newman's *Idea of a University* which embodied the principle of unity in education, in religion and in culture, Dawson devised a scheme that would be the Christian counterpart of the old system of classical studies, such as the School of *Litterae Humaniores* at Oxford. Just as classical history, philosophy and literature have been studied as an integrated whole, so Christian history, philosophy, literature and institutions might be studied in the same way.

Reactions were mixed to this idea, as Professor Bruno Schlesinger commented in an article contributed to a Dawson special issue of *The Chesterton Review*:[31] while some more enlightened spirits among the intellectual establishment – John Courtney Murray SJ, Thomas Merton and Jaroslav Pelikan, to name a few – welcomed the project, there was a barrage of protest from the Catholic educators, who had been teaching Thomist philosophy and theology as the core of the Catholic curriculum for years. They distrusted the historical approach and spoke of the danger of 'cultural relativism' in Dawson's ideas.

Dawson, himself, was amazed at the violence of the attacks on his proposal (mainly voiced in the columns of *Commonweal*) and wrote in reply that he certainly did not realize that 'there was an influential body of Catholics who reacted to the words "Christendom" and "Christian culture" in the same way as a bull reacts to a red cloth'. He realized that such people were the victims of an ancient error, believing that Christian culture is the same thing as medieval culture and that Christendom means the Christian empire. This error, I am afraid, still persists. Dawson painstakingly explained that he used the word 'culture' in the sociological sense so that Christian culture is the Christian way of life in its historical development and Christendom is simply the society which has been informed by the Church.

Dawson lectured extensively in America on this subject and while his lectures were packed out on some occasions and while he was hailed as one of the world's most distinguished historians and philosophers of history, there was only one taker among the Catholic colleges for his Christian Culture course. This was St. Mary's, Notre Dame. Its programme for Christian Culture was launched in 1956 under the Chairmanship of Professor Bruno Schlesinger, whose noble work through every vicissitude has enabled it to continue until this day under the new description of Humanistic Studies.

Dawson did not live to see that Catholic educationalists of the present *avant-garde* would consign Christian culture to the dustbin of history. But he did foresee that the Church might turn against its own cultural traditions and that we might have to survive for a time in a cultural vacuum.

There is no doubt that the world is on the move again as never before and the pace is faster and more furious. But there is nothing in this situation which should cause Christians to despair. On the contrary it is the kind of situation for which their faith has always prepared them and which provides the opportunity for the fulfilment of their message.[32]

So I return to the point with which I started, to Dawson's conviction that 'the society or culture which has lost its spiritual roots is a dying culture, however prosperous it may appear externally'.

NOTES

1   Horace, *Odes* Book 1.

2   Preface to *Enquiries into Religion and Culture* (London, 1933), p. vi.

3   Cf. Christina Scott, *A Historian and His World* (New Brunswick and London, Transaction Publishers, 1991), pp. 15, 228.

4   'Edward Gibbon: Annual Lecture on a Master Mind', *Proceedings of the British Academy*, vol. xx, 1934.

5   *The Decline and Fall of the Roman Empire* (Everyman edn, J. M. Dent, London, 1954).

6   British Academy Lecture, p. 4.

7   *Concise Cambridge History of English Literature* (revised edn, Cambridge, 1970), pp. 896, 924.

8   'The Problem of Metahistory', *History Today*, 1951, I, pp. 9–12.

9   'Edward Gibbon: Annual Lecture on a Master Mind', p. 12.

10 Introduction to *The Decline and Fall*, p. xi.

11 T. F. B., *A Monument to St. Augustine* (Sheed & Ward, London, 1930).

12 Ibid., I 'The Dying World', p. 38.

13 Ibid., II 'The City of God,' pp. 66, 67.

14 'H. G. Wells and *The Outline of History*', *History Today*, I, pp. 28–32. In *DWH*.

15 'Toynbee's Study of History: The Place of Civilizations in History', *International Affairs* (1955) xxxi, 149–58. In *DWH*.

16 *Antiquity*, December 1928.

17 Bernard Wall, *Headlong into Change* (Harvill Press, 1969), p. 89.

18 E. J. Oliver, *Christopher Dawson – Philosopher of History* (unpublished).

19   Introduction to *The Making of Europe* (London, Sheed & Ward, 1932), p. xvii.

20   Aldous Huxley, *The Spectator*, CXLIX (1932), p. 235.

21   J. M. Cameron, Lowell Lecture at Boston College, Mass., 26 April 1990. 'Christopher Dawson: A Retrospect.'

22   Christopher Hill, 'The Church, Marx and History', *Spectator*, 20 September 1957, p. 370.

23   John Carmel Heenan, *Cardinal Hinsley* (London, Burns, Oates & Washbourne, 1944), p. 183.

24   *Sword of the Spirit Bulletin*, No. 58, June 1943.

25   Correspondence, Cardinal Hinsley, Westminster Archive, 4 November 1941.

26   Robert Speaight, *Georges Bernanos* (Collins & Harvill Press, London, 1973), pp. 202–3.

27   Ibid., p. 202.

28   *Sword of the Spirit Bulletin*, No. 74, September 1944.

29   'The Living Tradition of Christianity', *Catholic Herald*, 10 October 1947.

30   *Understanding Europe* (Sheed & Ward, London, 1952), p. 227.

31   Bruno Schlesinger, 'Responses to Dawson's ideas in the United States', *The Chesterton Review*, Dawson Special Issue, Vol. IX, No. 2, May 1983.

32   *The Historic Reality of Christian Culture* (London and New York, 1960), p. 28. In *RWH*, pp. 265f.

DWH   *The Dynamics of World History* (Sheed & Ward, 1957).

RWH   *Religion and World History* (Doubleday, Image Books, 1975).

2

Christopher Dawson's Catholic setting

AIDAN NICHOLS OP

In 1920 there had been rather over two million Catholics in England and Wales. They were ministered to by a clergy some four thousand strong: double its figures in 1880. Four hundred thousand of their children received education in Church schools.[1] Their community was a complex, stratified affair. It was compounded of three main elements, the indigenous, recusant 'Old Catholic' element, at its strongest in west and north Lancashire and County Durham; the massive Irish immigration, beginning before Victoria's reign opened but continuing in force throughout our period till it dwindled to a trickle in the 1940s and 1950s; and the converts, of whom a minority constituted the nucleus for a Catholic intelligentsia.[2] The Old Catholics provided the socially most prestigious members of the Church, in the shape of the Catholic aristocracy and other landed families no less antique for lacking handles to their names. Their presence reassured those to whom it was important that to be Catholic was not to be non-English, and furnished the basis for an alternative genealogy of Englishness to that found in the Whig interpretation of history – or Protestant sentiment generally.

It would be a mistake, however, to think of the recusant Catholics as consisting entirely of nobs and swells; in the traditional heartlands of recusancy, Catholicism was 'the healthy religion of a normally structured society'.[3] Moreover, in the

English Midlands, where the Industrial Revolution had taken a more small-scale, but no less intensive or prosperous form, an indigenous Catholic middle class had already formed by the later decades of the eighteenth century. From the Old Catholics, the English Catholic community between the two World Wars inherited its major institutions: its seminaries, principal monasteries and leading Catholic independent schools.

The Irish (or, as intermarriage proceeded apace, *Anglo*-Irish) gave Catholicism what Anglicanism signally lacked and the Nonconformists would increasingly lose as the century progressed: a thorough rooting in the working class. It might even be said that it was the generous distribution of Catholicism among all the main social groupings of the inter-war years that made possible its conviction of a vocation to *change* England. Catholicism was a visionary, culture-transforming synthesis, made up of divine Revelation and human wisdom, intended redemptively to finish and perfect society. Yet English Catholicism could take seriously a mission not just to 'convert' England but to baptize its culture in the plenary grace of the gospel only because it was aware of its latent strength in such varied socio-economic strata.

The last strand in the weave of the community came from the converts, most of whom entered the Church through marriage, but some – and these the more influential – by a process of study and reflection on the state of contemporary thought and the contemporary world. Figures like the historian Christopher Dawson, the philosopher of mysticism Edward Watkin, the theological belletrist Ronald Knox, the art historian E. W. Tristram, the lay theologian and critic G. K. Chesterton, and the (Scottish) novelist Compton Mackenzie became Catholics because – and here generalization is not too hazardous – they saw the Church of Rome as enjoying legitimate authority in matters of faith and morals, and as representing not only a wider Christendom than that which they had inherited but a wider *humanitas* as well.

The Church they entered had become, in its own terms, a more effective body than in the age of Victoria, crucial though that latter period was for its revival.[4] Its network of parishes and schools was systematically in place, their running, if more routinized, better adjusted to the efficacious catechesis, sacramentalization and pastoral care of a growing population. As late as the 1950s, English seminarians in Rome could take pride in the thought of the peculiar compactness and vigour of their community, the close bonds which linked clergy and people, the business-like quality of parochial good management – and contrast the performance of the Latin lands.[5] If it was not a Church notable for theological achievement (in marked contrast to, for instance, its cross-Channel neighbour in France) the Society of Jesus, in particular, was taking giant steps to redeem the situation, with such ventures as Heythrop College, Oxfordshire (eventually a 'Pontifical Athenaeum', able to confer papal degrees), Campion Hall, a permanent private hall of Oxford University, and the annual Catholic Summer Schools in theology at Cambridge. The collected papers of the latter, organized around the main themes of dogmatics and edited by the indefatigable Fr Cuthbert Lattey SJ, constitute something of a multi-authored native *Summa Theologiae* of the 1920s.[6] Nor were there lacking individual priest-scholars of distinction among the diocesan clergy, such as the Orientalist and liturgist Adrian Fortescue,[7] and the metaphysician Canon D. B. J. Hawkins.[8]

However, the real intellectual strength of the English Catholic Church would lie in what I shall call its 'theology of culture': its willed act of presence in the variety of domains – from art to politics – where its most illustrious converts were already fully at home. Despite the notable attempts to Anglicize (both literally and metaphorically) the philosophical and theological achievements of French Thomism (and these were certainly not without a wider resonance among the non-Catholic public), its main claim to the attention of posterity lies in this resolute endeavour to bring a Catholic sensibility to bear on cultural life. Without any depreciation of the supernatural uniqueness of revelation and dogma – on the contrary, it was the recognition of the metacultural status of Catholic Christian faith which made the enterprise possible – theological concern was focused chiefly on man as the culture-dwelling animal. What Professor Hastings says of the convert writers and thinkers of the inter-war years could be extended to the Catholic intelligentsia as a whole: 'They found in it [Catholicism] a sure

framework for spiritual progress, literary creativity and political
stability, but also for an ordered and coherent view of the world
to replace the increasing intellectual and ideological confusion
evident outside the walls.'⁹ Their theological culture issued in a
theology *of* culture, a theologically informed programme for
culture's Christian revivification.

By the end of the 1930s, the English priesthood comprised
well over 5500 men, while the average annual intake of converts
amounted to some 12,000. In the suburbs and country towns
Catholic churches and chapels burgeoned, in many areas for
the first time since the Reformation. Moreover, the somewhat oppressive feelings of being generally on the defensive –
against Protestantism, whether refined or vulgar, or against
Modernism, whether scholarly or journalistic – had given way to
a greater serenity, and willingness to seize the initiative. We hear
the note struck at the end of Maisie Ward's *Insurrection versus
Resurrection*, written in 1937.

> The best Catholic thinkers of today are, like Newman, passionately
> orthodox. A Chesterton, a Claudel, realise that it is not by surrender
> to the passing enthusiasms of an hour that you really move men,
> that you really win them. The minor poet appeals to the little group,
> the genius speaks in the common speech of man and reaches the
> heart of the universe. The Modernist was like the minor poet: when
> he spoke of the modern mind he was thinking of a little group of
> Biblical critics or immanentist philosophers. But the Faith has a
> common speech to the heart of all mankind . . .

The writer's father, Wilfrid, had been Newman's biographer,
and a leading Liberal Catholic (but anti-Modernist) in the turn-
of-the-century doctrinal crisis; her mother, Josephine, divided
her energies between novel-writing and speaking for the
Catholic Evidence Guild. Maisie herself was Chesterton's
biographer while her husband, Frank Sheed, co-founded with
her the Catholic publishing house named after them and was a
lay theologian in his own right. Her testimony must count for
something, therefore, when she concludes:

> The long siege is over. For the siege implied coherent and
> successful human systems and a Church hemmed in and on the
> defensive. Today there are no such systems. Over against the
> Church stands chaos. The one great question that remains is which

shall prevail – chaos or the divine order eternally established by God.[10]

It should not be thought, however, that the Catholic community in England was entirely of one mind and will. In *Catholicism in England 1535–1935* David Mathew was at pains to stress that the Church converts entered was far from being in all respects a disciplined phalanx which could be relied on to have but one judgement in all things. First, there was a marked division among English Catholics where matters party political were concerned. The most prominent Catholics in public life – in administration and diplomacy as well as politics proper – were Conservatives. 'Sections' of the Catholic industrial population looked rather to Labour. Secondly, there were the less numerous, but highly vocal, adherents to a distinctively Catholic 'third way' in political judgement: the followers of Distributism, the adherents of the Land Movement, and, at the vortex of this activity, the fascinating figure of Eric Gill with his proposals for a root-and-branch reform of the shape and ethos of industrial society. Lastly, among the factors making for disunity, Mathew placed the 'strain' occasioned by the gap between Catholic life in its moral dimension and 'an increasingly alien social ethic' – he meant in regard to what is coyly termed 'family morality', notably, divorce and contraception. While an earlier generation of non-Catholics in England maintained, beneath the surface, a distaste for Rome ultimately founded on Protestantism, whether residual or full-blooded, a new generation objected mainly to moral teachings of the Church once shared with Protestantism (and indeed humanism) at large. And here 'the use of marriage' (that is, contraception) bulked largest. *Plus ça change* . . . an observer from the 1990s might well note.

> There was always a wall between us, but now it is crowned with glass. It is improbable that dissensions on such large questions as 'mariolatry' and papal infallibility would have the same effect of social disintegration as a divergent outlook on the most personal of all questions.[11]

The inter-war years had begun, after all, with a confident agnosticism settled firmly in the driving-seat of English society.

The umbilical cord had not so much snapped as wasted away for those who, in the last analysis, set more store by what the papers say: 'The families who completely subordinate their religious interests are naturally carried slowly outside the Catholic Church.' But if that description is not a thousand miles distant from the state of English Catholicism some half century and more after Mathew's writing, in his very next statement the sense of *déjà-vu* is utterly dispelled. For Mathew goes on: 'On the other hand, a quality of greater determination, sometimes aggressive in its manifestations, is becoming characteristic of the manner in which Catholicism is held by the large majority of its adherents.'[12] Despite the epithet 'aggressive', this is intended as an approbatory statement ('the life and its implications have penetrated deep'). A more assured and exigent Church than that which would succeed it in the 1960s, its presence was, for the 'born Catholic', hard to escape. The novelist Antonia White wrote of the Church in her barely fictionalized account of her childhood, *Frost in May*: 'Wherever she looked, it loomed in the background, like Fujiyama in a Japanese print, massive, terrifying, beautiful and inescapable, the fortress of God, the house on the rock.'[13]

The most important Catholic salon of the period was that which convened at the house of Charles Burns, doctor and psychologist, in St Leonard's Terrace, Chelsea. It was described in a number of autobiographies, or biographies, of figures of the period, perhaps most fully in Christina Scott's life of her father, Christopher Dawson. Here as in a kaleidoscope, a shifting galaxy of luminaries could be espied. Charles Burns himself brought a sympathy with the Viennese psychologists, but of no uncritical kind. His aim was to expel what was alien in their thought, while rendering their sanitizing perceptions congenial. Tom Burns, Charles' younger brother, later to be editor of *The Tablet*, was a publisher with the Catholic house Sheed & Ward. Though his enthusiasm for the Neo-Thomists was later to be qualified, he played a part in making their work, and notably that of Jacques Maritain, known in England. Maritain's *Art et Scolastique* had already been printed in English translation by H. D. C. Pepler's St Dominic's Press at Ditchling, where it much influenced Eric Gill.[14] But as Burns discovered on forays in the Parisian *Quartier Latin*, beyond that slight volume lay 'a whole *opus*, an invasion of all my chosen fields of thought'.[15] Gaining Maritain's friendship, Burns met thereby the social thinker Emmanuel Mounier, the dramatist and philosopher Gabriel Marcel, and a host of other figures of the French Catholic revival (Stanislaus Fumet, Henri Ghéon, Julien Green . . .), the contributors, both imaginative and philoso-phizing, to the series *Le Roseau d'or*. If later the French spiritual masters from de Caussade to Laberthonnière came to have more importance for Burns, his work of mediation nonetheless remained useful.

The poet and artist David Jones had a different mission. His work tried to re-relate his readers both to history and to their own human nature. In seeking the recovery of tradition, he aimed to foster not a sense of living in the past but of the past *living in us*.

> This sense of our past dwelling among us, not as a ghostly revival nor as documentation but as really present and as insistently demanding something of us, is communicated in the *Anathemata* over a vast range of what the poet calls 'our inheritance' . . .'[16]

However, as this critic points out, the lion's share of that patrimony is pre-Tudor and so pre-Reformation, a past (there-fore) medieval, Germanic, Celtic and Roman, whose perspec-tives are integrated by the principal mysteries of the Christian narrative, the Incarnation and the immolation on the hill, as well as by the universal sacrifice of the Mass.[17] Taking Jones's principal work, the epic-like *The Anathemata*, to be in the best and original sense a 'museum', or 'sanctuary of the Muses', David Blamires spoke of how the '"devoted objects" are collected and arranged with care that is more than careful of their mere beauty: they are set to some purpose, to illustrate the "inward continuities" of man's life as a "maker" and as a spiritual being'.[18] Jones's awareness of the vital meanings recuperable in the artefacts and mentefacts of the past led him on indeed to make the further philosophical claim that man is in a highly distinctively sense *homo faber*, 'man the maker'. He is man the maker *of signs*, *homo significator* – and it is through the awareness of embodied significance that an animal may simultaneously be a spiritual subject. Conjoining word and image, for he worked not only as poet but also as calligrapher, illustrator and engraver as well as in watercolour painting and drawing, Jones was peculiarly well placed to write about the relation of art to the Christian sacraments – themselves fusions of matter and form – as well as to the revelation made via a pattern of events and language which is their source.

In the Preface to *The Anathemata*, Jones singled out one man as, through his 'writings and conversation', the chief provider of the work's *materia poetica*. And this was the historian of culture Christopher Dawson, another regular participant in the Chelsea group.[19] Dawson was, in the period, its most influential member. Indeed, Eliot, on a lecture tour in the United States, some time after the publication of Dawson's *Progress and Religion* and *The Making of Europe*, when asked, in a peculiarly American question, who was 'the most powerful intellectual influence in England' at the time, is remembered as replying 'Christopher Dawson'.[20] Dawson, the offspring of minor Yorkshire land-owners and clerical patricians from the Welsh Marches, was an Anglo-Catholic influenced, while at Edwardian Oxford, by the religious philosophy of von Hügel (with its integration of institutional, theological and spiritual elements) and also by the historian of medieval political and social ideas, Ernest Barker. His conversion to the Church of Rome in 1913 was precipitated, however, by reading the concluding volume of Harnack's history of dogma, where the great Protestant scholar described Luther's attack, from the angle of his doctrine of justification by faith alone, on the Catholic understanding of Christian perfection. What to Harnack was a return to the primitive gospel was to Dawson an irreparable breach with the Christian past.

Dawson's earliest professional work was for *The Sociological Review*, the journal of Le Play House, inspired by the pioneering French sociologist Pierre Frédéric Le Play, whose six-volume *Les Ouvriers européens* (1855) analysed social structures – from the Steppes of Russia to the north of England – in terms of 'work, place and folk'. To these Dawson would add 'religion', for he had already accepted the dictum of the Liberal Catholic John Baron Acton, Regius Professor of Modern History at

Cambridge, that 'religion is the key of history'.[21] Academically
brilliant but unplaceable – history, religion and literature were
all, with sociology, grist to his mill – a post was created specially
for him as 'Lecturer in the History of Culture' at the University
College of the South-West (later Exeter University) in 1922. The
modest demands of his slight audience enabled him to begin
work on a mammoth cultural history, provisionally entitled 'The
Life of Civilizations': this was, after all, the age of Oswald
Spengler, author of *Der Untergang des Abendlandes. Umrisse einer
Morphologie der Weltgeschichte* (1918–20; 1922) and Arnold
Toynbee, brain-father of the twelve-volume *A Study of History*
(1934–61). It was also a period of Christian interest in the
theology of history of an intensity unprecedented since patristic
times.[22]

Progress and Religion (1929), intended as a summary synthesis
of the entire work, announces the principal theme of Dawson's
enterprise. A society's vitality is bound up with its religion. He
wrote elsewhere:

> The great civilizations of the world do not produce the great
> religions as a kind of cultural by-product; in a very real sense the
> great religions are the foundations in which the great civilizations
> rest. A society which has lost its religion becomes sooner or later a
> society which has lost its culture.[23]

And whereas Spengler, in his 'morphology' of civilizations,
treated each culture as a closed system, Dawson's chart was
based on a principle of spiritual fecundity whereby parent
cultures, in their deaths, give rise to offspring cultures which
can continue their genes. But as with his Russian Orthodox
contemporary Georges Vasileivich Florovsky (1893–1979), who
also attempted a Christian theology of cultural history, Dawson's
deeper presupposition here concerns human freedom, especially in its mode of creative victory over resistant materials, what
Florovsky termed *podvig*, 'ascetic achievement'.

> If man is not the slave and creature of time, but its master and
> creator, then history also becomes a creative process. It does not
> repeat itself meaninglessly: it grows into organic unity with the
> growth of human experience. The past does not die; it becomes
> incorporated in humanity. And hence progress is possible, since

the life of society and of humanity itself possesses continuity and the capacity for spiritual growth no less than the life of the individual.[24]

As the tone and substance of these comments suggest, Dawson had not only an analysis to offer, as historian; he also had a prescription, as lay prophet. As he wrote in his (immediately post-Second World War) Gifford Lectures:

> We are faced with a spiritual conflict of the most acute kind, a sort of social schizophrenia which divides the soul of society between a non-moral will to power served by inhuman techniques and a religious faith and a moral idealism which have no power to influence human life. There must be a return to unity – a spiritual integration of culture – if mankind is to survive.[25]

Indeed, for all his criticism of Spengler (and also of Toynbee, whom he chastised for too sharp a distinction between primitive and civilized societies, and too blunt a one between the higher religions and civilizations), Dawson defended the 'meta-historians' against the charge that prophecy and history were disreputably combined in their work.[26] Such creative vision, he held, typified great historians: witness Ranke and de Tocqueville. Dawson's own work is best thought of as a latter-day *City of God* (his favourite text among Christian sources), which tries to show the special history of Christian revelation confronting and transforming the general history of the world, while remaining conditioned by its possibilities and limitations.

A way out of the waste-land: this was what Dawson's work seemed to offer, at any rate in aspiration, and explains the attraction to him of Eliot who invited him to write for his journal, *The Criterion*, almost as soon as *Progress and Religion* appeared. But if, in Dawson's view, for sunlight culture needs to be open to the spiritual, it also requires rooting in the earth. This second, and complementary, conviction connects Dawson with D. H. Lawrence, whose view of sexuality as a cosmic mystery he shared.[27]

Through Burns – but also, via the fountainhead, Frank Sheed, the Australian-born lay theologian and apologist – Dawson early became a regular author with Sheed & Ward, who had persuaded him away from the old-established publishing house of John Murray. The enticement was not primarily financial. It was in the hope of servicing, and stimulating, the budding Catholic revival of the 1930s that a serious – yet adventurous – Catholic firm took the plunge into the uncertain waters of the market where before such grave companies as Longmans, Green & Co. had simply made space for some Catholic authors and books. After the ending of Burns' brief firework of a journal, *Order*, it was the Sheed & Ward series *Essays in Order* which led the way in the work of the spiritual reintegration of culture – on an ultimately Catholic Christian foundation – which Dawson desired.

A uniform cover, designed by David Jones, shows a unicorn, bearing a somewhat cocky expression, in a landscape of natural symbols. A text from a late-fifteenth-century German source, the *Itinerarium Hoannis de Hese presbyteri ad Hierusalem*, provides the explanation for the graphics. The priestly pilgrim to the Levant records that:

> Near the fields of Helyon there is a river called Marah, the water of which is very bitter, into which Moses struck his staff and made the waters sweet, so that the Children of Israel might drink. And even in our times, it is said, venomous animals poison that water after the setting of the sun, so that the good animals cannot drink of it; but in the morning, after the sunrise, comes the Unicorn and dips his horn into the stream, driving the poison from it so that the good animals can drink there during the day.

The moral is (fairly) plain: the contributors to *Essays in Order* would clarify – in the sense of purify – the waters of culture which, though life-giving of themselves, have become muddied and insanitary. The grace of the Saviour (typologically, the Unicorn) will achieve what is otherwise impossible by rendering culture salutary once more. To change the metaphor: Christianity can heal what is wounded in contemporary culture and raise it up so that it becomes a manifestation of the life of the children of God.

In the first volume, a translation of Maritain's *Religion et Culture*, Dawson offered a general introduction to the series which set its tone from the start.

> Catholicism stands essentially for a universal order in which every good and every truth of the natural or the social order can find a place . . . It is the Catholic ideal to order the whole of life towards unity, not by the denial and destruction of the natural human values, but by bringing them into living relation with spiritual truth and spiritual reality.[28]

He admits that, institutionally and even philosophically, Christianity at large has ceded large tracts of ground to the advance of secularism since the Victorian age. Conceding, then, that the slogan 'New Christendom *Now!*' would be altogether out of place, for its evangelical base is lacking, and that what is at issue must be, rather, matters of 'co-operation and of conflict' between the new human order and Catholicism, Dawson claims nonetheless that the present (1931) is a *kairos*, an acceptable time, a day of salvation. 'We feel the need for spiritual order far more acutely than did the prosperous and self-confident nineteenth century, but we no longer believe that it will be the inevitable result of the political and economic evolution of the modern world.'[29] The exaltation of man (with Rousseau) and the idealization of nature (in the Romantics) produced a depreciation of spiritual reality, to which Protestantism responded (in theological Liberalism) by the abandoning of metaphysics and dogma, and a seeking of refuge in 'ethical ideals'. The exhibition of the spiritual bankruptcy of this particular conversation in the history of ideas, and the story of sensibility, can make way for the 'return of Catholicism from exile' – a phrase Dawson borrows from the German philosopher Peter Wust.

> The attempt of the nineteenth century to prescribe spiritual ideals in literature and ethics, while refusing to admit the objective existence of a spiritual order, has ended in failure, and today we have to choose between the complete expulsion of the spiritual element from human life or its recognition as the very foundation of reality.

And Dawson concludes:

> In so far as the modern world accepts the latter alternative, it can no longer disregard the existence of the Catholic solution, for Catholicism is the great historic representative of the principle of the spiritual order – an order which is not the creation of the human mind, but its ruler and creator.[30]

If anyone in the Chelsea circle epitomized the desire for a new (Christian) Renaissance, synthesizing the main elements of contemporary understanding within the total framework of a Catholic metaphysic, that person was Dawson's best friend, and the contributor of the fourth *Essay in Order*, Edward Watkin. Watkin, born near Manchester in 1888, was received into the Church while an undergraduate at New College, Oxford, in 1908 – at Downside, to whose contemplative interpretation of the English Benedictine ethos he remained permanently indebted (his son, Dom Aelred, became headmaster). Mysticism constitutes perhaps the commonest theme of his writing, though he himself regarded *The Philosophy of Form* as his most worthwhile work.[31] It tried to reconcile two epistemological approaches normally regarded as competing: the view, namely, that truth is attained by intuition, and the position which would have it that truth is found only through reasoning. Watkin claimed that thought is either intuition or the 'discrimination' of intuitions – thus linking the quantitative apprehensions of natural science on the one hand (abstract and clear intuitions, and those of aesthetic experience (dimmer, but more concrete intuitions) on the other. Whatever the merits of this proposal as a thesis in epistemology, its admirable holism of approach was typical of Watkin's Catholicism in general,[32] and of his 'essay in order' in particular.

Then there were translators of distinction, who helped introduce an Anglophone audience to treasures of Catholic theology and literature from continental Europe. Alick Dru was perhaps best known as a translator of Kierkegaard (Catholic philosophers and theologians were just beginning to take a serious interest in this Danish Lutheran opponent of Hegelianism around this time). But he also Englished Ghéon's study of Mozart, and major works by Henri de Lubac, Hans Urs von Balthasar and Adrienne von Speyr. T. S. Eliot wrote an introduction to his version of Josef Pieper's *Leisure the Basis of Culture*.[33] His study of Charles Péguy, long matured, confirmed the well-foundedness of a favoured poet of *Blackfriars*.[34] In collaboration with the Downside monk Illtyd Trethowan, he sought to replace the somewhat desiccated apologetics customary in English Catholic manuals with a more generous fundamental theology inspired by a contemporary of Péguy's, Maurice Blondel.[35]

Barbara Lucas, granddaughter of the matriarchal Edwardian Catholic poet Alice Meynell, translated novels by Léon Bloy (who had been responsible for Maritain's conversion from agnosticism), François Mauriac and the lesser-known Yvonne de Bremond d'Ars, as well as studies of modern Italian painting and contemporary theatre – and later, the historical theology of the Oratorian convert from Calvinism, Louis Bouyer. Her husband, Bernard Wall, put into English major works by Maritain, Marcel and, subsequently, Teilhard de Chardin. He was, however, primarily an Italianist, with a major study of Manzoni to his credit.[36] Wall's interests were extremely wide-ranging and given expression in the journal of cultural affairs *Colosseum*, which he founded – like many 1930s journals, it would end ingloriously with the coming of war – as well as in an intellectual autobiography.[37] His account of immediately post-Civil War Spain helps to explain the passionate disagreements of informed English Catholics on the issue – of which more anon.[38]

If Jones was the chief literary artist in the group, he had an interpreter of brilliance in the fourth of the translators, René Hague. Hague would English a crop of intellectual fruits from French Catholicism – Marcel, de Lubac, Teilhard; but it was as elucidator of the often darkly riddling poetry of David Jones that his services were most demanded.[39] After Eric Gill's break with the co-founder of St Dominic's Press, Ditchling, Hilary Pepler, he found in Hague his closest collaborator. The printing press of 'Hague & Gill' would continue to use Gill's splendid type designs till its demise in 1956. Its production of Jones's *In Parenthesis* – probably the greatest poem produced by war in the English language –was both innovatory and fine.[40] Such services of mediation – translating, creative printing – are a good index of the concerns and enthusiasms that enlivened Dawson's 'Catholic setting'.

The London Catholic intelligentsia were primarily concerned with what, in the 1960s, came to be called 'indigenization', the giving of a local habitation and a name in England to the wider body of Catholic thought. In particular they sought to incarnate in English culture – at the level of philosophy, art and social thinking – the insights of the French Catholic revival, at once austerely Thomist and generously humane as, by the 1920s, that had become. The influence of Jacques Maritain, himself a pupil of the French Dominicans, was intellectually paramount, both through his writings and as mediated by occasional visiting French Dominicans such as Pères Auguste Maydieu and Marie-Dominique Roland-Gosselin. There was some early interest in the social philosophy of the *Action française*, but Maritain's *Things That Are Not Caesar's* was generally regarded as a convincing rebuttal of that movement's claims to Catholic allegiance.[41] But if France was the intellectual mainstay of the English Catholic intellectuals, another Latin country, across the Pyrenees, proved their Achilles' heel.

The mid-1930s confronted them with the issue of Spain. Like most English Catholics they were by and large pro-Franco but, unlike less well-informed opinion, far from favourable to the Franco excesses. Their opinions here were indebted to the convert poet and translator of John of the Cross, Roy Campbell.[42] However, this majority report failed to sway those who were horrified at any identification of the Catholic Church with the Francoist reaction: of these the most notable, and vocal, was Eric Gill. Gill was only an occasional conformist to the group's agenda of meetings. Still, he acted as a kind of elder statesman, if such a term can be used for one perpetually so dynamic and forceful. His conviction, largely achieved before the First World War opened, that art, philosophy and social politics are inextricably interrelated, and that the key to their unity belongs with religion, was the foundational *credendum* of the 1930s Catholic intelligentsia.[43] He preceded them, too, in his discovery of the serviceable qualities of the thought of Aquinas, especially as presented by the French Neo-Thomists, in this reconceiving of the world.

If the main non-Catholic participant in the Chelsea set was T. S. Eliot, in many ways its members echoed Eliot's basic themes: the reintegration of a fragmented cultural heritage, the overcoming of a diremption between thought and sensibility; the defence of the presence, within fine literature, of concepts drawn from metaphysics and religion, the reunion of rationality and mysticism, and the setting forth of the conditions for a new order in society, by way of a Christian sociology.[44] Swayed by Eliot's extraordinary prestige in the literary world of the day, they tended to suppose that the current of cultural history was flowing in their direction – towards a 'new Christendom'. The post-war world with its growing secularism, levelling democracy hostile to élite culture, and bureaucratization, would prove a sad awakening. This 'ministry of all the talents', considered as a corporate claimant for the intellectual leadership of English Catholicism, was more impressive than anything that had pre-ceded it – or would follow it. Not that it was all-embracing. It bore little relation, for example, to the parallel Catholic renaissance (both Roman and Anglican) then proceeding in the senior of the ancient universities, and associated in par-ticular with the 'Inklings' (C. S. Lewis, Charles Williams, J. R. R. Tolkien, et al.), with the Oxford Dominicans and with the brilliantly imaginative apologist Ronald Knox, the University's Roman Catholic Chaplain from 1926 to the eve of war.

All these Christian intellectuals in Dawson's milieu were operating at an apparently providential time. The intensified economic and political pressures of the years after the Great War (the lion caged in Bolshevism, stalking the land in Fascism), together with the manifest human insufficiency of much in the artistic and philosophical worlds of the time (formalism and nihilism in aesthetics, logical positivism in philosophy), com-bined to raise the question, 'Is liberalism enough?' In the novel form, Evelyn Waugh and Graham Greene were concerned simply to write good books – but the effect was that of an assault, mounted from different starting-points, on the complacencies of bourgeois liberalism: Waugh through the portrayal of a Catholic aristocracy whose sins are covered by acceptance of faith's paradoxes, Greene by attempting to see society through very different eyes, those of criminals and exiles. Looking back on the phenomenon of the English Catholic novel to mid-century, Fr Gerald Meath OP commented:

> Proust and Virginia Woolf are the products of a world which has been driven in on itself and condemned to self-conscious art because it has lost the pattern of God's planning. The loss of this sense means a loss of faith, and it has produced the excessive

concern with techniques and experiment that is so common today and has made the modern novel etiolated and narrow . . . [Catholic novelists'] greatest temptation may be to overemphasise the pattern, but undoubtedly their infallible method will be to keep out of God's light and allow him to appear through their 'mirrorings', and the last thing they will worry about will be 'edification'.[45]

The wider cultural context gave such writers the confidence they needed to persist in their literary strategies, rebarbative to modernism as these might seem. The 1930s witnessed what Hastings termed 'a breakdown of the agnostic consensus of the enlightened and . . . the growing sense that a belief in supernatural religion really was an intellectual option for modern man'.[46] The novelist Compton Mackenzie summed up at the end of the decade:

> Communism or Fascism – they may be mutually destructive, but they are both expressions of distrust in the individualism which has made such a mess of the world. We are watching now, I fancy, the beginning of the end of an epoch which started with the Renaissance and the Protestant Reformation and the discovery of America and the conception of England as an extra-European State.[47]

It was not, then, liberalism only – literary and cultural, social and political – against which such writers defined themselves. The attempt of the Papacy of John Paul II to outline a 'third way' outside the camps of both socialism and capitalism was widely anticipated in the period. As another wartime commentator remarked, à propos of the genesis and development of Belloc's social philosophy:

> The rise of Socialism was not merely disastrous in itself, in that it harnessed many fine and disinterested minds to a false philosophy, but it also manoeuvred into the defence of the capitalist regime, almost the whole of those forces which should have been led in the attack on it.[48]

As so often, the episcopate was only dimly aware of these creative stirrings in the Christian imagination, the Catholic intelligence. With the deaths of such late Victorian bishops as Henry Edward Manning, John Cuthbert Hedley and William Robert Brownlow, the age of the writing bishop was past.[49] Their worries lay elsewhere. David Mathew's chief cause for complaint was directed against the 'more sophisticated sections of the Catholic body'.[50] In the 'smart set' to whom Evelyn Waugh's Father Rothschild sj ministered with such omniscience and discretion, Mathew discerned a frame of mind of 'almost nominal Catholicism which is unwilling to move even slightly against the stream', an 'indifference', an 'impatience with the clergy'. A later historian, Dr Edward Norman, called the Catholic *ecclesia episcoporum* of this period 'a Church which had become confident and routinised; splendid in its pastoral machinery, but lacking the genius of inventiveness'.[51] Mathew's remarks do not smack of over-confidence. But then again, he was hardly a typical bishop. Certainly, the salon at St Leonard's Terrace would have considered itself reformist. If pressed, they might have identified their enemies as 'pietism' and 'separatism': a refusal to marry the heart's devotion to hard thinking, on the one hand, and, on the other, a quasi-sectarian indifference to the fate of the wider culture.[52]

But for the principal exception to Norman's strictures we must look elsewhere: Mathew's study was finished in the year (1935) that the safe but unexciting Cardinal Francis Bourne was succeeded at Westminster by an archbishop, Arthur Hinsley, who would do much for the revival of Catholic social thought. Hinsley was in that domain both patron and facilitator of the work of Dawson and his younger colleague Barbara Ward. The spread of Fascism well beyond the confines of Italy in the later 1920s had been followed by the dizzy rise of Hitler to the Chancellorship of Germany in 1933. Invited, initially, by the *Catholic Times* to comment on 'The Church and the Dictators', Dawson began to give serious attention to the role of the Church *vis-à-vis* contemporary politics. *Religion and the Modern State* (1936) proposed a choice between the 'mechanical order of the absolute State' (whether nominally Fascist or Socialist) and a recovery of the Christian elements in Western culture by way of a return to a spiritual order with a quite different ethos for civil society.[53] *Beyond Politics* (1939) opined that the Church's greatest task in the service of Western civilization was the preservation of her own inheritance and a refusal of instrumentalization by any political movement, whatever its name.[54] These works commended themselves to the newly enthroned archbishop. Hinsley, aware that Dawson had been refused a chair in the philosophy and history of religion at Leeds, owing to (it would seem) anti-Catholic prejudice, and so was out of a job, offered him two.

The *Dublin Review* had been founded by the first holder of the see of Westminster, Cardinal Nicholas Wiseman; Dawson had already written much in its pages, thanks to his good relation with his fellow-convert editor, Algar Thorold, an expert on the history of mysticism and son of the Anglican Bishop of Winchester. Now it could be his organ at a time of national emergency unparalleled since the Revolutionary and Napoleonic Wars.

Sword of the Spirit, by contrast, was an organization launched by Hinsley himself, with a view to creating a new domestic and international order once peace had come again.[55] Its vice-presidency (Hinsley himself being president) remained in Dawson's hands as long as the cardinal lived. The movement's aim was to unite all men of good will (but notably Christians) in a struggle against totalitarianisms of both Left and Right, and for the unity of the centre, what Dawson called 'principles far more vital than the issue of the Left/Right party dog-fight'.[56] In both cases, Barbara Ward – the future economist and human rights activist Baroness Ward – was to be found at Dawson's side, as assistant editor at the *Dublin Review* and as board member (and, effectively, administrator) at the Sword.[57] Unfortunately, the other Catholic bishops (with the exception of David Mathew) objected to what they considered the ecumenical dalliance of Sword of the Spirit. Hinsley rejoined that the movement aimed at practical co-operation with a view to realizing the papal social encyclicals – not at interventions in the realms of doctrine and discipline. Rome came down on the side of the collegial consensus. Father John Carmel Heenan, eventually his successor, commented shortly after Hinsley's death, with characteristic *suavitas*:

> In his moments of depression the Cardinal was sometimes inclined to believe that there was in some Catholic quarters a lack of good will. But he thought along these lines only in moments of

depression. In his heart he knew that his position and personality enabled him to go much further along the road to co-operation than would be possible for other members of the hierarchy. They always spoke as diocesan bishops. Cardinal Hinsley often spoke as a national leader first. He did not, of course, ever make utterances incompatible with the dogmatic character of the teaching Church but often he spoke not as a bishop teaching his own flock but as a Catholic Englishman testifying to his sense of spiritual communion with Englishmen outside the fold.[58]

The decision to divide into Catholic and non-Catholic branches inevitably made for loss of momentum – although by this time significant differences of opinion between Catholics and High Anglicans on the one hand, Broad and Free Church-men on the other, over the issue of natural law, had already created difficulties. After Hinsley's death in 1943, Dawson was removed from the *Dublin Review* editorship as (in effect) one too closely identified with the late cardinal's stand. However, their collaboration stimulated the writing of his *The Judgement of the Nations* (1942) with its plea for a post-war European unity,[59] while, as pointed out in a lengthy *Times* debate on 'Catholicism Today' in November 1949, the ten points of social and international order which the original Sword took as its agreed principles retained both validity and useful-ness.[60] In the later transformation of Sword of the Spirit into the Catholic Institute for International Relations, a much greater professionalization of social fact-finding was accom-panied by a new focus of concern on human rights and their abuse – a concept at once wider and narrower than that of order, but recommended by the usage not only of international organizations but of the Papacy itself from the 1960s onwards. In the post-conciliar world, too, Catholic identity would prove harder to sustain.

After the Second World War, English Catholicism was by no means as sclerotic and dull as is sometimes alleged. Institu-tionally, indeed, it went from strength to strength, and was strongly, even effortlessly, convinced of its future.[61] It continued to attract converts of the greatest intellectual distinction, whether prospective or already achieved: the philosopher Elisabeth Anscombe, the anthropologist E. E. Evans-Pritchard, the poet Edith Sitwell. To some degree, however, it suffered a closing in of cultural horizons.[62] Its very success as a creator of new parishes, schools, missionary training houses, encouraged it to become more activist and clerical in orientation. As early as 1942, Dawson could be found complaining that 'a belief in effecting things by organization and formulas, etc., etc., [is] growing rather than lessening'.[63] The generosity of temper of an older generation, the conviction that Catholicism was, thanks to the renewing power of the supernatural for nature, a culture-transforming force of unlimited significance, was less in evidence now. 'If brilliance there was, it was largely the autumnal maturity of a generation formed well before the Second World War.'[64] Dawson's disappearance over the American horizon in 1958 and the (as it may yet prove, temporary) eclipse of his reputation in England were pre-monitory signs of a setting sun.[65]

NOTES

1   A. Hastings, *A History of English Christianity, 1920–1985* (London, Collins, 1986), p. 134.

2   For the background, see E. I. Watkin, *Roman Catholicism in England from the Reformation to 1950* (London, Oxford University Press, 1957); J. Bossy, *The English Catholic Community, 1570–1850* (London, Darton, Longman & Todd, 1975).

3   A. Hastings, *English Christianity*, p. 133.

4   E. R. Norman, *The English Catholic Church in the Nineteenth Century* (Oxford, Clarendon Press, 1984).

5   A. Kenny, *A Path from Rome: An Autobiography* (London, Sidgwick & Jackson, 1985), p. 55.

6   Beginning in 1922 they continued publication till 1940.

7   J. G. Vance and J. W. Fortescue, *Adrian Fortescue: A Memoir* (London, Burns, Oates & Washbourne., 1924).

8   Hawkins's work may be described as an attempt to commend to those raised in British empiricism the merits of Scholastic philosophy and the service it could perform for Christian doctrine: see E. A. Sillem, 'Hawkins, Denis John Bernard' *New Catholic Encyclopaedia* 6 (New York, McGraw-Hill Book Company, 1967), p. 954.

9   A. Hastings, *English Christianity*, pp. 279–80.

10   M. Ward, *Insurrection versus Resurrection. The Wilfrid Wards and the Transition*, *II* (London, Sheed & Ward, 1937), pp. 550–1.

11   D. Mathew, *Catholicism in England 1535–1935. Portrait of a Minority: Its Culture and Tradition* (London, Longmans, Green, 1936), p. 253.

12   Ibid.

13   A. White, *Frost in May* (London, D. Harmsworth, 1933). For Fr Victor White's role in bringing back this formidable lady to the Church, see S. Chitty, *Now to My Mother* (London, Weidenfeld & Nicolson, 1985), p. 135.

14   J. Maritain, *Art et Scolastique* (Paris, Librairie de l'art catholique, 1920); ET *The Philosophy of Art* (Ditchling, St Dominic's Press, 1923), with an Introduction by E. Gill.

15   T. Burns, *The Use of Memory: Publishing and Further Pursuits* (London, Sheed & Ward, 1993), p. 24.

16   H. Grisewood, *David Jones* (London, BBC Publications, 1966), p. 13.

17   On David Jones: D. J. Blamires, *David Jones, Artist and Writer* (Manchester, Manchester University Press, 1971); T. Dilworth, *The Shape of Meaning in the Poetry of David Jones* (Toronto, University of Toronto Press, 1988). Professor Dilworth is now preparing a study of Jones's painting as exhaustive as this work is for his poetry.

18   D. Blamires, *David Jones*, p. 195.

19   [M. D. Knowles,] E. I. Watkin [with J. J. Mulloy], 'Christopher Dawson, 1889–1970', *Proceedings of the British Academy* LVII (1971), pp. 439–52.

20   C. Scott, *A Historian and his World: A Life of Christopher Dawson, 1889–1970* (London, Sheed & Ward, 1984), p. 210.

21   Ibid., p. 49.

22   J. M. Connolly, *Human History and the Word of God: The Christian Meaning of History in Contemporary Thought* (New York and London, 1965).

23   C. Dawson, *The Dynamics of World History* (New York, 1957), p. 128.

24   Idem, *Enquiries into Religion and Culture* (New York, 1933), p. 252.

25   Idem, *Religion and Culture* (London, 1948), p. 217.

26   Thus 'The Problem of Meta-History', in idem, *Dynamics of World History* (London and New York, 1957). For a spirited modern defence, see C. T. McIntire and M. Perry, 'Toynbee's Achievement', in C. T. McIntire and M. Perry (eds), *Toynbee: Reappraisals* (Toronto, 1989), pp. 3–31.

27   C. Scott, *A Historian and his World*, p. 94.

28   C. Dawson, 'General Introduction' to J. Maritain, *Religion and Culture* (ET, London, Sheed & Ward, 1931, = *Essays in Order*, 1), pp. viii–ix.

29   Ibid., p. xvii.

30   Ibid., p. xxv. One is reminded of C. S. Lewis's devastating comment on the critical approach of F. R. Leavis: 'Leavis demands moral earnestness; I prefer morality.' Cited by H. Carpenter, *The Inklings* (London, George Allen & Unwin, 1978), p. 64, in the course of a discussion of Lewis's *The Personal Heresy.*

31   E. I. Watkin, *The Philosophy of Mysticism* (London, Grant Richards, 1920); idem, *Poets and Mystics* (London, Sheed & Ward, 1953); idem, *The Philosophy of Form* (London, Sheed & Ward, 1935; 1938; 1950).

32   E. I. Watkin, *The Catholic Centre* (London, Sheed & Ward, 1939) gives this holism a theocentric and doxological rationale: following the French Carmelite spiritual theologian Elizabeth of the Holy Trinity, 'Catholic praise' has its 'circumference' in the utmost limit of creation and its 'centre' in God, p. 247.

33   J. Pieper, *Leisure the Basis of Culture* (London, Faber & Faber, 1952).

34   A. Dru, *Péguy* (London, Harvill Press, 1956); cf. *Blackfriars* XXVIII, No. 333 (1947), with essays by Robert Speaight and Liam Brophy.

35   A. Dru and I. Trethowan (eds), *Blondel's 'Letter on Apologetics' and 'History and Dogma'* (London, Harvill Press, 1964).

36   Bernard Wall, *Alessandro Manzoni* (Cambridge, Bowes & Bowes, 1954); and more widely, *Italian Life and Landscape* (London, Paul Elek, 1950–1); *Italian Art, Literature and Landscape* (London, William Heinemann, 1956); *A City and a World: A Roman Sketchbook* (London, Nicolson, 1962). Worth mentioning here are his 'Vaticanological' explorations in *Report on the Vatican* (London, Weidenfeld & Nicolson, 1956) and (with his wife) *Thaw at the Vatican* (London, Victor Gollancz, 1964).

37   Bernard Wall, *Headlong into Change: An Autobiography and a Memoir of Ideas since the Thirties* (London, Harvill Press, 1969). This took further the comments in *These Changing Years: Notes on Civilization and Revolution* (London, Harvill Press, 1947).

38   Bernard Wall, *Spain of the Spaniards* (London, Sheed & Ward, 1938). The editorial policy of *Blackfriars* favoured the *de jure* (Republican) government; soon after the war ended, however, there emerged from Blackfriars, Oxford, John-Baptist Reeves's *Dominican Martyrs in Red Spain* (Oxford, n.d. but 1939), which gives an account of thirty-one Dominicans who apparently died for the faith, including the former Master of the Order, Bonaventura Garcia de Paredes.

39   R. Hague, *A Commentary on the 'Anathemata' of David Jones* (Wellingborough, Christopher Skelton, 1977); idem (ed.), *Dai Greatcoat: A Self-Portrait of David Jones in his Letters* (London, Faber & Faber, 1980). Hague also reconstructed from fragments a poem cycle left unpublished on Jones's death as *The Kensington Mass* (London, Agenda Editions, 1975).

40   Bernard Wall, *René Hague: A Personal Memoir* (Wirral, The Aylesford Press, 1989), pp. 17–19.

41 J. Maritain, *La Primauté du spirituel* (Paris, Plon, 1927); ET, *The Things That Are Not Caesar's* (London, Sheed & Ward, 1930). The point of the (original) title was that *Action française* asserted 'La politique d'abord!', holding that only when a proper ordering of civil society had been restored in France could the religious question usefully be addressed. Both 'sides' made appeal to Thomism, something rather obscured in A. Maydieu OP, 'The Influence of St Thomas on French politics', *Blackfriars* XXVIII, no. 330 (1947), pp. 395–405. Only Eliot, exempted by his Anglicanism from attention to papal *volte-faces*, never withdrew explicit allegiance to Maurras. 'Throughout his life, Eliot would continue to support Maurras, and his philosophy was to enter the fabric of Eliot's own concerns', so P. Ackroyd, *T. S. Eliot* (London, Cardinal, 1984), pp. 41–2.

42 R. Campbell, *Light on a Dark Horse: An Autobiography, 1901–1935* (London, Hollis & Carter, 1951), pp. 308–47.

43 M. Yorke, *Eric Gill: Man of Flesh and Spirit* (London, Constable, 1981), pp. 73–98.

44 S. Spender, *Eliot* (London, Fontana Collins, 1975). For Eliot's new Christendom writing, see T. S. Eliot, *The Idea of a Christian Society* (London, Faber & Faber, 1939); idem, *Notes towards the Definition of Culture* (London, Faber & Faber, 1948); and R. Kojecky, *Eliot's Social Criticism* (London, Faber & Faber, 1971).

45 G. Meath OP, 'The Catholic Novel', *Blackfriars* XXXII, no. 281 (1951), p. 609.

46 A. Hastings, *English Christianity*, p. 291.

47 C. Mackenzie, *West to North* (London, Rich & Cowan, 1940; 1942), p. 297.

48 B. Jerrold, 'The Influence of Hilaire Belloc', in D. Woodruff (ed.), *For Hilaire Belloc: Essays in Honour of his 72nd Birthday* (London, Sheed & Ward, 1942), p. 11.

49 P. Hughes, 'The Bishops of the Century', in G. A. Beck A.A. (ed.), *The English Catholics, 1850–1950* (London, 1950), p. 192.

50 D. Mathew, *Catholicism in England*, p. 259.

51 E. R. Norman, *Roman Catholicism in England from the Elizabethan Settlement to the Second Vatican Council* (Oxford, Oxford University Press, 1985), p. 109.

52 Their criticisms of the weaknesses of many clergy and laity in this regard, as well as – it must be conceded – their failure to note some careful distinctions worked out in the theology of the schools (the laymen among them had no formal theological training), could make relations with ecclesiastical censors unpredictable. For Watkin's experience, see M. Goffin, 'Fighting under the Lash', *Downside Review* 113. 392 (1995), pp. 203–18.

53 C. Dawson, *Religion and the Modern State* (London, Sheed & Ward, 1936).

54 C. Dawson, *Beyond Politics* (London, Sheed & Ward, 1939).

55 For Hinsley's role, see J. C. Heenan, *Cardinal Hinsley* (London, Burns, Oates & Washbourne, 1944), pp. 182–210. The movement took its title

from that of his BBC Radio broadcast to the nation on 10 December 1939: see ibid., pp. 87–8.

56 Cited C. Scott, *A Historian and his World*, p. 139.

57 For an example of her thinking in this period, see her 'The Incarnation and the Human Order', *Blackfriars* XXI, no. 249 (1940), pp. 694–700.

58 J. C. Heenan, *Cardinal Hinsley*, p. 209.

59 C. Dawson, *The Judgement of the Nations* (London, Sheed & Ward, 1942).

60 Letter of 8 November 1949 by Professor A. C. F. Beales, author of *The Catholic Church and International Order* (Harmondsworth, 1941). For the ten principles, see J. C. Heenan, *Cardinal Hinsley*, pp. 180–1.

61 A. Hastings, *English Christianity*, pp. 473–5.

62 The difference in tone is detectable in the French collection of essays by exclusively British Catholic authors: D. Mathew et al., *Catholicisme anglais* (Paris, Editions du Cerf, 1958), for example at p. 55.

63 In R. Hague (ed.), *Dai Greatcoat*, p. 112.

64 A. Hastings, *English Christianity*, p. 487. Anscombe and Evans-Pritchard (other names could be mentioned) are, evidently, exceptions to this rule.

65 This chapter was not delivered as a paper at the Centre for Faith & Culture conference but is an expanded version of material published in Aidan Nichols' *The Dominican Gallery: Portrait of a Culture* (Leominster, Gracewing, 1997).

3

Christopher Dawson and Europe

FERNANDO CERVANTES

I

Our century began with a revolt against history. 'In most fields of intellectual activity', wrote Carl E. Schorske in a memorable passage, 'twentieth-century Europe has proudly asserted its independence from the past'.[1]

It is true that this development is not wholly new in European culture. Already in the eighteenth century the word 'modern' had acquired its characteristic connotations as a rallying-point for any movement opposed to the legacy of Classical antiquity. The 'modern' was anything and everything opposed to the 'ancient'. It was the representative of progress and enlighten-ment against stagnation and obscurantism. But however familiar the concept might be, the way in which 'modernity' has developed in the twentieth century differs in a substantial sense from the eighteenth-century urge to oppose the past or to define the present in opposition to the past. To quote Schorske again,

> [I]n the last one hundred years . . . the word 'modern' has come to distinguish our perception of our lives and times from all that has gone before, from history as a whole, as such. Modern architecture, modern music, modern philosophy, modern science – all these define themselves not *out* of the past, indeed scarcely *against* the past, but in independence of the past. The modern mind has been growing indifferent to history because history, conceived as a continuous nourishing tradition, has become useless to it.[2]

This development is all the more remarkable and paradoxical when we consider that there has seldom been an age when more energy was spent in reconstructing past ages and when interest in history was more alive. Nevertheless, no matter how remarkable the achievements of twentieth-century historical scholarship may be or how much our knowledge of the past may have increased, there is no doubt that the modern study of history is fundamentally opposed to an understanding of the past as an organic, intelligible whole. Metahistory[3] is even more discredited than metaphysics. True history is meticulous and specialized. If it can lay a claim to any value or significance beyond mere reconstruction, such a claim must be strictly practical and utilitarian. It is not, therefore, the vision of Spengler or Toynbee, much less that of Christopher Dawson, that appeals to the modern mind, but the practical and secular outlook of a Paul Kennedy or a Henry Kissinger or a Winston Churchill.

Beneath the flood of monographic history, therefore, the revolt against the past with which our century began has persisted and endured. And it is not now so much a revolt as an attitude of aloofness and indifference, one in which the vision of the past as *tradition* is in danger of being lost. As Christopher Dawson wrote in 1948, 'the changes that have been taking place in the present century . . . have caused a loss of social tradition and a dislocation of human experience such as no previous generation has known since the beginning of history'.[4] This sense of loss was felt by Dawson more acutely and realistically than by almost any other writer of the period, for he intuited it from his own personal experiences and family background as much as he understood it from a scholarly and intellectual perspective. Through his parents, he tells us, he had learnt the

> essential connection between *story* and *history,* so that I came to know the past not so much by the arid path of *The Child's History of England,* as through the enchanted world of myth and legend. In this way I discovered very early that history was not a flat expanse of time, measured off in dates, but a series of different worlds and that each of them had its own spirit and form and its own riches of poetic imagination . . . This was the old road which carries us back not merely for centuries but for thousands of years; the road by

which every people has travelled and from which the beginnings of every literature have come. I mean the road of oral tradition. It may be that the changes of our generation . . . have closed this road for ever. But if so, those of us who remember the world before the wars have witnessed a change in human consciousness far greater than we have realised, and what we are remembering is not the Victorian age but a whole series of ages – a river of immemorial time which has suddenly dried up and become lost in the seismic cleft that has opened between the present and the past.[5]

Dawson's vision of Europe and the importance which he attached to the European tradition cannot be separated from this preoccupation. It was far from being a narrow or 'Eurocentric' concern, for it was a natural extension of his notion of *Pietas*, in the classical sense of the word, 'which is the cult of parents and kinsfolk and native place as the principles of our being' and which far from being 'a matter of sentiment or social tradition' is in fact 'a moral principle that lies at the root of every culture and every religion, and a society that loses it has lost its primary moral basis and its hope of survival'.[6]

At the time when Dawson began to write, moreover, there could have been little doubt among most of his European contemporaries about the privileged position of Europe as the pinnacle of human achievement, both materially and culturally. It was only during the aftermath of the Great War, with the decline of faith in Progress and the shattering of European complacency, that a period of questioning began in which the future of Europe and of European world hegemony became the central themes. The bulk of the analyses, as one would expect from a secular and utilitarian age, centred on the economic, political and strategic elements of the problem. It was precisely the undue emphasis given to these elements that Dawson saw at the root of the recurring misunderstandings of the historic reality of Europe. 'The failure of the European system', he diagnosed in the early 1950s, 'has been primarily due to the unlimited and unrestricted development of the principle of sovereignty'. This, too, had been the main reason why the existence of a European commonwealth of nations had never been fully recognized or given an adequate institutional expression. For the development had eclipsed the existence of

Europe as a 'society of peoples', which in turn obscured the fact that the viability of any European state does not so much depend on its military power, or even on its juridical status as a sovereign state, but rather on its historic place in the structure of European society and its partnership in 'the European cultural community'. Consequently, the viability of an international European order required a revision of the modern conceptions of the external conditions of sovereignty. In this revision, Dawson argued that the medieval conception of Europe as a 'commonwealth of Christian peoples' was not only more adequate, but also 'more true to the historical and sociological realities' than the Renaissance ideal of absolute sovereignty and rationalized power politics which had dominated and divided modern Europe.[7]

This was a rare and lonely voice in the Anglo-Saxon world of the early 1950s, and with hindsight it is not difficult to understand why it met deaf ears. It was a voice crying in the wilderness: the voice of perhaps the last of the great historians who, in the works of Dom David Knowles, 'saw the development of Europe steadily and saw it whole'.[8] But above all it was the voice of the author of *The Making of Europe*, a brilliant and now regrettably neglected book subtitled 'An introduction to the history of European unity', without which Dawson's vision of the importance and significance of Europe and the European tradition would be impossible to understand.

II

A central reason for the reluctance of modern critics to be persuaded by Dawson's interpretation of European history is his insistence that the true 'making' of Europe should be located in the period AD 400–1000, in other words, the period that only until a few years ago was known as 'the Dark Ages'. What could modern, cosmopolitan Europe, the champion of secular, liberal democracy, possibly derive from this remote and obscure period? Were not the Renaissance and the Reformation, the Enlightenment and the social revolutions much closer and more fundamental to the foundations of Europe as we know it today?

Dawson, of course, was far from belittling or disregarding the importance of these movements, and he addressed them specifically and at length in subsequent learned works.[9] But his vision was much wider and all-encompassing, while his emphasis on the importance of the spiritual element in culture allowed him to see with staggering and unrivalled lucidity that all the elements that are fundamental to what we understand as Europe today were not only present, but already expressed in a genuinely European consciousness, by the eleventh century. To ignore this formative period in European history was, therefore, not only misleading but fundamentally erroneous, particularly when it went hand in hand with the modern cult of nationalism and its distortion of the common cultural and spiritual inheritance of Europe. For Europe, however familiar the term might be, was a particularly elusive notion. 'From the geographical point of view', Dawson writes,

> Europe is simply the north western prolongation of Asia and possesses less physical unity than India or China or Siberia. Anthropologically it is a medley of races, and the European type of man represents a social rather than a racial unity. And even in culture the unity of Europe is not the foundation and starting point of European history, but the ultimate and unattained goal towards which it has striven for more than a thousand years.[10]

This last point is important, particularly in the context of a number of criticisms that were levelled against Dawson for allegedly exaggerating the notion of European unity along the lines of the nineteenth-century romantics who looked back to medieval Christendom as a golden age of religious fervour and unity.[11] That Dawson thought European unity to be important did not mean that he conceived it as an objective and quantifiable reality. European unity was 'the ultimate and unattained goal'; a goal, however, that was at the centre of the organic development of that complex and diversified cultural tradition to which he was profoundly conscious of belonging.

In *The Making of Europe* Dawson singles out four fundamental elements in the formation of Europe, without which no notion of European unity could begin to make sense. The first of these is the Roman Empire. It was to Rome that Europe was

indebted for the preservation and transmission of the civilization of ancient Greece, from which all the most distinctive
elements in Western culture derive – science, philosophy,
literature, art, political thought and ideas of law and freedom.
And it was to Rome too, and particularly to the work of Julius
Caesar, that continental Europe owed its incorporation into the
Mediterranean cultural unity. Thus, from Rome Europe
inherited a sense of unity based on common laws and a common
culture, as well as a notion of universalism where the local
citizenships and allegiances might be subordinated to the wider
membership captured in the notion of the *oecumene*, which
viewed the empire as the representative of civilization, justice
and freedom.[12]

Now Rome had won her empire by her genius for military
and political organization, which led to a high level of material
culture and to an admirable development of public spirit on
the part of the citizens, but the process was also accompanied
by the virtual disappearance of the religious element which had
inspired the civic patriotism of the fifth and sixth centuries BC.
The culture of the empire had become almost entirely
secularized, and the proliferation of mystery religions is proof
of the religious vacuum that led people to seek spiritual life
outside contemporary society. Into this ailing world, Christianity
came as a breath of fresh air. The new religion derived its
strength from a sense of historic continuity with the Jewish
tradition and of social solidarity. It appealed to the poor, the
oppressed, the underprivileged and to all those who revolted
against the spiritual emptiness and corruption of the age. It
thus became the focus of the forces of opposition to the *status
quo* in a much more effective way than any political or economic
movement. It found inspired expression in the Apocalypse and
in a passionate exaltation of the ideal of martyrdom which
became the ultimate stronghold of spiritual freedom and
'rendered plain the fact that Christianity was the one remaining
power that could not be absorbed'.[13]

But in the Catholic Church the Christian religion also
possessed a system of ecclesiastical organization and a principle
of social authority without which the new religion would in all
likelihood have been drawn into the emerging religious

syncretism that characterized Gnosticism and Zoroastrianism. These special characteristics allowed the Catholic Church under the later empire gradually to take the place of the old civic organization as the organ of popular consciousness. It is no accident that the bishops soon became the most important figures in city life as the representatives of the community.[14]

Thus, Dawson singled out the Catholic Church as the second fundamental element in the making of Europe. But at no stage did he lose sight of the significance and vitality of the Eastern Christian tradition, as expressed in the monastic movement, the new liturgical poetry and art and, above all, in the Greek philosophical culture and the scientific theological systems that it inspired. It was thanks to the work of the Greek fathers that 'the Church was able to formulate a profound and exact intellectual statement of Christian doctrine and to avoid the danger of an unintelligent traditionalism on the one hand, and on the other, that of a superficial rationalisation of Christianity, such as we find in Arianism'.[15] This Greek tradition was introduced into the West by the Latin Fathers who, with the exception of St Augustine, remained essentially the pupils of the Greeks. Nevertheless, they contributed an element of moral strength and social discipline which brought theology into line with the cause of tradition and unity. This gave the Latin Church enormous resilience, and when the empire fell the Western Church remained, while in Byzantium the Church lost its unity as a result of the reaction of the oriental nationalities to the centralization of the State.

Apart from providing a principle of unity, therefore, in the West the Catholic Church became to the Classical tradition what Rome had been to the tradition of ancient Greece. But the Classical tradition was an independent element which Dawson singles out as the third fundamental constituent in the making of Europe. 'If Europe owes its political existence to the Roman Empire and its spiritual unity to the Catholic Church', he writes, 'it is indebted for its intellectual culture to a third factor – the Classical tradition', which has been the constant foundation of western letters and western sciences.[16] For this reason, the reconciliation of Christianity and the Classical tradition between the third and the fifth centuries, which

Dawson recounts with incomparable learning and elegance, had a profound effect upon the formation of the European mind. Without it, Europe would have had no tradition of secular learning, no secular literature (save that of the minstrel and the saga writer), and none of the elements that led to the development of its characteristically rational and critical attitude to life and nature.

The three elements mentioned so far were the *formative* influences which shaped the material of Europe. The *material* itself was to be found in what Dawson called 'the obscure chaos of the barbarian world'. This characterization might seem unacceptable to our 'politically correct' age. Yet Dawson was in fact one of the first historians to assess the importance of the barbarians in the formation of Europe. Far from being a passive and negative background for the creative activities of the higher culture of the Mediterranean, the barbarian peoples had their own cultural traditions which stretched back to the Bronze Age and which became fundamental to European culture. To give but one example, the principle of kinship, as opposed to citizenship and the emphasis on the authority of the State, contributed to the development of the European ideals of personal freedom and self-respect based on a spirit of loyalty and devotion to the community. Thus the barbarians, whom Dawson calls the *gentes*, as opposed to the *imperium* and the *ecclesia*, became the fourth element in the making of Europe: the source of the national element in European life.[17] And what we know as Europe today emerged out of the laborious fusion of these four elements – the Roman Empire representing the political element, the Catholic Church the spiritual, while the intellectual and the local elements were represented respectively by the Classical tradition and the barbarian nationalities.

Dawson dedicated the last chapters of *The Making of Europe* to explaining the consolidation of this process of fusion, a process already discernible in a preliminary stage in Gaul at the time of Clovis and St Gregory of Tours. In this, the importance of the rise and expansion of monasticism would be difficult to exaggerate. For the primarily urban nature of Western Christianity – in sharp contrast with the situation in the East where the peasants were, if anything, more Christian than townspeople – contained a danger of secularization to which the bishops were especially prone. Monasticism thus became the new order that allowed Christianity to permeate the countryside. In a remarkable way, the monastery came to replace the bishopric throughout Celtic Europe and the development led to a unique fusion between the Church and the Celtic tribal society where the hierarchical episcopacy was completely subordinated to the monastic system. The impulse that this process gave to monastic activity can be gauged from the indelible traces that the wandering Irish monks of the sixth and seventh centuries left throughout central Europe. 'The successors of the martyrs were the ascetics',[18] writes Dawson, and their presence must have impressed the mind of the European peasants with the sense of a new power that was stronger than the nature spirits of the old religion. Indeed, it is remarkable that it is just in those regions where the external survival of pagan customs was most noticeable, as in Brittany and the Tyrol, that the Christian ethos affected the life of the peasant most deeply. And it was precisely this continuity between the new and the old, involving the Christianization of sacred sites and menhirs, which opened the peasant mind to Christian influences that it could not receive in any other way.[19]

But it was above all St Benedict who 'applied the Latin genius for order and law to the monastic institution and completed that socialization of monastic life that had been begun by St Pachomius and St Basil'.[20] The influence of Benedictine monasticism, which also inherited the learned tradition of the Roman civil service, whose best representative is Cassiodorus, is especially clear in the Anglo-Saxon culture of the seventh century. The establishment of monasticism in the north of England under St Wilfrid and St Benedict Biscop marks the beginning of the new Anglian[21] art and culture, a genuinely original movement and yet equally indebted to Celtic monasticism and to the Roman Benedictine mission. And it was from here that the conversion of Germany and the reformation of the Frankish Church were undertaken. The Anglo-Saxon influence, in fact, is responsible for the first beginnings of a vernacular culture in Germany. The very idea of a vernacular culture was alien to the traditions of the continental Church and was the characteristic product of the Christian cultures of England and Ireland, whence it was transmitted to the continent by the missionary activity of the eighth century. It was thus the Anglo-Saxon monks, and above all St Boniface of Crediton – a man, writes Dawson, who 'had a deeper influence on the history of Europe than any other Englishman who has ever lived'[22] – who 'first realised that union of Teutonic initiative and Latin order which is the source of the whole mediaeval development of culture'.[23]

The process found its most characteristic expression in the Carolingian period, whose ideal of unity Dawson regarded as 'the foundation and starting point of the whole development of medieval Western civilization',[24] an opinion which triggered the most recurrent criticisms of *The Making of Europe*. And indeed, when read out of context, some of Dawson's opinions about the period do seem somewhat overstated. At the beginning of chapter 12, for instance, we read:

> The ideal of the medieval empire, the political position of the papacy, the German hegemony in Italy and the expansion of Germany to the east, the fundamental institutions of medieval society both in Church and State, and the incorporation of the classical tradition in medieval culture – all have their basis in the history of the Carolingian period.[25]

In its proper context, however, the judgement is perfectly balanced. For Dawson was under no illusion about the weakness and intrinsic fragility of the Carolingian empire, a 'shapeless and unorganised mass with no urban nerve-centres and no circulation of economic life', which had 'more in common with the ephemeral empires of the Huns and the Avars and the West Turks than with Rome' and which transformed the Augustinian ideal of the City of God into 'something dangerously similar to a Christian version of Islam with Charles as the Commander of the Faithful'.[26]

The importance of the Carolingian period lay not in its political or economic or even its cultural achievements, but rather in its embodiment and representation of an ideal of unity which already incorporated the four elements which Dawson singled out as fundamental to the making of the European tradition. This ideal survived the collapse of the empire and the second 'dark age', and it re-emerged when Otto I recovered the Carolingian tradition and united it with the tribal patriotism of the Saxons. His coronation in 961 brought northern Europe once more into contact with the world of the Mediterranean and initiated a process whereby the empire became less Saxon and more international. Otto married the Burgundian-Italian Adelaide and Otto II the Greek princess Theophano. Thus, by the time of Otto III, the emperor could claim to unite in his person the twofold tradition of the Christian empire in its Carolingian and Byzantine forms. Although Otto III's close collaboration with Pope Sylvester II, with a view to carrying out the renewal of the empire and the restoration of Rome to its rightful place as the centre of Christendom, was of little political importance, it had enormous historical significance, for it marked 'the emergence of a new European consciousness'. In Dawson's words

> All the forces that went to make up the unity of medieval Europe are represented in it: the Byzantine and Carolingian traditions of the Christian Empire and the ecclesiastical universalism of the papacy, the spiritual ideals of monastic reformers . . . and the missionary spirit of St Adalbert, the Carolingian humanism of Gerbert and the national devotion of Italians like Leo of Vercelli to the Roman idea . . . It looks back to St Augustine and Justinian and forward to Dante and the Renaissance.[27]

From the practical point of view, moreover, the results were not entirely sterile; for the short years of Otto and Sylvester's joint rule saw the rise of the new Christian peoples of Eastern Europe. It was at this time that the Poles and the Hungarians were freed from their dependence on the German church-state and given their own ecclesiastical organization, which was the indispensable condition for the independence of their national culture. The unity of Christendom, therefore, was not conceived as the unity of an imperialist autocracy. Christendom was essentially a society of free peoples under the presidency of pope and emperor; and whereas hitherto conversion to Christianity had been inseparable from political dependence and the consequent destruction of the national traditions, the close of the tenth century saw the birth of a new series of Christian states extending from Scandinavia to the Danube. In this way, by the beginning of the eleventh century the foundations of the modern world by the formation of that society of peoples which we know as Europe were already firmly laid.[28]

III

The Making of Europe does not bring us very close to the modern world of secular nation-states and liberal democracies. But it does allow us to reach a more adequate understanding of Dawson's devastating criticisms of the nationalist interpretations of European history and of the unrestricted development of the principle of sovereignty. For, much more than a collection of independent and sovereign nation-states, Europe 'is the most interdependent and interrelated group of states that exists'; and 'this diversity and interdependence has always been an essential condition of European culture and the source of its strength as well as of its weakness'.[29] 'In old Europe', Dawson continues,

> the status of the lesser states did not depend merely on their military and economic resources but on their historic rights and their cultural achievements. For in Europe the centres of power and the centres of culture did not necessarily correspond . . . the main artery of European life was not dominated by any great state, but passed through a series of small independent states and confederations from the Italian city-states in the south to the United Provinces in the north, with the Swiss Confederation dominating the mountain barrier in the centre . . . the cities that were most characteristically European, with the exception of Paris, were not the capitals . . . but the independent or semi-independent centres, like Rome and Florence, Geneva, Zürich and Basle, Augsburg and Nuremberg, Ghent and Bruges, Leiden and Amsterdam, Bremen and Lübeck, and, far to the east, Novgorod, the last representative of free Russia . . .
>
> And this tradition of pluralism and diversity is still maintained . . . by the smaller states, which therefore represent a far more important element in European civilization than we can assess by material standards.[30]

Consequently, the cornerstone of any reconstitution of Europe must be 'the rights and responsibilities of the relatively small peoples, which form the most typically European units and on which the future of European culture so largely depends'.[31]

This was far from being the narrow or romantic vision of Europe that some of Dawson's critics thought he was proposing. Nor was it especially 'Eurocentric'. It is true that Dawson had centred his account of the rise of European unity in the Latin West, but, as we have seen, this was because it had been in the West, and especially during the Carolingian period, that a fusion of the four elements that he had singled out as fundamental to the 'making' of Europe had been achieved. Meanwhile in Byzantium, the stress on centralization and the development of a state-church (a process which Dawson put in the context of similar developments in contemporary Eastern civilizations – e.g. the Sassanian Persians among whom Zoroastrianism became the religion of the State), led to the alienation of the eastern provinces, which in turn contributed to the great social and spiritual changes from which Islam was to emerge.

But nowhere did Dawson lose sight of the importance and significance of the Byzantine and Islamic traditions, to which he dedicated one-third of *The Making of Europe*. He underlined, for instance, that Byzantine culture was far from being a mere decadent survival from the Classical past, as Gibbon had claimed, but that it was 'a new creation, which forms the background of the whole development of mediaeval culture, and to some extent, even that of Islam'.[32] It is true that it was primarily in the sphere of religion and art, rather than in that of its political and social achievements, that the importance of Byzantium lay. But it was also in Byzantium that the survival of secular culture and the scientific tradition that would eventually come to the West through Islam found their origin. Consequently Dawson repeatedly emphasized the importance of the contact between the medieval culture of the Latin West and the 'higher civilisation' of the Islamic and the Byzantine worlds as 'a decisive influence on Western Europe and one of the most important elements in mediaeval culture'.[33] Without it there would have been no aristocratic courtly culture, no assimilation of the Graeco-Arabic science and a much poorer vernacular literature.[34] Moreover, these influences continued in the ascendant until they were checked by the Renaissance and by the Turkish invasion which brought about the final separation of Western Europe from the Islamic world, just at the time when the medieval unity was beginning to wane.

Now it is true that with the passing of the medieval unity and the shift from the Mediterranean to the Atlantic, Western culture became more autonomous, more self-sufficient and more 'occidental' than ever before, so that it is understandable that most historians should see this period as much more relevant to the modern situation than that covered by *The Making of Europe*. Moreover, a real and effective cultural unity was kept very much alive after the division of Christendom through a firm allegiance to the Classical tradition and humanism. And this secular cultural tradition is naturally more appealing to the modern mind than the religious tradition of Christianity. Already by the early eighteenth century, the latter had been rendered increasingly less persuasive as a result of the post-Reformation doctrinal hardenings and the subsequent wars of religion which inevitably weakened religious convictions before the self-confident rationalism of an emerging lay intellectual tradition.

Yet Dawson also saw in this process a sharp dualism between religion and culture which was at the root of the secularization, and consequently the devitalization, of Western culture,[35] and which was 'largely responsible for the separation of higher education from its spiritual roots in the life of people, so that our idea of culture has become a sublimated abstraction instead of the expression of a living tradition which animates the whole society and unites the present and the past'.[36] However reluctant to admit it, Europeans have been conscious of the inadequacy of this situation for more than a century. Matthew Arnold in England, Renan and Saint-Beuve in France, and even Americans like Emerson and Henry James and Henry Adams, were all profoundly conscious of the mutilation and impoverishment that the acceptance of an exclusively secular and utilitarian outlook entailed. Yet, as genuine representatives of their time, they failed to transcend the dualism between religion and culture. Although they were aware of the importance of religion, they did not have a religious attitude to life, and thus they were unable to stand on common ground with ordinary people before the mystery of faith, as even the most high-brow of Christian teachers had done in the past. As Dawson put it, it is the mystery of faith which alone 'brings all men together at the heart of life and reduces the differences of culture to insignificance. Faith is therefore the beginning and end of Christian culture as it is the beginning and end of Christian morals.'[37]

Consequently, Dawson had no doubt that Europe could only achieve a reintegration of its cultural and spiritual heritage by restoring the Christian faith to its rightful place as the principle of cultural unity and the creator of moral values. And this was a problem of re-education in the widest sense of the word. For Christian education cannot be adequately conveyed through words or study alone, since it is not merely an initiation into a Christian way of life and thought, but, more fundamentally, an initiation into a new life and into a *mystery*. It has, therefore, always involved a discipline of the whole person; 'a process of catharsis and illumination which centred in the sacred mysteries, and which was embodied in a cycle of symbolism and liturgical action'.[38] Our modern education, and this includes religious education, has proved fundamentally defective here, for it conveys no sense of *revelation*. Above all it has lost sight of a fundamental ideal, shared by the Eastern and Western traditions, which regards contemplation and spiritual vision as 'the supreme end and justification of all human culture'. For 'all true religious teaching leads up to the contemplation of the divine mysteries, and where this is lacking, the whole culture becomes weakened and divided'.[39]

However impractical these considerations might seem to the modern mind, there can be little doubt that it is only through a religious attitude to life that proper grounds can be established for an effective reintegration of culture. And this is even more obvious today than when Dawson was writing, for the Europe of today has not only lost, but consciously disowned, any claims it might have had in the past to cultural or spiritual leadership. The cultural leitmotif of modern Europe, and indeed of the modern West *tout court*, is a secular pluralism based on a relativistic toleration of anything, so long as it does not threaten the values of liberal democracy. The obvious irony is that this kind of 'liberal' or 'secular fundamentalism' – which proved so patently inadequate during the Salman Rushdie affair[40] – is much more superficial and narrow, and indeed 'Eurocentric', than the acceptance of the historic reality of Christendom. For it is the product of a much more recent and superficial synthesis which, as Dawson wrote of the liberal-deist compromise of the nineteenth century, has only 'succeeded in uniting the etiolated ghost of historic Christianity with the phantasm of pseudo-scientific rationalism'.[41] Like its nineteenth-century counterpart, modern secular fundamentalism professes to base itself on purely rational grounds, when it really draws its spiritual vitality from the religious tradition that it rejects. It is 'neither truly religious nor completely rational', and thus it risks being 'rejected alike by the most living religious traditions and the most serious scientific thought of the age'.[42]

Without a religious attitude to life, moreover, there is little hope of meeting one of the most urgent challenges facing the Western world today: that of establishing a genuine and effective dialogue with non-European cultures. As Dawson insisted, 'it is only when the religions of different cultures come into touch with one another . . . that real contact is made with the spirit of the alien culture'.[43] This was far from being a pious hope. It was based on a lifetime of dedicated, sympathetic and profound study of the religious foundations of human culture from prehistoric to modern times. If one thing is becoming increasingly clear, it is that the secularization of modern culture has done nothing to diminish the religious instincts in human nature. If left unsatisfied, they will seek expression either in a rejection of the Christian tradition which bows to the apparently stronger and more vital traditions of Hinduism and Islam, or in more narrow threatening movements which revert to a superficial paganism or even to irrational fanaticism. But such phenomena could only occur in a context of profound ignorance among the peoples of the West, and among Christians in particular, about the vitality and richness of their sacred tradition. As an antidote to this danger, the work of Christopher Dawson is one of the most remarkable scholarly achievements in our age.

NOTES

1 Carl E. Schorske, *Fin de siècle Vienna: Politics and Culture* (Cambridge, 1981 edn), p. xvii.

2 Ibid.

3 This was the most famous subject of a debate between Dawson and Lord (then Mr Alan) Bullock. On the term 'metahistory' Dawson writes: 'I take it that the term was coined on the analogy of Metaphysics . . . When Aristotle had written his books on Physics, he proceeded to discuss the ultimate concepts that underlie his physical theories: the nature of matter, the nature of being and the cause of motion and change. In the same way, Metahistory is concerned with the nature of history, the meaning of history and the cause and significance of historical change.' *History Today*, vol. I (June 1951), pp. 9–12.

4 Christopher Dawson, *Memories of a Victorian Childhood* (an autobiographical memoir first published under the title 'Tradition and Inheritance' in *The Wind and the Rain*, v & vii (Spring, 1949, no. 4; Summer, 1949, no. 1), p. 9.

5 Ibid., p. 27.

6 Ibid., pp. 10–11.

7 Christopher Dawson, *Understanding Europe* (London, 1952), pp. 59–64.

8 See his introduction to Dawson's *The Dividing of Christendom* (London, 1971).

9 The most significant of these are *The Dividing of Christendom* (London, 1971), which deals with the Renaissance and with the Reformation and its aftermath; *The Gods of Revolution* (London, 1972), a posthumous publication of his exceptionally perceptive, and regrettably unfinished, study of the French Revolution; *Understanding Europe* (London, 1952) and *The Movement of World Revolution* (London, 1959). Also of relevance are his wartime analyses of the European crisis: *Religion and the Modern State* (London 1936); *Beyond Politics* (London, 1939) and, above all, *The Judgement of the Nations* (London, 1943).

10 Christopher Dawson, *The Making of Europe* (London, 1932), hereafter *TME*, p. 3.

11 See, for example, Geoffrey Barraclough, *European Unity in Thought and Action* (London, 1961).

12 *TME*, pp. 3–24.

13 Ibid., p. 30.

14 Ibid., pp. 26–38; and see also 'St Augustine and his Age', in *Enquiries into Religion and Culture* (London, 1933), pp. 198–223.

15 *TME*, p. 40.

16 Ibid., p. 48.

17 Ibid., pp. 67–100.

18   Ibid., p. 196.
19   Ibid., pp. 200–4; on this see also Christopher Dawson, *Religion and the Rise of Western Culture* (London, 1950), pp. 32–43.
20   *TME*, p. 204.
21   Now more commonly referred to as Northumbrian.
22   *TME*, pp. 210–11.
23   Ibid., p. 213.
24   Ibid., p. 286.
25   Ibid., p. 214.
26   Ibid., pp. 256–7, 219.
27   Ibid., pp. 281–2.
28   Ibid., pp. 282–3.
29   *Understanding Europe*, p. 49.
30   Ibid., pp. 50–1.
31   Ibid., p. 64.
32   *TME*, p. 103.
33   Ibid., pp. 288–9.
34   These themes were treated in detail in *Medieval Religion* (London, 1934) and *Medieval Essays* (London and New York, 1953). See especially his essays on the scientific development and the origins of the romantic tradition. The oriental and Islamic elements in the rise of vernacular literatures is dealt with in *TME*, pp. 207–8: the Arab invasions brought an influx of refugees to the West 'who played somewhat the same part in the seventh century as the Greek refugees from Constantinople in the fifteenth'.
35   It is not possible to treat this aspect of Dawson's thought in this space. It is the central thesis which animates his whole work and it was admirably summarized in *Religion and Culture* (London, 1948). I have attempted a short summary of the thesis in 'A Vision to Regain? Reconsidering Christopher Dawson', *New Blackfriars*, vol. 70, no. 831 (October, 1989), pp. 437–49; see especially pp. 439–40.
36   *Understanding Europe*, p. 9.
37   Ibid., p. 250.
38   Ibid., pp. 243–4.
39   Ibid., pp. 244–7.
40   See, for example, Gavin D'Costa, 'Secular Discourse and the Clash of Faiths', *New Blackfriars*, vol. 71, no. 841 (October 1990), pp. 418–32.
41   *Progress and Religion* (London, 1929), p. 243.
42   Ibid.
43   *Religion and Culture* (London, 1948), p. 104. See also *The Age of the Gods* (London, 1928), p. xx.

4

Christopher Dawson and the Catholic idea of history

DERMOT QUINN

I

Christopher Dawson was this century's most distinguished English Catholic historian but for all his distinction he remains a puzzle. To examine his work is to become aware that paradox lies at the heart of it, that no simple statement captures the totality of his achievement. In an elegant revisionist essay, James Hitchcock has shown how consistently Dawson seems to confound expectations. Rural in taste, he was 'the most cosmopolitan of scholars';[1] devoutly English, he accepted a Harvard chair in late middle age, leaving his homeland; a critic of American industrialism and individualism,[2] he came to love America, and remains more admired there than in England; remote from intellectual companionship for much of his life and temperamentally anti-modern, he was daring in historical methodology; a conservative Christian, he acknowledged nevertheless the 'Kingship of Christ' as a principle 'of revolutionary importance for the political as well as the moral order'.[3] His variegated life, in other words, seems to resist the shapeliness of biography. The conventions are mocked by eccentricities; unexpectedness keeps breaking through. Dawson looks like the best kind of nonconformist: one who does not conform even to his own nonconformity.

These ambiguities do not exhaust his complexity. To call Dawson significant among Catholic historians is itself puzzling, and part of the puzzle has to do with a manner of thinking – call it 'Catholic history' – as much as the man himself. Certainly there is no doubt of his distinction. His Oxford tutor Ernest Barker thought him unequalled among those he had taught, 'a man and a scholar of the same sort of quality as Acton and Von Hügel'.[4] David Knowles thought him 'in his field the most distinguished Catholic thinker of this century'.[5] Yet the testimonials draw attention only to the fact that Dawson as historian is largely forgotten. Fashion has passed him by. Perhaps his insistence that religion lies at the heart of culture seems reductive or confessional. Perhaps the anti-modernism seems precious or overdone. Perhaps his belief in Europe as 'a spiritual unity [with a] common system of moral values'[6] is too Eurocentric for our Europhobic or multicultural day. More likely, though, is that fashion has passed him by because it never embraced him in the first place.

Indeed, Dawson seems not of this century at all. The comparison with Acton is apt: both private scholars devoted to large themes convinced that the study of history was a deeply moral enterprise. Yet the linkage with Acton seems to confer on him a Victorian *gravitas* separating him from contemporaries. Dawson came to maturity after the Great War, when the Actonian mind – confident, liberal, progressive, rational – had perished in the trenches. After Passchendaele and the Somme, the world grew suspicious of the politician as preacher, the historian as homilist. Dawson continued to see pattern in history long after others could only see absurdity. And in another sense he sits ill as an English historian. If history-writing discloses national style, then there is more Germany than England in him, more Mommsen than Maitland, more Spengler than Stubbs. Monographic miniaturism did not appeal to him: landscape did. His preoccupations were the nature of culture and civilization, progress and religion, the pattern of history itself: metaphysical questions far removed from *quo warranto*, the reign of King Stephen, and the rise of bastard feudalism. His methodology was always empirical: in that at least he was English. But 'metahistory' bulked much larger with him than others. It was in fact his stock-in-trade:

The academic historian is perfectly right [he wrote] in insisting on the importance of the techniques of historical criticism and research. But the mastery of these techniques will not produce great history, any more than a mastery of metrical technique will produce great poetry. For this something more is necessary. The experience of the great historians such as Tocqueville and Ranke leads me to believe that a universal metahistorical vision . . . partaking more of the nature of religious contemplation than of scientific generalisation lies very close to the source of their creative power.[7]

The defence bears examination. 'Universal metahistorical vision' sounds like the continental school at its vaporous worst. But fire is best fought with fire. Dawson knew whereof he spoke. Think of his criticism of Spengler, whose continentalism was matched only by his relativism.[8] Spengler's keenness to describe civilizations was unsustained by any belief in 'Civilization' itself. At bottom, he dissolved 'the unity of history into an unintelligible plurality of isolated and sterile cultural processes'.[9] Dawson's insistence on metahistory thus showed the flaws of that school better than simple reliance on empiricism which, for all its attractions, could never prove anything outside itself.

So far, then, a few puzzles. Dawson was an Englishman who wrote in the German manner; a nineteenth-century figure cast adrift in the twentieth; he was *rus in urbe*; a conservative revolutionary. They are all serviceable conceits. But the most telling paradox has yet to be explored. Dawson was a *Catholic* historian; and Catholicism lay at the core of his identity. What does this mean? At one level the implications seem clear. 'Catholic historian' implies both conjunction and contra-distinction. To be Catholic, to write *inter alia* of Catholic matters, to do so sympathetically but without abandonment of critical faculty: that seems unobjectionable, a conjunction without controversy. But contradistinction also lurks. Why speak of Catholic historian unless to suggest a double identity, a split loyalty? The Catholic follows different rules and answers to a higher judge, the argument goes. He pretends to be a pluralist but in the end only Mother Church matters. It is the old Augustinian anthem turned strident by secularism. But consider its assumptions. If there are indeed two cities as Augustine describes them, notice how odd that it is the secularist who demands (in the name of pluralism) that the Catholic should live in only one of them. In any divided loyalty, he asserts, sacred claims should be first abandoned, as making real pluralism impossible. But this is, of course, arbitrary, uncritical and itself anti-pluralist: not a double identity but a double standard. As an earlier writer put it,

> to demand from the ecclesiastical historian an absence of all antecedent views is not only entirely unreasonable, but an offence against historical objectivity . . . It could be maintained only to the hypothesis that the end of scientific investigation is not the discovery, but merely the seeking after truth without ever finding it . . . [a hypothesis] quite impossible to defend, for the assertion that supernatural truth, or even plain objective truth of any kind is beyond our reach, is itself an antecedent hypothesis.[10]

Before the Catholic historian need defend himself against charges of anti-pluralism, in short, he is entitled to demand a similar defence (if not an apology) from his accusers.

It is erroneous, then, to imagine 'Catholic history' as special pleading or the abrogration of critical judgement. That way lies poor history. More to the point, that way also lies poor Catholicism. In the first instance, the academic historian is 'perfectly right' to insist on techniques of historical criticism and research. Without them he is nothing. Dawson's point was that they were insufficient, not that they were unnecessary. Of course, this does not solve the dilemma of double loyalty, but reinforces it by implying the inadequacy of purely historical means of understanding history. But it does no injury to professional integrity to suggest that 'truth' may reside somewhere beyond empiricism. The Catholic holds a distinctive view of the world. That does not imply the impossibility of pluralism: logically, indeed, it implies its necessity. Nor is it reasonable to imply (as Kingsley famously did of Newman) that the Catholic is not interested in the truth as such. On the contrary, the Catholic shows his Catholicism by telling the truth. Should even this be doubted, then we must conclude that no conversation is possible between sacred and secular.

All of this ought to be obvious, and indeed if 'Catholic history' were only the chronicle of a people and their faith there would be no difficulty in employing conventional methods to make sense of it. Those methods are not 'positivist' but are simply applications of human reason to concrete problems. Nor should the charge of metahistory be a cause for alarm. As Hans Urs von Balthasar reminds us, the historian's quest is that of Everyman: 'to grasp things by distinguishing . . . the factual, singular, sensible, concrete and contingent [from] the necessary and universal . . . which has the validity of a law rising above the individual case and determining it'.[11] Thus any discrete historical statement contains a statement about history itself: only in that way does it become persuasive. Likewise the historian who has not generalized has not said anything at all. He has gathered facts mistakenly believing they speak for themselves. The particular and universal do not exist as separate elements but are intimately joined in every historical moment. The question of historical laws arises from this. Between the radical view that there are no historical laws and the equally radical view that all history is ruled by laws, the Catholic historian steers a middle way. On the one hand, the denial of historical law falls retortively: to claim there are no historical laws itself amounts to one. But this in itself does not justify the grandiose historicism of (say) Hegel or Marx, for any scheme which attempts to understand the particular with an elaborate architecture of 'laws' or 'forces' often denies the very particularity it seeks to explain.

Is this, then, the distinctive problem of 'Catholic history'? No. To account for contingency within teleology is not a peculiarly Catholic problem. Even historians who deny design face that difficulty: their anti-teleology is equally schematic, their radical contingency equally a statement about historicity and thus history itself. The Catholic historian's problem is rather his providentialism. He must make a case for design, also for divine purpose enshrined in it. This is possible, but the messiness of history often gets in the way. Think of Bishop Bossuet, whose great scheme of universal history 'drawn from Holy Scripture' achieved harmony only at the expense of historical particularity. The result was unsatisfactory, not only from the historian's but also from the theologian's point of view. In deposing contingency, the concreteness of the here-and-now, he deposed history itself, thus injuring his own incarnational scheme. Christ did indeed become Lord of history but it was an empty domain, a meaningless sovereignty. Bossuet seemed to regard history as a drama whose outcome was already known, and history-writing as a branch of apologetics which had to apologize for nothing. His teleology required a knowingness that was too optimistic and a determinism that was too pessimistic. It is a trap which still awaits the unwary.

This is not to say that providential history is impossible. On the contrary, such a reading poses difficulty precisely because it is necessary. Without acknowledgement that Christ is Lord of history, that all history is summed up and takes its meaning from the Incarnation, the Catholic historian differs in no significant way from the secular historian who attempts to write universal history from a purely material perspective. But if the Catholic sees history as revelation of a divine economy of salvation, then his project has become theological. Crucially, however, this does not annihilate historical norms or methods. As von Balthasar reminds us, 'we cannot allow the secular disciplines to be absorbed by theology as though it alone were competent in all cases because Christ alone is the norm. Precisely because Christ is the absolute he remains incommensurate with the norms of this world'.[12] The task of the Catholic historian is thus not to write 'good history' either from a Catholic or non-Catholic perspective: it is rather to decide the extent to which his historical project is more or less open to theological norms which he acknowledges in acknowledging his Catholicity. Perhaps Bossuet's failure was the failure to distinguish properly between the two, to the disappointment of both.

II

These, then, are the problems Christopher Dawson poses. But to understand Dawson the historian we must understand Dawson the man. The two did not exist separately but were integrated at a profound level of his personality. Yet he makes severe demands of the biographer, who must fashion a story from the slender excitements of provincial scholarship and decent obscurity. Dawson's life is a study in anonymity. Bookish youth, Oxford, exiguous existence in Exeter for a while, back to Yorkshire as a scribbling squire, Harvard at the end: hardly the stuff of Richard Hannay or Dornford Yates. Yet a life so solitary and so resolutely of the mind yields its own evidence. Books and articles reveal both the contours of a sensibility and the experiences which formed it. The writings themselves provide the autobiography. We are fortunate, too, that Christina Scott has provided a superb account of her father. In it, she records Dawson's earliest memories of Hay-on-Wye and Yorkshire, of landscapes shot through with history. As a child he 'liked the freedom and absence of restraint in the wild moorland country', as if the very wilderness linked him to the world of myth and legend. That mythic world – 'half history and half poetry' – formed a landscape powerful in its appeal. He seemed to see in it 'the old road which carries us back not merely for centuries but for thousands of years; the road by which every people has travelled and from which the beginnings of every literature have come'.[13] So it was that he came to acquire a 'love of history [and an] interest in the differences of cultures'.[14] His imagination was primarily visual. History was not an abstraction but a thing to be seen, in churches and graves, in the soil itself. This is surely suggestive. He became a visionary historian, imaginatively aware of great movements of people and civilizations, because he began as a visual one. To adapt the poet Thomas Hardy, 'he was a man who used to notice such things'.

No subsequent reflection eradicated this experience of history as a tangible thing. 'The past does not die', he was fond of quoting from St Augustine. 'It becomes incorporated in humanity.'[15] Here was an almost mystical sense that, in the face of 'laws of history' which explained or explained away the past, 'there always remains an irreducible element of mystery'.[16] It began in the imaginative world of childhood and was linked to a powerful intellect which, in exploring connections between landscape and history, also intuited a relationship between time and eternity. Dawson's career in Oxford (a virtually autodidactic one) refined his intellect. So also did conversion to Catholicism, which owed much to a historical temper engaged by the drama of the Christian past given actuality in the Christian present.[17] After Oxford, the turn of his mind became more contemplative.

'I found [him] full of mysticism and history', wrote his friend
E. I. Watkin, 'busy with an essay on the religious significance of
history'.[18] 'He finds in revelation', Watkin added, 'the necessary
key to the interpretation of history.' Notice the interplay of two
ideas: revelation alone as making sense of history, history itself
as part of unfolding revelation.

Dawson never abandoned these preoccupations: on the one
hand, the relationship between culture and religion, on the
other the role of revelation in history and history in revelation.
From *The Age of the Gods* in 1929 to *The Gods of Revolution* in
1972, published two years after his death, they constituted a
life's work. With Acton he held that religion offered the key to
history. No other principle – economic, social, cultural –
matched its explanatory power. 'However far back we go in the
history of the race, we can never find a time or place where man
was not conscious of the soul and of a divine power on which his
life depended.'[19] Moreover, religion was the key to culture: the
extent to which a culture secularized was the extent of its
decline. Dawson avoided the claim that longevity alone provided
proof of religious truths. Nor did he conflate numinosity – a
vague impulse to spirituality – with religion itself. But the sheer
scale of the religious experience of man moved him greatly: 'a
massive, objective, unquestioned power that entered into
everything and impressed its mark on the external as well as the
internal world'.[20] It gave a kind of insurance that 'however dark
the prospect' there was sense in the senselessness, pattern in
the chaos.[21]

This quest for a universal historical principle is evident in all
of Dawson. One idea – one word – runs through his work as a
leitmotif: 'unity'. The writing is suffused with language of
harmony and consonance, a symphonic sense of history as a
dance to the music of time requiring overarching melody to
save it from cacophony. Look at *Progress and Religion* (1929), his
most important book: 'The Nation as a Spiritual *Unit*'; 'cultural
units . . . [as ideas] dictated by material conditions'; 'religious
belief a source of *disunion*' after Descartes; 'the *unity* of
European culture re-established on the basis of international
science' in the eighteenth century; 'need of social and moral
unification' in contemporary Europe; 'intellectual and spiritual

disunion' since the Reformation; '*divorce* between religion and social life fatal to civilization'; 'Christianity and international *unity*'. Theme and variation are impossible to miss.

Why the preoccupation with unity? It represented a quest for the principle of integration. Societies and civilizations hold together: it is in their nature to do so. History, too, must be coherent, otherwise providentialism is absurd. And so, a unifier (and related unities) must be found. Four 'unities' engaged Dawson most: of society, culture, Europe and civilization. Each was important. Together they formed a fifth unity: history itself. As a schema, this had something of the confidence of the Great Chain of Being, that Elizabethan world-view wherein every object, smallest to greatest, found its place. Dawson's outline was less grand, but was every bit as assured. But what *was* the unifying principle? Dawson believed that religion supplied it:

> Every living culture must possess some spiritual dynamic, which provides the energy necessary for that sustained social effort which is civilization. Normally this dynamic is supplied by a religion, but in exceptional circumstances the religious impulse may disguise itself under philosophical or political forms.[22]

Epigrammatic, learned and serene, the insight was typical. It derived from three sources – knowledge of world religion, an anthropologist's ability to categorize types and forms, and recognition of the inadequacy of non-religious accounts of historical processes. Consider these sources for a moment. The scholarship was extraordinarily wide. Dawson was at home with Julian the Apostate and Julian of Norwich, the gospel of Mark and the gospel of Marx. He could range from the shamans of Siberia to the Pueblo Indians of Arizona, from Isis and Osiris to Confucius and Lao Tzu. There is a polymathic quality to his work which delights as it staggers. As for anthropology, that too was authoritative. Dawson wrote of totems and totemism, of cults and cultures, of higher and lower civilizations, of true and false religion, with great care. To be sure, he realized the theoretical deficiencies of anthropology, in particular its uncritical Darwinism and indifference to the actual processes of historical change. 'By and by anthropology will have the choice between being history and being nothing', he thought.[23] But his insights into primitive culture owed much to it. And it had another value. He saw how anthropology 'undermined Enlightenment assumptions in one important way – "primitive" beliefs could not merely be dismissed as absurd and irrational but were shown to have profound meaning within their particular cultures'.[24] Dawson's critics thought him anti-relativist, even anti-historical:[25] not so on this evidence. Primitive religion was an important rebuke to those who would deny man's spirituality. For all its 'obscurity and apparent illogicality'[26] it possessed depth and psychological richness where rationalism offered only hubris and superficiality. 'The higher [the rationalist] builds his tower of civilization the more top-heavy it becomes, for his nature remains essentially the same as that of primitive man.'[27]

I shall have more to say of the Enlightenment in a moment. Let us return to the theme of unity, particularly that of human societies. Dawson had a powerful sense that the stability of any human organization derived from its organic identity. It was a living thing. It has rhythm and seasonality. It grew slowly. It respected the constraints of human and physical geography. Listen to a passage from *Progress and Religion* in which Dawson examines the capacity of cities to lose economic and vital contact with their regions:

> [T]his process of urban degeneration . . . is one of the greatest sources of weakness in our modern European culture. Our civilization . . . has lost its roots and no longer possesses vital rhythm and balance . . . Just as a mechanical, industrial civilization will seek to eliminate all waste movements in work, so as to make the operative the perfect complement of his machine, so a vital civilization will cause every act to partake of vital grace and beauty . . . Why is a stockbroker less beautiful than a Homeric warrior? Because he is less incorporated with life; he is not inevitable, but accidental, almost parasitic. When a culture has proved its real needs and organized its vital functions, every office becomes beautiful.[28]

Much of Dawson is here: breadth, aesthetic sense, apparent anti-modernism, moral passion. 'The perfection of a culture', he argued, is 'measured by its correspondence with its environ-ment'.[29] That, by the way, was why urban industrial life seemed so false. 'The medieval artisan had no high standard of life', Dawson wrote, 'but at least he shared in the living organic life of his city; the gulf between his existence and that of the collier or cotton spinner of the later eighteenth century is almost that which separates civilization from barbarism'.[30]

This was unity at the simple level of a culture at home with itself. But unity was also about continuity and collective memory, the shared and conscious history of spiritual oneness by which great civilizations are known. Europe exhibited such unity, and Dawson devoted much of his writing to its examination. Making sense of Europe was indeed his significant achievement. But what *was* Europe? More, certainly, than a geographic expression:

> Europe is a community of peoples who share in a common spiritual tradition that had its origins 3,000 years ago in the Eastern Mediterranean and which has been transmitted from age to age and from people to people until it has come to overshadow the world . . . What we call 'Europe' in the cultural sense is really only one phase of this cultural development . . .[31]

Dawson's Europe was a society of regionally diverse, geographically mixed, historically variegated peoples. But there was nothing ramshackle about the diversity, nor any merely notional unity found in shared variety. The unity was a substantial thing. Its basis was the Christian Church. In no trivial sense the Church was Europe and Europe was the Church. Here was a spiritual confraternity transcending racial and political division, offering even in decline the *memory* of oneness, the *remembrance* of a common citizenship. 'What have we done with this inheritance?' Dawson used to ask. 'At least we have *had* it. It has been part of our own flesh and blood and the speech of our own tongue.'[32] That plangent longing which critics have heard in Dawson may be heard here, not however as nostalgia but as a call for action. As he wrote he saw threats to European unity in the form of war, totalitarianism and materialism. The rediscovery of Europe's spiritual identity was not historical reverie but a matter of urgent necessity.

Dawson made due acknowledgement of Europe's Greek roots. Without Platonism and its elaborations 'Europe' as an ideal would have been impossible. But Christianity above all changed Europe, turning a philosophically finite Hellenism into a culture with extraordinary powers of adaption, expansion, self-understanding, and capacity for the infinite. The Incarnation was all. Revelation was revolution. Both East and West were transformed by it. The manner of that transformation differed in each place. In the East (under the influence of Neo-platonism) the Incarnation was respiritualized, the Godhead losing the flesh it briefly assumed. In the West (influenced by Augustine) the spiritual order developed 'not as a static metaphysical principle, but as a dynamic force which manifests itself in human society'.[33] This Augustinian insight was profoundly important for the Christian Church, and pivotal for Dawson's understanding of the West. Through it, the integrity of Christianity as incarnational was preserved. Through it, the world of finite being could be understood not as static or illusory but as spiritually charged and dynamic.[34] Through it, a new social order could arise based on 'the only true citizenship . . . membership of the Church'.[35] Augustine showed through his understanding of Incarnation as an event in time and beyond time that Church and sacrament made manifest on earth a heavenly world of which they were both foretaste and fulfilment.

Dawson believed this spiritual oneness to have been most nearly achieved in the Europe of the Middle Ages. Medievalism bulks so large in his writing – and in criticism of it – that it is important to know what he meant by it. Simpler perhaps to say what he did *not* mean. It was not perfection, or heaven on earth, or 'some ideal pattern . . . by which existing societies can be judged'[36] or even especially pleasant.[37] It was, however, an age in which the implications of spiritual unity were worked out and made manifest in the life of a society. In the secular sphere, 'a new democratic spirit of brotherhood and social co-operation' arose, along with growth in communal and corporate activity. In the ecclesiastical sphere, the Church became responsible for education, art, literature, the care of the poor, the comfort of the dying: not institutional obligations but the duties felt by men towards men. Naturally so dominant an ideal could turn to theocracy. But medieval spirituality joyfully embraced the goal of Christian brotherhood: witness the writing of St Bernard, the life of St Francis. Separation between faith and life, or between the spiritual and the material was avoided, 'since the two worlds [had] become fused together in the living reality of practical experience'. Francis made that Augustinian fusion a reality, St Thomas gave it philosophical authority. It was Aquinas who recognized the autonomy of natural reason in epistemology, ethics, and politics, precisely because he recognized the incarnational implications of that autonomy. Dawson summarized his insights with economy and sympathy:

> [Man] is the point at which the world of spirit touches the world of sense, and it is through him and in him that the material creation attains to intelligibility and becomes enlightened and spiritualized ... Thus the Incarnation does not destroy or supersede nature. It is analogous and complementary to it, since it restores and extends man's natural function as the bond of union between the material and the spiritual worlds.[38]

This was the medievalism Dawson celebrated: an era and a people transformed by the power of the gospel. Here was no exercise in mere *pietas*, no lament for lost centuries. The importance of those centuries was 'not to be found in the external order they created or attempted to create, but in the internal change they brought about in the soul of Western man'.[39] Dawson loved Langland's great visionary poem *Piers Plowman*, thinking it 'the last . . . most uncompromising expression of the medieval ideal of the unity of religion and culture'. Notice the implication: culture was not swallowed up by religion but was transformed by it, religion was not swallowed up by culture but transformed and transcended it, so that Incarnation itself begins to be understood in and through culture, not apart from it.

> For Langland the other-world is always immediately present in every human relationship, and every man's daily life is organically bound up with the life of the Church. Thus every state of life in Christendom is a Christian life in the full sense – an extention of the life of Christ on earth. And the supernatural order of grace is founded and rooted in the natural order and the common life of humanity ... He realized more clearly than the poets and more intensely than the philosophers that religion was not a particular

way of life but the way of all life, and that the divine love which is 'the leader of the Lord's folk of heaven' is also the law of the life upon earth.[40]

Langland's eloquence is richly echoed in his expositor.

I have suggested that there were three grounds for Dawson's emphasis on religion as the basis of culture. So far we have looked at two: his knowledge of world religion, his ability to distinguish types and forms of religious or quasi-religious belief. Let us consider now the third: the inadequacy of non-religious explanations of historical processes, especially those offered by Enlightenment and post-Enlightenment thinking. Dawson was an exceptionally astute critic of the Enlightenment, primarily because the weapons he deployed against it – an appeal to reason and to history – were its own. His objection was that as an account of man and his world it was unpersuasive, and that it supplanted a far more persuasive one. It would not be difficult, in fact, so see the 'age of reason' as an age rather of multiple intellectual discontinuities. Consider a few of them. First came Descartes' divorce of mind and body which entailed a celebration of reason independent of physical existence, and truth independent of experience or authority.[41] Then came social contract theory's divorce of individual and 'society' which replaced communities with self-conscious states and created persons fearful for rights only when they realized they had them. And it continued. Hobbes summoned the omnipotent state to protect 'rights' and the protection was so complete the rights themselves disappeared. Locke separated the person from the body and the separation was so effectual that the individual 'owned' himself as a piece of property, presumably diminishing in personhood with amputation, tooth loss or encroaching baldness. Rousseau separated humanity from human beings and the chasm was so wide that the former was to be worshipped, the latter despised. There was something radically broken about all of this, as if a culture or a manner of thinking had become disconnected from its own source. Dawson captured it brilliantly. 'The abstract ideal of "civilization"', he suggested, 'took the place of the historic tradition of European culture . . . [The] concepts of Reason and Truth and Civilization [were used] as weapons to attack every truth and to undermine the foundations on which the . . . structure of European culture rested.'[42]

The division between Europe before and after the Enlightenment can be overdrawn, but one contrast captures the difference. Consider Thomism and Cartesianism. The first offered the Godhead in contemplation of itself. The second offered the mind in contemplation of nothing but itself: a startling declension. Dawson held, with good reason, that there stood only a short distance from Descartes to Robespierre's irrational worship of rationality[43] and Darwin's gloomy optimism. Take a memorable passage in which he showed how the confident ideal of perfectibility met its *quietus* in Natural Selection.

> The eighteenth-century philosophers, even . . . materialists, placed man in a category above and apart from the rest of nature. But the new evolutionary theory put man back into nature, and ascribed his development to the mechanical operation of the same blind forces which ruled the material world . . . It was a law of Progress, but blind non-ethical Progress in which suffering and death played a larger part than foresight or co-operation . . . [Thus] Cartesian reason, which had entered so triumphantly on its career of explaining nature and man to itself by its own unaided power, ended in a kind of rational suicide by explaining itself away.[44]

It was a striking phrase; versatile, too. The 'rational suicide' of Cartesianism did not end with the French Revolution or Darwinism but metastisized into new forms which sought to dispense with religion or replace it with quasi-religious ideology. One was nationalism. Another was liberalism. Both were dangerous. As for the first, Dawson saw how it could end in particularism 'even more dissolvent [of] the European tradition than the French Revolution itself'.[45] As for the second, it produced in its economic form extremes of wretchedness and wealth, in its political form an incoherent erastianism which replaced the confessional State with an anti-confessional one offering only conventional morality because convention itself had become the moral code. Dawson chronicled these pathologies with the grim knowingness of a man watching an accident about to happen. As he approached his own century he could see the secular impulse, the rationalist self-immolation, gallop towards insanity. In totalitarianism it reached its apogee as states attempted 'to eradicate the very roots of man's spiritual freedom and make society a smoothly functioning mechanism planned and controlled by experts in the name of social efficiency'.[46] The liberal alternative was little better. 'We can either remain in the half-way house of liberal democracy', Dawson urged, 'striving desperately to maintain the higher standards of economic life which are the main justification of our secularized culture; or we can return to the tradition on which Europe was founded and set about the immense task of the restoration of Christian culture'.[47] That was his final injunction, to his own world, and to ours.

III

This account of Dawson's historical understanding has been brief, perhaps bald. It should prompt in us, however, some broader reflections both on his vision of history and on the Catholic historical enterprise in general. Central to that vision – it should be obvious by now – was religion: 'the massive, objective, unquestioned power that entered into everything', and impressed its mark on everything. Now, this is controversial and Dawson's critics have not been slow to say so. What form does the criticism take and how powerful is it? We should distinguish two objections: the first resists *any* unifying historical principle; the second resists the particular principle, religion, that Dawson favours. The distinction is important but largely ignored by critics themselves. Thus, if they fall into the first category, they tend to deny metahistory but defeat themselves retortively, the argument itself being metahistorical; or (if they fall into the second) they deny religion only to replace it with some crypto-religion of their own, more often than not secular humanism.

But consider these twin criticisms more closely. Listen again to Dawson's unifying principle. Every living culture must possess some spiritual dynamic, he claims, normally supplied by a religion. In exceptional circumstances, however, the religious impulse may disguise itself under philosophical or political forms. There may be two kinds of circularity here. On the one hand, if Dawson is indeed steeped in the history of religion it may be that he overstates its importance to history: everything seen through that prism is distorted by it. On the other hand, it seems to allow him the claim that certain ideologies may be bastard religions (and open to criticism as such) while also preserving religion itself from the accusation of being a bastard ideology. These difficulties are not trivial: nor however are they insurmountable.

The first answers itself. That expertise should be proof of disproportionate understanding is an odd idea, indeed a circular one. Dawson emphasized the importance of religion in history not because he was steeped in it: he was steeped in it because it was important. The second criticism, however, needs careful examination. Perhaps its most sophisticated version was offered by Hayden White in 1958. White objected on five grounds to Dawson's entire project. First, he claimed Dawson was unwilling to admit that historical dialectic may proceed beyond a point reached by Christianity at a given stage of its development. Like an earlier version of Fukuyama and the 'end of history' school, Dawson offered the medieval Catholic Church as the only carrier of all that was genuinely spiritual in the West: after that history 'stopped' or went into decline.[48] A variant of this is that Dawson's construction of sociological types was flawed. 'For him', White argues, 'a civilization may be considered healthy only if and when it conforms to a type which existed at a given time and place . . . Those which have not developed . . . a priestly caste he dubs primitive; those which have rejected [one] he calls decadent.'[49] White's second objection is that 'Dawson's sociology of culture is not that at all but a sociology of religion'.[50] A third is that Dawson's schema (precisely, it seems, because it is schematic) fails to 'do full justice to the multiplicity of human creativity'.[51] The fourth objection is that Dawson denies secular culture any positive value. Finally, he argues that Dawson is really *anti-historical*, holding as he does that some 'insights into the historical picture . . . require special forms of understanding',[52] by which he meant, simply, that only Catholics could grasp the true meaning of European history.

What are we to make of this? It seems like a sober assessment, scrupulous in method and motive. In fact, much of it is wrong;

even wrongheaded. Some of it, to be sure, need not be taken
too seriously. To suggest that Dawson's sociology of culture is
nothing more than a sociology of religion seems to miss the
point rather comprehensively. Likewise the notion that he fails
to recognize the multiplicity of human creativity or – it amounts
to much the same thing – is inclined to disparage secular
culture. A glance at *Progress and Religion* might suggest otherwise. To conflate a unified historical schema with the multi-
fariousness of history itself is a category mistake which Dawson
avoided even as White did not. Equally curious is the claim
that Dawson made a fetish of medievalism, as if his work
were a long lament for a vanished Eden. But Christ was Lord
of *all* history. If history and culture are indeed incarnational,
then that kind of yearning is a kind of despair. After all,
nostalgia is simply Manichaeanism in a maudlin mood. Its
desire for a lost world is a contempt for earthly things, a loathing of the contemporary because a loathing of temporality
itself. The Christ who entered history entered all of it. 'We
see *again and again*', Dawson wrote, 'the miracle of divine
creativity and a new spiritual harvest springing from the old
soil of human nature'.[53] He was no nostalgist. He condemned
the cult of progress as a perversion of Enlightenment
perfectibility because he recognized it for what it was:
Manichaeanism in another guise – distaste for the here-and-
now expressed as a desire for the future rather than the past.
He did not desire the past because he despised the present. To
imagine that he regarded it as a museum wherein to take
residence as a form of escape is to misunderstand his notion of
history itself.

But White is wrongheaded as well as wrong. The pose of
academic neutrality conceals a highly partisan dissent
from Dawson's work, particularly its Catholicism. 'It is very
difficult for anyone who is not a Catholic', White quotes
Dawson as arguing, 'to understand the full meaning of
[European history]', 'full meaning' implying a truth requiring not human or historical ability but a special epistemological dispensation.[54] The logic is weak. 'Very difficult' is not
the same as 'impossible': on the contrary, it implies possibility.
That aside, it is clear that White, not Dawson, demands

epistemological privileges. Listen to the peroration, a parody of secular scientism:

> If earlier societies seemed better adjusted or more harmonious, it was because Church and State acted together to destroy individual responsibility rather than encourage it. For good or evil, modern science has broken through these older compulsives and offered to man responsibility for everything he does. Religion must offer, like science, philosophy, a truth that admits the possibility of revision. [Then] it will have no need of sedatives.

But this is incoherent. History itself is absolutized, granted authority it cannot possess. Historical judgement is deemed to be somehow self-ratifying, in need of no further argument or proof. In the same way as conventional morality collapses – because convention itself becomes the moral code – so historical understanding informed only by an absolutized 'History' is no understanding at all. To adopt the critic's own terminology, it becomes a truth that admits no possibility of revision, a species of historicism opening into an empty room. It creates the past as sanction or norm but provides no grounds other than itself for doing so. The historicist who argues for the invincible 'pastness' of the past renders meaningless any judgement – even that judgement – which he cares to make of it. If it *is* a foreign country, if they *really* do things differently there, the historian cannot know it or even know that he cannot know it.

The second charge of circularity thus falls in the same way as the first. Dawson does not invent religion as the key to historical processes, then discover bastard religion – ideology – as proof of the prior claim. On the contrary, he is careful in his definition of both, and in the evidence he offers for both; more careful than his critics. Besides, his notion of religion in history is more subtle than theirs. It is not the all-explainer of some crude determinist teleology – serving the function for the believer that economics (say) serves for the Marxist or the libido for the Freudian. If history is incarnational, then it is religiously charged in an entirely different way; and notions of past, present and future are obliterated in the central reality of Christ, Alpha and Omega, who is the Lord of all history.

And so we approach the heart of the matter. Dawson liked to quote Edmund Burke on the emptiness of historicism. 'Burke wrote very truly and finely', he said, 'that the so-called laws of history which attempt to subordinate the future to some kind of historical determinism are but the combinations of the human mind. There always remains an irreducible element of mystery.'[55] The point is well taken. As systems expand, so paradoxically they contract: the attempt to explain everything ends by explaining nothing. But where does this leave Dawson himself? Is not his own quest for a unifying principle equally objectionable? Not quite. The irreducible element of mystery which mocked the pretensions of determinists – and also became a dangerous gnosticism for anti-determinists – became for him a kind of epiphany: 'To the Christian the mystery of history is not completely dark, since it is a veil which only partially conceals the creative activity of spiritual forces and the operation of spiritual laws.'[56] Von Balthasar offers a similar insight. 'Any attempt to interpret history as a whole', he wrote, 'if it is not to succumb to gnostic myth, must posit some subject which works in and reveals itself [as] a being capable of providing general norms'. For him, as for Dawson, that subject is Christ, whose life is 'the norm of every historical life, and so of every history whatsoever'.[57]

Thus, we begin to grasp more completely Dawson's vision. It was shaped by that Augustinian sense of a past not dead but incorporated into all of humanity. At one level this seems like a call for metahistory, a simple acknowledgement that the Catholic historian necessarily does things differently:

> Whereas the secular historian is in no way committed to the cultures of the past, the Catholic, and indeed every Christian, is bound to recognize the existence of a transcendent supra-temporal element at work in history. The Church exists in history, but it transcends history so that each of its temporal manifestations has a super-natural value and significance. To the Catholic all the successive ages of the Church and all the forms of Christian culture form part of one living whole in which we still participate as a living reality.[58]

But there is more to this transcendence than meets the eye. The notion that history is not complete, that we participate in it and are creatively transformed by it, is as much theological as historical, though no less historical for being theological. As von Balthasar memorably puts it, 'all our destinies are interwoven; and until the last of us has lived, the significance of the first cannot be finally clear'.[59] For Dawson too, the 'communion of saints' was actual, not abstract. And as we participate in history we participate in the Christ who entered it and is Lord of it. But understand well what this means. The historical Christ is the norm of all history not simply because he is Christ but because he is historical. Historicity – the actual, the concrete, the particular – is not obliterated but given new meaning in him. Von Balthasar puts it thus: 'As the end of history, the *eschaton*, he is present at its centre, revealing in this one particular *kairos*, *this* historical moment, the meaning of every *kairos* that can ever be.'[60] But as Dawson reminds us 'God not only rules history, he intervenes as an actor in history'.[61] He is Lord of history but also Lord in history. Thus 'the meaning of history in Christ is not to be understood as though created nature had no immanent meaning, no intelligibility of its own, but only in Christ . . . [for otherwise] there could be no true incarnation, no possibility of God's becoming man'.[62] The logic of history is not suspended by him but acknowledged in the very act of his becoming historical.

Thus we end, as we began, in paradox. But some paradoxes are worthier than others. The puzzles of Dawson are only the puzzles of any decently complex life. Rusticity and urbanity, companionship and solitude, continuity and change: in truth they hold together perfectly well. Dawson the historian offers more impressive challenges – to the intellect, the imagination, even the soul. The measure of his achievement should not be in the poundage of books or papers or scholarship, formidable and abidingly important though these are. Rather it should be in a scale of a different sort. He proposed a real paradox, not a trivial one, and explored it with consummate skill: that for a historical faith the past is everything and yet, in another sense, it does not exist at all but is bound up in present and future, in the world that is and is to come. Its laws are human but also divinely touched, its meaning accessible to reason but also irreducibly mysterious. Such was his vision and his faith: such should be the vision of all Catholic historians.

NOTES

1 James Hitchcock, 'Christopher Dawson: A Reappraisal', in *The American Scholar*, vol. 62, 1993, p. 111.

2 That conjunction was itself paradoxical, as Dawson noticed: industrialism and individualism often cancel each other out.

3 Christopher Dawson, *The Sword of the Spirit* (Catholic wartime pamphlet), 1942, p. 4.

4 Quoted in Christina Scott, *A Historian and His World* (London, 1984), p. 110.

5 Ibid., p. 210.

6 Christopher Dawson, *Understanding Europe* (New York, 1960), p. 6.

7 Christopher Dawson, *The Problem of Metahistory* (1951).

8 Christopher Dawson, *Progress and Religion* (New York, 1929), p. 38.

9 Ibid., p. 43.

10 J. P. Kirsch, 'History', in *The Catholic Encyclopedia*, vol. VII (New York, 1910), p. 367.

11 Hans Urs von Balthasar, *A Theology of History* (New York, 1963), p. 5.

12 Ibid., p. 14.

13 Scott, *A Historian and His World*, p. 27.

14 Ibid., p. 15.

15 Quoted in ibid., p. 99.

16 Christopher Dawson, *The Historic Reality of Christian Culture* (New York, 1960), p. 18.

17 See Scott, *A Historian and His World*, p. 63. 'Like Newman his approach to Catholicism was through history. "The fathers made me a Catholic," Newman once wrote . . . and, on another occasion, "To be deep in history is to cease to be a Protestant" . . . that is, the cumulative evidence of the Christian past led him to a full acceptance of the Catholic present.'

18 Quoted in ibid., p. 57.

19 Dawson, *Religion and Culture* (London, 1948), p. 41.

20 Christopher Dawson, quoted in Scott, *A Historian and His World*, p. 15.

21 *The Sword of the Spirit*, p. 4.

22 Dawson, *Progress and Religion*, p. viii.

23 Ibid., p. 50.

24 James Hitchcock, 'Christopher Dawson: A Reappraisal', p. 112.

25 See, for example, Hayden V. White, 'Religion, Culture and Western Civilisation in Christopher Dawson', in *English Miscellany* (Rome, 1958), pp. 247–87.

26 John J. Mulloy, 'Christopher Dawson and a Christian Apologetic', in *The Dawson Newsletter*, Fall 1987, p. 3.

27 Christopher Dawson, *Religion and Culture*, p. 28, quoted in Mulloy, op. cit., p. 3.

28 Dawson, *Progress and Religion*, p. 68.

29 Ibid., p. x.

30 Christopher Dawson, *Dynamics of World History* (New York, 1957), p. 192.

31 Christopher Dawson, *Understanding Europe* (New York, 1960), p. 32.

32 Christopher Dawson, *Religion and the Rise of Western Culture* (London, 1950), p. 273.

33 Dawson, *Progress and Religion*, p. 164.

34 Ibid., p. 164.

35 Ibid., p. 166.

36 Christopher Dawson, *The Historic Reality of Christian Culture* (New York, 1960), p. 14.

37 Dawson, *Progress and Religion*, p. 167.

38 For this paragraph, see Dawson, *Progress and Religion*, pp. 168–75.

39 Christopher Dawson, *Religion and the Rise of Western Culture*, p. 274.

40 Ibid., pp. 270–2.

41 Dawson, *Progress and Religion*, p. 10.

42 Christopher Dawson, *Understanding Europe* (New York, 1960), p. 192.

43 Arnold Toynbee, Introduction to Christopher Dawson, *The Gods of Revolution* (London, 1985), p. x.

44 Dawson, *Progress and Religion*, pp. 18–22.

45 Dawson, *Understanding Europe*, p. 193.

46 Christopher Dawson, 'Newman and the Sword of the Spirit' (*The Sword of the Spirit*, August, 1945) in *The Dawson Newsletter*, Spring/Summer 1991, p. 13.

47 Christopher Dawson, *The Movement of World Revolution* (New York, 1959), p. 65.

48 White, 'Religion, Culture and Western Civilisation', p. 277.

49 Ibid., p. 278.

50 Ibid., p. 278.

51 Ibid., p. 281.

52 Ibid., p. 285.

53 Christopher Dawson, *The Historic Reality of Christian Culture*, p. 14.

54 White, 'Religion, Culture and Western Civilisation', p. 283.

55 Dawson, *The Historic Reality of Christian Culture*, p. 18.

56 Ibid., p. 18.

57 Hans Urs von Balthasar, *A Theology of History* (New York, 1963), p. 21.

58 Dawson, *The Historic Reality of Christian Culture*, p. 58.

59   Von Balthasar, *A Theology of History*, p. 73.
60   Ibid., p. 86.
61   Dawson, *The Sword of the Spirit*, p. 4.
62   Von Balthasar, *A Theology of History*, p. 112.

5

Dawson and 'economic man'

RUSSELL SPARKES

DAWSON'S ACHIEVEMENT

There is no doubting the magnitude and permanence of Dawson's achievement in mapping out the beginnings and growth of Europe. For roughly a thousand years, AD 400–1400, Europe meant Christendom, and Christendom was based on, though not identical to, the Catholic Church. A similar argument had been developed a few years earlier by Hilaire Belloc in *Europe and the Faith*, but whereas Belloc's book was based on rhetoric and assertion, Dawson's great works such as *The Making of Europe* are grounded in deep scholarship.

Yet the medieval period is alien to most of us now, and Dawson's thought can wrongly be put aside as of interest only to the specialist. In fact, his work has very real relevance to the problems facing us today, and it is on this basis that I want to examine his treatment of the very different culture of ancient Rome, which in its pagan flaunting of sexual depravity, contempt for human life, and worship of wealth and power has far closer parallels to the late twentieth century than anything which has come in between. Likewise, his analysis of the 'crisis of capitalism' in the 1930s can be regarded as a powerful critique today. We find ourselves in the apparent paradoxical position that we live in the 'triumph of free market capitalism', following the collapse of Communism, but that this triumph is associated with the disintegration of society. I find Dawson's

93

thought a useful guide as to why this is neither paradox nor coincidence.

This paper also aims to show some examples of Dawson's prescience. People like Shaw and Wells are generally thought of as the prophets of what was to come, but actually the majority of their forecasts were wrong. Dawson, on the other hand, like Chesterton before him, was rooted in the tradition and thought of the Church, and therefore his knowledge spanned centuries rather than a few years of this century. People are beginning to realize how accurate a prophet Chesterton was, but the same is true of Dawson, although this is not yet generally accepted. Lastly, I aim to introduce the simple figure of Piers Plowman, and what might have been.

In the 1920s and 1930s Dawson was one of the few Westerners to observe that classical economics is both intimately based on, and used as an argument for, liberalism in politics. (This had not escaped the notice of a German scribbler in the British Museum called Karl Marx.) Economics may claim to be a value-free science, although its larger assertions fail Karl Popper's touchstone of what constitutes a science, and its claimed area of influence becomes the larger as its forecasting ability and obvious usefulness seem to decline. (I note that a recent Nobel Prize for economics was awarded for a study analysing the family in terms of a cost benefit programme for each individual member!) As Dawson stated, 'Capitalism is nothing else but economic Liberalism, and . . . it has a very close relationship not only with political Liberalism, but also with liberal philosophy and liberal idealism'.[1] Such Liberal ideas seemed to disappear after the near collapse of capitalism in the 1930s, and the need for universal support for the 'people's war' in the 1940s. Yet they have re-emerged since the 1970s, emerging from the world of economics via Milton Friedman, and taken up by right-wing or free-market Conservatives in the UK, and neo-conservatives in the US. Of course, 'free markets' is nothing more than a translation of the phrase universally used in the nineteenth century, '*laissez-faire*', or 'let markets be free'.

The 'Golden Age' of classical *laissez-faire* economics was the nineteenth century. It was commonplace to note in the early part of that century that a Virginian slave planter had an interest in the health and well-being of his slaves, whereas a Lancashire mill owner was only concerned in getting labour as cheaply as possible – if workers became injured, there were always new ones who could be hired. Aquinas would have protested at the idea that an economic situation where a rich employer negotiates a wage with a poor man, who needs the wages that day to pay for his food and shelter, is or ever could be in any sense fair. In a startling parallel with our own time, women were found to be more docile and cheaper than men, who became 'unemployed' for the first time in history. The first survey of the factories in 1844 under the new Factory Act discovered that of 420,000 workers in the cotton mills, less than 100,000 were grown men, and 242,000 were women and girls, often working in the most appalling conditions. As the historian Sir Arthur Bryant noted, the promotion of *laissez-faire* ideas led to the idea of the poor as no longer people, but a mere factor of production which had to be worked hard if Malthus's fear of starvation for all was to be avoided:

> The most one could hope for was that the poor should be fed at all. Hardships suffered by them in the course of obtaining food were in reality blessings, since without them they and all mankind would starve. This belief was widely held by humane and enlightened reformers who were passionately anxious to eradicate ancient abuses, of which there were many, and to mitigate human suffering. The English individualists who subscribed with such uncritical zeal to the doctrine of *laissez-faire* in economic matters were among the world's greatest humanitarians ... These humanitarians rigidly opposed the infliction of all needless pain except in the factories and mines of England. For here, in their view, it could not be avoided.[2]

Hence thinkers like J. S. Mill were personally kind men who believed that the world had to be centred around money, and believed that if it was not based on the iron laws of *laissez-faire* capitalism, it would collapse into the mass starvation which Malthus had predicted. Thus these reformers replaced the old poor-law system of parish relief by that of the workhouse. The poor had to be punished for their need, and many of the old and the sick preferred death to the cruelty of the workhouse.

The liberal State claimed to be minimal, and treat all equally – a dubious claim, of course. As Dawson noted:

> [T]he liberal democratic ideal of absolute equality . . . ignores the very idea of status and regards society as a collection of identical units. But the result of this denial of status is not to make men really equal but only to leave them at the mercy of economic forces. A man is judged . . . by what he has, and since the worker has nothing he has no real share in the Capitalist state. Against this, Catholic social philosophy maintains that a man's rights depend not upon his wealth, but upon his social function.[3]

The modern economy seems to be rapidly overthrowing the post-war settlement, and reverting to a nineteenth-century model. Yet at the same time there is an explosion of sexual immorality, violence and crime which was unknown to the Victorians. Is the increased worship of wealth connected with the revival of paganism? Dawson's knowledge of history convinced him that it was so, but to demonstrate this we need to go back to the ancient world.

MONEY IN THE ANCIENT WORLD

> And what manner of government do you term oligarchy? A government resting on a valuation of property, in which the rich have power and the poor man is deprived of it.[4]

Some of the oldest books of the Old Testament on the Jubilee law and in Leviticus are concerned with the moral use of property. From the early days of the Church to the Reformation private property was sanctified as part of the community order, and there were strict prohibitions on such things as usury – charging an excessive rate of interest. This reached its intellectual height in the work of St Thomas Aquinas, but was part of a great tradition of Natural Law with God at the apex descending through man to the world. Man did not own the land, he was merely the steward of it, and his rights were defined in terms of the community. Four hundred years before Our Lord's birth, and at the very dawn of Western society, Plato wrestled with the problems of money and society. As he said then:

The accumulation of gold in the treasury of private individuals is the ruin of honest government; they invent illegal modes of expenditure; for what do they or their wives care about the law? And then one, seeing another grow rich, tries to rival him, and so the great mass of citizens become lovers of money, and so they grow richer and richer, and the more they think of making a fortune the less they think of goodness; for when riches and goodness are placed together in the scales of the balance, the one always rises as the other falls . . . And here is another defect . . . the inevitable division: such a State is not one, but two States, the one of the poor, the other of rich men; and they are living on the same spot and always conspiring against another.[5]

These considerations became very relevant in the following centuries, as the rise of the Roman Republic led to vast fortunes being created at the same time as a large mass of the urban poor. Since ancient Rome believed in absolute property rights, unrestricted by tradition, custom, or religion, the economic situation was perhaps more similar to the present time than the intervening centuries. We are well aware of the hatred of tax-collectors in the New Testament, and much of this was, of course, the natural resentment of paying taxes to an occupying power. Yet they were also hated for their venality. They were tax-farmers, who bought the right to collect taxes in an area (often corruptly), and then used all manner of extortion to make as much profit as possible for themselves. When cities could not pay, the tax-collector would advance the money at an extortionate rate of interest. We should remember that property rights included those over people as slaves. As Dawson wrote in *Enquiries into Religion and Culture* in his great chapter on 'St Augustine and his age',

[Rome] organised the world only to exploit it. Roman capitalists, money-lenders, slave-dealers and tax-gatherers descended on the East like a swarm of locusts and sucked the life out of the dependent communities. Every Roman, from the aristocratic capitalist like Brutus or Lucullus down to the meanest agent of the great financial corporations, had his share in the plunder. It is characteristic that Brutus, who was regarded in later times as a model of republican virtue, quarrelled with Cicero because the latter was forced to reduce the interest on Brutus's loans to the impoverished cities of Cilicia from 48 per cent to a beggarly 12 per cent! The age of the

Republic culminated in an orgy of economic exploitation which ruined the prosperity of the subject peoples and brought Rome herself to the verge of destruction. The crisis was averted by the foundation of the Empire.[6]

The Emperor was initially just a chief magistrate and head of the army, but as time went on he became increasingly a despotic ruler served by a huge bureaucracy, like the former empires of the East. 'Rome had done great things for the world . . . yet they had only been purchased by war and slavery and the oppression of the weak . . . and they had been used for evil rather than for good: to serve the senseless luxury of the rich and the brutal passions of the mob.'[7] The old Roman values of stoicism, patriotism, and pride in civic virtue slowly withered to be replaced by the pursuit of pleasure. At the very beginning of the Empire, the Stoic philosopher and historian Seneca deplored the unrestrained pursuit of wealth and pleasure, noting that appetite grows faster than enjoyment, and the result is world-weariness, despair, and sometimes a longing for death. Seneca may not have known the term 'Existentialism', but he was acquainted with those who 'do not want to live, and do not know how to die', who felt life to be totally meaningless and superficial. Two millennia before Freud, he spoke of unsatisfied desires leading to the *libido moriendi*, or death instinct.

The result was debauchery and brutality. The essence of paganism was not admiration of the ancient civic gods of Greece and Rome, nor admiration of the beauty of nature, but rather the worship of sexuality in all its most perverse and bizarre forms, of power and lust, and the inhuman savagery of the gladiator. Dawson quotes John Cowper Powys who felt the evil power of paganism in

> those symbols of pure lust on the sinister red-brick walls of the scoriac streets of ancient Pompeii; and you only have to enter one of the little Byzantine churches in Rome we know today to realize what a rainy dew of freshness must have fallen upon the jaded sexuality of the ancient world.[8]

Or as Chesterton put it:

> In the Roman Empire, long before the end, we find nature worship inevitably producing things against nature. Cases like that of Nero

have passed into proverb, when Sadism sat on a throne brazen in the broad daylight ... what had happened to the human imagination was that the whole world was coloured by dangerous and rapidly degenerating passions; by natural passions becoming unnatural passions. Thus the effect of treating sex as only one innocent natural thing was that every other innocent natural thing became soaked and sodden with sex ... the moment sex ceases to be a servant it becomes a master.[9]

We may briefly remember the Empress Messalina, who shocked the hardened whores of Rome, of Nero who became so bored with ordinary orgies that he forced his mother into incest before murdering her. We may remember the 'mystery religions', and Emperor Eglabalus who had an operation to make him both male and female. I do not mention this just to recoil at these horrors; it just seems no accident that, as in our own time, worship of money and of degeneracy are combined. The Church has always defined unrestrained sexual appetite as concupiscence, and we may define the essence of paganism as this, that it worshipped what the Church calls man's fallen nature. The good things of this world are limited in their physical enjoyment, but the potential appetite for sex and money are unique as potentially insatiable. It was also true that in belief and morals Rome was pluralistic and tolerant, but only as long as the beliefs were not firmly held. Gladstone noted 150 years ago:

> Rome, the mistress of state-craft, and beyond all other nations in the politic employment of religion, added without stint or scruple to her list of gods and goddesses, and consolidated her military empire by a skilful medley of all the religions of the world. Thus it continued while the worship of the Deity was but a conjecture or a contrivance; but ... the religion of Christ became, unlike other new creeds, an object of jealousy and of cruel persecution, because it would not consent to become a partner in this heterogeneous device, and planted itself upon truth, and not in the quicksand of opinion.[10]

Gladstone's words upon the 'quicksand of opinion' seem very relevant to a modern society desperately trying to rebuild ethics upon the shifting sands of individual self-interest, and again it is striking that a society based upon wealth and power used tolerance as a political device. Divide and rule indeed.

At the end of the fourth century St Augustine wrote in *De Civitate Dei*:

> They do not trouble about the moral degradation of the Empire; all that they ask is that it should be prosperous and secure. 'What concerns us', they say, 'is that everyone should be able to increase his wealth so that he can afford a lavish expenditure ... Let the poor serve the rich for the sake of their bellies and so that they can live in idleness under their protection ... Let the laws protect the rights of property and leave men's morals alone. Let there be plenty of public prostitutes for whosoever wants them ... Let there be gorgeous palaces and sumptuous banquets, where anybody can play and drink and gorge himself and be dissipated by day or night.[11]

Let me repeat one sentence: 'Let the laws protect the rights of property and leave men's morals alone.' Does it not sound like Milton Friedman or Margaret Thatcher? There are indeed many parallels between ancient Rome and modern industrial society. Like the modern West, ancient Rome was an urban society based on a money economy and the specialization of labour capable of producing artefacts of very high quality. If the modern world has virtually unlimited mechanical power, the ancient world had the practically unlimited supply of slave labour. Like the modern era, it facilitated the production of large quantities of industrial goods traded over a large geographic area. Finally, and probably most relevantly, ancient Rome believed in absolute property rights, the latter a concept alien outside Western Europe, and believed to be illegitimate there until the Enlightenment of the eighteenth century.

The late Empire's political and economic problems may also have relevance for modern times. Having been partially reversed in the early Empire, the trend towards a concentration of wealth in the hands of a few accelerated in the late Imperial period. The era also saw declining economic output and high inflation, with money almost becoming worthless; this combination was not seen again in the West for another 1600 years, when economists proclaimed the 'stagflation' of the 1970s a unique occurrence in human history. The political establishment became regarded as increasingly venal and irrelevant to most men's problems; educated gentlemen like Ausonius retreated to their estates. What political authority there was increasingly derived from the moral authority of the Christian Church, and bishops found themselves forced to exercise temporal as well as spiritual power. The economic disintegration of the Empire was clear in the fourth century as the money became almost worthless, which in turn led to the decline of urban civilization. Increasingly draconian measures were decreed by the State to raise revenue as what would now be called its tax base shrank. Men moved into the countryside where the very rich had enormous estates around their villas, foreshadowing the feudal system to come. In Gibbon's famous phrase, fewer and fewer of the Empire's people had any reason to defend her. Of course, shortly after Augustine's words were written the Western Empire collapsed and Rome itself was sacked by Alaric the Goth in 414, as the Book of Revelation had prophesied: 'The merchants of these wares, who gained wealth from her, will stand far off, in fear of her torment, weeping and mourning aloud. "Alas, alas, for the great city . . . in one hour all this wealth has been laid waste."'

THE MEDIEVAL ESTABLISHMENT

When economic life revived after the subsistence farming and famine of the Dark Ages it was founded on a totally different basis. With the collapse of political authority, the only thing that just managed to hold civilization together was the Church, which used its great moral authority to impose its views on the way the economy should work. The feudal system was essentially a land-based barter system which did not need money. However, in the twelfth century trade and the use of money revived, and the greatest mind of the age turned his attention to it. St Thomas Aquinas's reasoning appears alien to the modern mind, resting as it did on an odd idea of Aristotle's that money is a 'fungible' commodity like food: it is something destined to be consumed. Added to this were a number of Old Testament passages such as Exodus 22:25, Deuteronomy 23:20–1, and Leviticus 25:35–6, which could be read in two ways. The first would be totally to deny the right to charge interest on any loan, which would be the sin of usury. The second, which seems a better translation of two separate Hebrew words *neshek* and *tarbit* (as was pointed out by Calvin), is to distinguish between loans to the poor and needy, often called 'your brother' in the texts, and other more general loans where it is acceptable.

Aquinas taught that where an investor shared the risk of capital loss, for example, in funding a ship trading with the East, a high return was quite acceptable. What was not acceptable was demanding a high return where the capital was guaranteed, for example, by a debenture secured on a property. In other words, sharing the risk via equity and getting a high return was quite acceptable; this was known as *periculum sortis* (risking the capital). Looking at pure loans, he considered two cases where interest might be charged. The first was compensation that might be due for any loss made in making the loan, known as *damnum emergens* (evident loss). The second ground for interest on a loan was the possible profit foregone in making it, i.e. what economists today would describe as the opportunity cost in making it, which was known as *lucrum cessans* (wealth lying idle). Aquinas ruled against *lucrum cessans*, but his successors disagreed. This was no empty philosophical matter; until the Reformation and up to the end of the seventeenth century people who charged what was regarded as an excessive rate of interest could find themselves hauled before the courts and charged significant fines, hence this complex system was as much a matter of practical law as of theory.

Medieval economic life was an integrated expression of the Church's teaching. It rested on two key themes, a ban on excessive interest payment policed by the Church courts, and a theory of the just price which was carried out by the guilds. Relics of the guilds survive in elements of modern trade unions, but also in the grand livery halls of the City of London, and both may give a misleading impression. Generally speaking, they were groups of craftsmen in medieval England and elsewhere who submitted themselves to a system of mutual aid, but also of mutual discipline. They were not what we understand by communes; each workshop was led by a master who worked for his own profit. The nearest modern analogy would be the farmers of Denmark and the Netherlands, who own their own land and take the profit thereof, but who market their produce through great co-operatives. The guilds, however, were much more than that. No one could become a member of a guild without serving a long apprenticeship, and only the members of the guilds (the masters) had a say in the running of it. Each master was assisted by journeymen (skilled workers paid by the day, from the French *journée*) and by apprentices. No master was allowed to employ more than a certain number of apprentices or journeymen, and to ensure that trade was fair there were restrictions on production. For example, it was forbidden to work by artificial light. The scale of the workshops was very small, perhaps on average a master, a journeyman, and one or two apprentices. In Paris in 1300 there were 5000 masters and 7000 journeymen, while in 1387 in Frankfurt 1500 masters employed only 800 journeymen.

While this was the case in England, France and much of Germany, things were rather different in northern Italy and Flanders. Bruges and Florence bestrode the major trade route of the period, and so while in most medieval towns trade was a local affair, substantial riches did accumulate in these cities. Moreover, and this is particularly true of cities like Florence, the guilds became embroiled in a political struggle for power. According to Dawson,

> Italy was unique, inasmuch as the nobles . . . from the first took a leading part in the common life of the city, and the gilds to which they belonged, such as the bankers, the merchants and the lawyers, inevitably possessed a much greater social prestige and political influence than the gilds of the craftsmen and shopkeepers.[12]

Italy was also unique in that there was no central authority, however weak, to prevent ultimate authority arising from control of the town.

In the modern world, at least in the rich North, there is an *abundance* of goods and services. Any control of production, as was practised by the guilds, can only be to create a 'cartel' in order to raise prices and increase profits. In the medieval world drought, plague, or war could, and often did, lead to hunger and famine. The Middle Ages lived on the edge of constant starvation. In such a background of *scarcity*, the guilds not only maintained standards of quality but insisted that goods should be freely and fairly available, so that craftsmen could not extort undue prices from their customers. In many cases the guilds enforced the sale of goods only in public markets, so that less aware buyers could not have their ignorance abused. The practice of 'forestalling', of buying goods before they were brought to market, was prohibited, as was 'regrating', buying things in a market and selling them again for a higher price. 'Engrossing', the idea of buying up goods with a view to restrict supply and force up price, was particularly despised. The system was meant to be fair to both buyers and sellers, quite unlike the rapacious tax-collectors of ancient Rome or the admired entrepreneurs of modern capitalism. In Merrie England, unlike its modern successor, *caveat emptor* was not required.

To sum up, the medieval achievement was, in Dawson's words,

> that it was the medieval city which first provided the favourable conditions for a thorough-going christianization of social life such as had existed neither in the city culture of the ancient world, which was based on slavery, nor in the feudal agrarian society which had been built up so largely by the strong at the expense of the weak.[13]

We should note that city life as it re-emerged in the twelfth century was based, dominated, impregnated with the Christian faith. Men formed 'confraternities' dedicated to a particular saint; towns formed part of the concept of the commune, an association where all men, not just merchants, vowed to work together. As he saw, 'it was the religious confraternity or "charity" which was the seed of the great flowering of communal life in the merchant and craft gilds which were the most striking feature of medieval urban society'. The gild's 'intense solidarity made its membership more important in the life of the individual than the city itself, since it was through the gild that the ordinary man exercised and realised his citizenship'.[14]

The importance of the gilds lay in the fact that they formed a non-political hierarchy regulating the economic life of the town, but the regulation was one of local self-discipline, rather than the massive rule-book of ancient Rome or modern states.

> In this way the medieval city succeeded in reconciling the interests of the consumer with the corporate freedom and responsibility of

the producer . . . it was this integration of corporate organization, economic function and civic freedom which makes the medieval city the most complete embodiment of the social ideals of the Middle Ages, as we see them in their most highly developed form in the writings of St Thomas and his contemporaries.[15]

The medieval world in many senses appears alien to us, but if respected contemporary theorists such as Peter Drucker and Charles Handy are right in their view that the modern world is at the beginning of a 'discontinuity shift' which will make the 2020s unrecognizable to the 1980s, then it may have useful guidance for us. First is the dominant medieval idea of natural law, that man is but one part in the chain of being of the natural world. Growing ecological awareness in the 1980s and 1990s has reintroduced the idea of man as just one part of the cycle of life on Earth. This has important moral implications, and for the first time in 300 years people are questioning the claim of economics to be a self-sufficient science in its own right, and insisting as did the medieval schoolmen that economic conduct is just a branch of human conduct in general, and therefore subject to general rules in the interests of society. Second, medieval society, like Asia for much of its history, was stuck in Malthus's trap of population density absorbing all resources, and the vast majority of people living on the edge of real want and near starvation. Western Europe since the Industrial Revolution has escaped this trap through technological development, and has forgotten what it was like.

If environmental pressures do put a cap on growth, as seems inevitable, we may have to relearn these lessons. The speculator will become the despised 'spiv' of the Second World War who knew how to avoid rationing at a high price, the lender the modern loan shark who lends to the very poor at extortionate rates of interest. Tawney captured the medieval world-view:

> Loans are made largely for consumption, not for production. The farmer whose harvest fails or whose beasts die, or the artisan who loses money, must have credit, seed corn, cattle, raw materials, and his distress is the money-lender's opportunity. Naturally, there is a passionate popular sentiment against the engrosser who holds a town to ransom, the monopolist who brings the

livings of many into the hands of one, the money-lender who takes advantage of his neighbours' necessities to get a lien on their land and foreclose.[16]

THE REFORMATION AND THE RISE OF CAPITALISM

After the Reformation, all this changed. As Tawney said in his great work, *Religion and the Rise of Capitalism:*

> It was the contraction in the territory within which the writ of religion was conceived to run . . . What requires explanation is not the view that these matters are part of the province of religion, but the view that they are not. When the age of the Reformation begins, economics is still a branch of ethics . . . the appeal of theorists is to natural law, not to utility, the legitimacy of economic transaction is tried by reference, less to the movement of the market, than to moral standards derived from the traditional teaching of the Christian Church.[17]

William Temple, Archbishop of Canterbury in the 1940s, was of the same mind:

> The Puritan simplification of religious teaching . . . had the effect of breaking up a tradition derived from Biblical teaching as a whole. That teaching certainly included the reality and rightfulness of private property; but it also contained provisions which made the actual rights of property conditional rather than absolute . . . The Puritans' fundamental individualism, which brought a fuller sense of personal responsibility to God, also at the same time undermined the appreciation of wealth as essentially social and therefore subject at all points to control in the interests of society as a whole . . . Calvin set the door ajar, and the pressure of life would open it so widely, that Calvinism, which began as a system of regimentation, where economic activity was subject to severe moral restraint, became ultimately the mainspring of unrestricted enterprise and competition.[18]

This also resulted in a total change in the view of the State. In the 1620s and 1630s Archbishop Laud, who was as well-meaning but also as politically maladroit as his master Charles I, had used his Court of the Star Chamber to prevent economic injustices; in particular to force landowners to give back common lands that they had 'enclosed'. Laud was perhaps the last Archbishop of Canterbury to hold the essentially medieval belief that Church and State must work together: 'Both Commonwealth and Church are collective bodies, made up of many into the one; and both so near allied, that the one, the Church, can never subsist but in the other the Commonwealth.' The basis of the State was social justice. 'God will not bless the state, if kings and magistrates do not execute judgement, if the widow and the fatherless have cause to cry out against the "thrones of justice".'[19] The rising merchant class forced Charles to execute Laud, before turning on and destroying the King himself.

Within fifty years men no longer saw things this way, and invented the idea of the State as the result of some form of social contract. John Locke's thoughts in 1690 would not appear strange to a modern liberal audience: 'The great and chief end of men uniting into commonwealths is the preservation of their property.'[20] Locke is the father of modern economics, for like all faiths it requires an absolute, in this case the absolute, inviolable nature of private property. As the economist Barbara Ward noted, 'the chief purpose of government is to protect private property, which now enjoys the divine right once claimed by kings'.[21] Despite thousands of the moderately wealthy being ruined by the South Sea Bubble, while the King and Prime Minister made millions, 'speculation continued to be an inevitable adjunct of property and in its turn acquired the Lockean sanction of inviolable private ownership and control'.[22]

THE RISE OF ECONOMIC MAN

Dawson saw that Liberalism was based on the eighteenth-century ideas of the English philosophers like David Hume and French Rationalists like Voltaire, whom Dawson described as seeing nothing in Christianity but a 'mass of grotesque and repulsive absurdities', and as having described the Bible as 'a monument of the most outrageous folly', the Psalms as 'Barrack Room Ballads'. (Plato, of course, is a 'madman' and Shakespeare a 'low savage'.) But the 'great prophet and true founder' of the Liberal movement was Rousseau – a movement which, Dawson adds, 'continued to grow with the expansion of European civilisation in the nineteenth century', and 'is at present the established religion of the U.S.A.'[23]

It was no accident that modern capitalism, and Liberalism itself, grew up in England. The Reformation freed men from the authority of the Church; but the heirs of the Reformers were 'rebels and individualists in revolt against any kind of social discipline and external compulsion ... their hostility to marriage springs from a romantic idealisation of sex, and a desire to free their emotional life from all social constraints'.[24] Let us contrast this with 'the medieval idea of liberty ... which was not the right of the individual to follow his own free will, but the privilege of sharing in a highly organized form of corporate life which possessed its own constitution and rights of self-government'.[25]

Dawson rightly saw the growth of economics as perhaps the major force behind this movement. The claim, as described earlier, was that economic laws were as deterministic and necessary as the physical laws discovered by Newton. Just as the economists of the 1990s urge birth control upon the poor countries of the world, so their spiritual fathers in the nineteenth century declaimed that society had to be based, not on tradition, patriotism, legitimacy or faith, but solely on money. This was the only way to maximize the wealth of the country and avoid sinking into the slough of mass poverty which Malthus had predicted. In this way secularism was as assertive and triumphalist as Communism was later to be.

I earlier mentioned Voltaire's description of Christianity. David Hume is generally regarded as the father of British 'empirical' philosophy, but look at the unbalanced and emotive tone of his magnum opus, *An Enquiry Concerning Human Understanding*:

> If we take in our hand any volume; of divinity or school meta-physics, for instance; let us ask, *Does it contain any abstract reasoning concerning quantity or number?* No. *Does it contain any experimental reasoning concerning matter of fact and existence?* No. Commit it then to the flames, for it can contain nothing but sophistry and illusion.[26]

As Bacon noticed 350 years ago, 'A little philosophy inclineth man's mind to atheism, but depth in philosophy bringeth men's minds to religion.'

It is a pity that so few people apart from professional economists have ever studied the subject of the beginning of economics, for public ignorance has allowed dubious assertions to be advanced unchallenged. What happened briefly was this. In the eighteenth century the notorious libertine and son of the Enlightenment Jeremy Bentham invented his so-called system of ethics called utilitarianism. Instead of any general spiritual, or even general moral principles, utilitarianism was the 'ethics' of individual self-interest. Fifty years after Smith's *Wealth of Nations*, utilitarian philosophers like David Ricardo and J. S. Mill universalized self-interest as a theoretical framework for economic life – so-called perfect competition. For non-economists probably the typical sign of economics is the classic demand curve, still explained by older textbooks in terms of marginal utility. (In a curious way this is like a perverted imitation of Kant's Categorical Imperative, with self-interest substituted for duty.) However, the great minds of economics have always realized that the subject is based on this implausible and thin basis of utilitarianism. Joseph Schumpeter described utilitarianism as 'the shallowest of all conceivable philosophies of life', while Keynes called it 'the worm which has been gnawing away at the inside of modern civilization and is responsible for its present moral decay'.[27]

It is generally stated that Adam Smith is the father of economics, and that his observations of the 'invisible hand of the market' were the fundamental basis which others later developed. This is at best a half-truth, and since Dawson clearly believed the conventional wisdom I will briefly state the grounds of my opposition to it. Adam Smith was a pragmatist, an observer, it is true, of the economic life of his time, and he may be accorded the title 'father of political economy'. It is true that he once used the phrase 'invisible hand', and that he introduced the concept of specialization of labour, but he never made the vaunting claims about the sphere of economics which those who take his name in vain are apt to do. Throughout the nineteenth century there was a great tension between such descriptive political economy, and quantitative analysis following Ricardo's attempts to base all economics on mathematical universalization of utilitarian principles. There also came a clever side-step, whereby the increasing use of mathematical symbols was felt to demonstrate that economics was a pure science free of political or ethical content. As Jeavons put it in the 1870s, 'economics, if it is to be a science at all, must be mathematical science, and moral values have nothing to do with this'.[28]

The same sentiments were stated by Lord Beveridge in 1937, in an address read by millions of economic students as the preface to Lipsey's best-selling *An Introduction to Positive Economics*. 'If the charge of barrenness of realistic economics in the past were justified completely, that would not be a reason for giving up observation and verification. It would only be a reason for making our observations more exact.'[29] By the end of the period, economics with the spurious certainty of its elegant equations had almost destroyed the former practice of political economy. The physicist Walras produced a mammoth set of equations to describe the economy, while the Italian Pareto did the same in the field of 'welfare economics', essentially defining the economist's Utopia as one where no one can be made better off without making anyone else worse off, the rationalist, utilitarian scheme taken to its ultimate conclusion. Modern welfare economics is based on the concept of Pareto optimality, yet as Amartyo Sen remarked, 'Pareto optimality can come "hot from hell" because a state can be Pareto optimal with some people in extreme misery and others in luxury *so long as the miserable cannot be made better off without cutting in to the luxury of the rich*' (my emphasis).[30]

Yet a few mavericks remained, including Barbara Ward and Fritz Schumacher who both stressed the moral basis of economic life. Not the least of Dawson's importance is the way he inspired such people, despite the disapproval of their peers. Barbara Ward was a distinguished economist who wrote a number of influential books on development and the environment such as *Progress for a Small Planet*, and who quite explicitly recognized her debt to Dawson. (In July 1940, when Catholics in England were publicly accused of being in sympathy

with Fascism, Dawson inaugurated a group called The Sword of
the Spirit, with Cardinal Hinsley as President and Ward as
Secretary, to work for 'the restoration in Europe of a Christian
basis for both public and private life' and which expressed its
total and utter opposition to Nazism. The new movement played
a significant part in the war effort, and laid the foundation stone
of then unprecedented ecumenical co-operation. The Sword of
the Spirit was the precursor to the Catholic Institute for International Relations, and it is generally believed that, as Michael
Walsh wrote, 'Cardinal Hinsley and the war-time members of
the Sword executive helped to make the Catholic Church part
of English national life. It came to enjoy a status in the country
greater than ever before in modern times.'[31])

It is also worth noting that Smith's *Wealth of Nations* was
written in the 1770s before the dawn of mass industrialization.
The economy he knew was still the traditional one of small
cottage industry, where buyer and seller were of equal weight,
and his modern acolytes forget that he therefore opposed
limited liability companies where the weight of capital could
overcome the excellence of a small company. His work can be
seen as a plea for freedom for small communities from excessive
State power, but the negative conception of liberty to mean
simply the absence of legal restrictions on contracts or
interference on trade owes much more to Bentham than to
Smith. Although Smith's 'invisible hand' is very well known, its
continuation is not, where he describes how society uses esteem
and trust in complex relationships: 'We trust our health to the
physician; our fortune and sometimes our life and reputation
to the attorney. Such confidence could not safely be reposed in
people of a very mean or low condition. Their reward must be
such, as may give them that rank in society which so important a
trust requires.'[32]

Adam Smith is so often quoted as the advocate of free-market
economics that it is worth remembering that this gives a
distorted view of his work. That great economic treatise, the
Wealth of Nations, was a defence of individual enterprise against
the corporate State established in France at the end of the
seventeenth century by Louis XIII's minister Colbert, and the
'mercantile' theory that international trade should be regulated

by the State. It seems likely that Adam Smith would have been shocked by the claims sometimes given by neo-conservatives using his name that there is *nothing but the free market*. Smith's other great work is the *Theory of Moral Sentiments* in which he emphasizes that societies where men are guided by a moral sense of duty to help each other will flourish: 'All members of society stand in need of each other's assistance . . . where the necessary assistance is reciprocally afforded, the society flourishes and is happy.'[33] Ranking *below* this is the society based on self-interest and legal rights (here called justice), which is only 'a mercenary exchange of good offices according to an agreed valuation'. Since free-market apologists have distorted the accepted interpretation of Adam Smith, I want to quote Professor Andrew Skinner of Glasgow University, a leading expert on him:

> The advocate of liberty and freedom of choice did so in the belief that our actions are and should be subject to the constraints which are represented by accepted rules of behaviour (which include the rules of justice), and further that all our activities are open to the scrutiny of our fellows . . . Our choice of butcher, brewer or baker may be affected by judgements as to their behaviour on matters other than quality or price. Whom we buy from is as interesting a decision as what we buy . . . Smith's emphasis upon the central issue of propriety may find some interesting applications in addressing the wider questions of choice in the sense that 'economic' decisions may and should be socially constrained.[34]

Classical economics may claim that it has the answer to all our problems, that the perfect resource allocation can be achieved only by its iron laws of supply and demand, but the fact is that the perfect competition it glorifies has never existed. On the contrary, the evidence suggests that economic life has a tendency to oligopoly, where a small group of producers exploit the public, but this was and is ignored by such theorists. Nevertheless, because their arguments suited the emerging industrial classes of the period, they became dogma and public policy. Exactly the same arguments are now being used in the UK and the US as to why wages must be cut and health and safety abandoned on the same spurious grounds of expediency to 'meet global competition'.

Let me describe a few of Dawson's forecasts of the way society might develop. His first book *Progress and Religion* was published in 1929, but prophesied the decline of the British Empire, then at its political if not economic height. He forecast that modern society's attack on traditional morality and marriage would lead to a collapse of the family, but,

> as Leo XII pointed out, the alteration of the fundamental laws that govern marriage and family will ultimately lead to the ruin of society itself. No doubt the state will gain in power and prestige as the family declines, but state and society are not identical. In fact, the state is often most omnipotent and universal in its claims at the moment when society is dying, as we see in the last age of the Roman empire.[35]

In Rome, as the civic spirit declined, the claims of the State became more and more oppressive, but the demands of the citizens of Rome to be fed for nothing, and to be entertained, grew steadily up to the moment of abyss. In the last century of this bureaucratic tyranny, very similar in its methods and claims to modern Communism, the only centre of independent life was the Christian bishop: 'He alone stood between the people and the oppression of the bureaucracy . . . On one occasion a praetorian prefect was so offended that he declared that he had never been spoken to in such a manner. "No doubt", replied St Basil, "you have never met a Bishop."'[36] The Church also began its work of charity, supporting the poor on the basis of local people and real need.

As Dawson stated: 'If religion loses its hold on social life, it eventually loses its hold on life altogether. And this is what has happened in the case of modern Europe. The new secularized civilization is not content to dominate the outer world and to leave man's inner life to religion; it claims the whole man.'[37] He was confident that the West would be unlikely to fall for the attractions of either Fascism or Communism, which was not a popular view in the 1930s, but warned that even in the West the obtrusive State would invade the workplace, the school, and finally the family:

> The State of the future will be not a policeman, but a nurse, and a schoolmaster and an employer and an officer – in short an earthly providence, an all-powerful, omnipotent human god – and a very

jealous god at that ... [it] will make as just as large a claim on the life of the individual as do [Communism and Fascism] and will demand an equally whole-hearted spiritual allegiance.[38]

It is worth mentioning that crime in the United States is highly correlated with single-parent families; since 1960 the proportion of children born outside wedlock has risen from 8 per cent to 25 per cent but within the Black community, the numbers are a rise from 26 per cent to 68 per cent over the same period!

He thought the businessmen and trade unionists of his day would be replaced in politics by professional politicians, skilled in argument and promises, but basing their policies on nothing more than short-term expediency. I understand that opinion polls regularly give politicians the poorest ratings for all types of occupation; so who is to say that Dawson was wrong when he declared 'We are beginning to breed professional politicians with no social responsibilities, like the class that has destroyed representative institutions on the Continent.'[39] Man's search for fulfilment, rather than being focused on eternity, becomes a desperate race for pleasure in this life. As Leo XIII wrote in *Rerum Novarum* in 1890, in such a secular society 'tranquillity no longer prevails either in private or public life and the human race has been hurried on almost to the verge of ruin'.[40]

THE QUESTION OF CAPITALISM

At the beginning of Dawson's 1935 book, *Religion and the Modern State*, there is a striking illustration by Eric Gill. The Latin reads: 'The woman which thou sawest is that great city, which reigneth over the kings of the earth' (Revelation 17:18).

And who is this mysterious woman who rules over the kings of the earth? Of course she is ancient Rome, but it is interesting that in Revelation St John represents Rome not as a great tyranny, or military machine, but as the whore of Babylon. Babylon was the previous great imperial capital where anything could be bought or sold, and it is in this capacity that the Book of the Apocalypse sees Rome as the great enemy of the Church.

As Dawson says, this book is the culmination of the Jewish apocalyptic tradition, and the first Christian vision of history. Before the Kingdom of God can be established on earth,

> the mystery of iniquity must fulfil itself on earth and the harvest of human power and pride must be reaped. This is the significance of the judgment of Babylon ... as the embodiment of material civilization and luxury, the great harlot, whose charms bewitch all the nations of the earth, the world market whose trade enriches the merchants and the shipowners.[41]

One of Dawson's greatest insights lies in his book *Religion and the Modern State*, where he discusses the nature of capitalism: 'The fact is that the word Capitalism is commonly used to cover two entirely different things, and consequently responsible for an endless series of misunderstandings and confusions of thought.'[42] The first usage is to describe the role of private property in the economic process, and in this sense it has always been judged licit by the Church, just as it has been deemed advantageous by Adam Smith. The second usage covers the economic system which grew up in the nineteenth century where capital 'money' became the driving force behind businesses, which were bought and sold like commodities. We might well use 'private property' for the former, and 'Big Business' for the latter, rather as Chesterton and Belloc used to do.

There is a huge difference between a small workshop owned by its proprietor, who lives and works there, and knows well his small workforce, and the giant multinational conglomerate which devours small companies. It can do this via quick takeovers on the stock exchange, or simply by using its enormous financial muscle to drive small firms out of business, as the British supermarket chains appear to have done to the corner shop. Men who used to own their own business have become employees of such supergrocers, and most people have no alternative but to be an employee to survive.

Dawson seems to argue that this confusion is inadvertent, but I believe that he is being too charitable. The purveyors of modern capitalism know full well what product they are pushing. Adam Smith in particular is misused; the neo-conservatives who invoke his name so frequently do not appear to have read the *Wealth of Nations,* or if they have, they are deliberately ignoring much of it. It is worth coming back to the question of the limited liability company and its role in society. Created during the seventeenth century, it was effectively banned in the 1720s in the aftermath of the South Sea Bubble when it was thought that such a permanent corporation was an incentive to speculation. Fifty years later, Smith's view was that the benefits of economic specialization or 'efficiency' derived from the individual's pride in his own business, and the knowledge that this business would be likely to prosper with him the only beneficiary if it produced quality goods. If the business did not make goods of sufficient quality, it would fail, and the big loser would be the owner. He contrasted this adversely with a joint-stock company with absentee owners, and salaried employees with much less interest in what they produced: 'The directors of joint-stock companies being the managers rather of other people's money than of their own, it cannot be well expected that they should watch over it with the same anxious vigilance with which the partners in a private copartnery frequently watch over their own.'[43]

What Adam Smith did not and could not foresee, was that the introduction of limited liability a century later (the Companies Act 1862) might give a well-capitalized and large company the ability to drive smaller companies out of business even though its products and efficiency were inferior. This might be done by cutting prices to such an extent that everyone made losses, which only the large company could sustain over any length of time. In the modern era mass-advertising probably takes the place of predatory pricing, but the effects may be the same. The point is that once the large company has driven other producers out of the market, it can corner the market, or in economists' jargon 'enjoy monopoly profits', i.e. charge high prices for inferior goods.

Dawson found the second usage of 'capitalism' an octopus almost impossible to pin down in terms of definition, but easy to recognize by its consequences:

> Broadly speaking it may be described as the economic aspect of that philosophy of liberal individualism which was the religion of the 19th century . . . It is a philosophy of separation and irrespon-

sibility which breaks up the moral organism of society into a chaos of competitive individualism . . . It makes self-interest the supreme law in economics, the will of the majority the sovereign power in the State, and private opinion the only arbiter in religious matters.

It is a system which 'finds a fitting expression in the nineteenth century manufacturing town with its dark factories, its squalid slums, its mean public places, its gin palaces and music halls'.[44]

'The real cause of the evils of industrialism was . . . the spirit which sacrificed the individual to the economic process.'[45] The Age of Enlightenment attacked what it saw as the overbearing power and dogma of the Church, and in the nineteenth century, with the exception of a few Evangelical reformers like Wilberforce and Shaftesbury, men saw religion as a private matter, occupying a few hours on Sunday, while business demanded the rest. Yet it seems a peculiar feature of tolerant and pluralistic societies, that they will tolerate everything except faith. This must be attacked at every opportunity, not with the prisons of the totalitarian regimes, but with all the propaganda force of the media and a modern education system. In Britain, since the 1994 Sunday Trading Law was passed, many Christians have lost their jobs for insisting on their right to attend church. This was not declared as an anti-Christian measure, but rather justified by the new god of 'economic efficiency'. Political and economic liberalism 'lives on the spiritual capital that it has inherited from Christian civilization, and as this is exhausted something else must come to take its place'.[46]

THE VISION OF PIERS PLOWMAN

Was there any alternative? Did this capitalist paradise have to occur? Towards the end of the fourteenth century the English language again became the speech of the whole country, after three centuries of surviving as a peasant dialect. Two great poets appeared; Chaucer is universally recognized, but his contemporary Langland has been almost totally forgotten, yet the latter had a vision of what Christian society should be. (Like Chaucer, Langland's English has become unintelligible to the general reader, so here when I am quoting Langland, I am using

Dawson's modernization.) Langland is one of those peculiarly English figures, a conservative revolutionary, like Bunyan, Cobbett, or Chesterton. A revolutionary since he is disgusted at the society in which he finds himself and which he desires to change; a conservative since his beliefs are based on morals rather than politics or class envy, and he looks back to the past for inspiration. Compare Cobbett's complaint about the horrors of industrialization for the poor with Langland's verses.

> When *master* and *man* were the terms, every one was in his place; and all were free. Now, in fact, it is an affair of *masters* and *slaves* . . . There are hundreds of thousands of the people of England who never taste any food but bread and vegetables, and who scarcely know what it is to have a full meal even of these. This is *new*, it was not so in former times, it was not so even till of *late* years.[47]

Langland is similar:

> And in the apparel of a poor man and a pilgrim's likeness
> Many times has God been met among poor people . . .
> And in a friar's frock once was he found
> But it is far ago in St Francis time.[48]

Langland was horrified by the emerging social dualism between Church and State which was to provide one of the major forces behind the Reformation. The prestige of the Papacy had suffered greatly by its 'Babylonian Captivity' at Avignon, and increasing wealth was leading to great pressures on the medieval settlement. Yet Langland never lost sight of the medieval vision of society as a unity, where all have different status within a hierarchy, but are all servants and children of one father.

Langland's great poem contrasts two figures, Lady Meed and Piers Plowman. Lady Meed represents the power of money, the ability of gold to buy the favours of kings and priests, in fact money as the basis of society, and she dominates the first part of the poem.

> Trust in her treasure betrayeth full many,
> She hath poisoned Popes, and impaired Holy Church.
> Monks and minstrels are among her lovers,
> Both learned men and lepers in hedges.

Summoners and jurymen are such as prize her,
She is with the sheriffs who rule the shires;
For she robs men of their lands, and their life as well,
And giveth the gaoler gold and silver,
To unfetter the false, to fly where he will.[49]

Accused of betraying Christ's Kingdom, Lady Meed defiantly sets forth the argument for self-interest and expediency, that money is needed to make the world go round.

It becometh a king that keepeth a realm,
To give Meed to men, who serve him meekly,
To aliens and to all men, to honour them with gifts,
Meed maketh him beloved, and esteemed as a man . . .
All kinds of craftsmen crave Meed for their prentices;
Merchants and Meed must needs go together
No wight as I ween without Meed may live.[50]

Nevertheless Meed is overthrown by the simple figure of Piers Plowman, initially a poor man, the ploughman or peasant on whose basic and unending toil the world depends. 'He is the true economic foundation of society, as opposed to Meed, which is the false economic motive.' Later it is obvious that as well as this he represents Our Lord himself, and lastly he is the Church carrying on its work of salvation. 'Langland's social conscious-ness is rooted in religious faith and finds its ultimate ground in the doctrine of Christian brotherhood.' He calls for nothing less than a spiritual renewal of both economy and society on the basis of Christian brotherhood:

For we are all Christ's creatures, and of his coffers rich,
And brethren of one blood, as well beggars as earls,
For on Calvary of Christ's blood Christendom gan spring,
And blood brethren we became there, of one body won . . .
No beggar or serving-boy among us, save sin made us so.[51]

Dawson ends his book *Religion and the Rise of Western Culture* with these words:

Yet Langland's poem is itself a proof that all was not lost; that the labour of seven hundred years had not been in vain. For if the barbarians of the west had learnt to think such thoughts and speak such a language, it shows that a new Christian culture had been born which was not an alien ideal imposed externally, but was the common inheritance of Western man.

What have we done with this inheritance? At least we have had it. It is part of our own flesh and blood and the speech of our own tongue.[52]

Modern economics is a philosophy of fantasy; it bases the whole of life on the fragile and theoretically infinite concepts of labour and capital. It sees land as inexhaustible and takes no account of the damage done to the water we drink or the air we breathe. Yet environmental considerations are driving all of us to reconsider Burke's dictum that politics is a spiritual community: 'a partnership not only between those who are living, but between those who are living, those who are dead, and those who are yet to be born'. As I mentioned earlier, the concept of natural law provides a fruitful framework for the analysis of such problems. It is seems obvious that a society based on aggressive self-interest must disintegrate, like bricks made without straw.

In the same decade as Luther pinned his theses to the doors at Wittenberg, Erasmus saw at Strasbourg one of the last examples of the guild system in full operation. 'I saw monarchy without tyranny, aristocracy without factions, democracy without tumult, wealth without luxury ... Would that it had been your lot, divine Plato, to come upon such a republic!'[53]

NOTES

The works of Christopher Dawson cited in this chapter:

ENQ   *Enquiries into Religion and Culture* (Sheed & Ward, 1933).
RMS   *Religion and the Modern State* (Sheed & Ward, 1935).
MR   *Medieval Religion* (Sheed & Ward, 1935).
RWC   *Religion and the Rise of Western Culture* (Sheed & Ward, 1950).

1   *RMS*, ch. IV, 'The Conflict Between Christianity and Communism', pp. 60–1.

2   Arthur Bryant, *English Saga* (Collins, 1943), ch. 2, 'Dark Satanic Mills', pp. 53–4.

3   *RMS*, ch. VIII, 'The Catholic Doctrine of the State', pp. 134–5.

4   Plato, *The Republic* (tr. Jowett, Oxford University Press, The World's Classics, 1940).

5 Ibid. I have replaced Jowett's term 'timocracy' with 'honest government'.

6 *ENQ*, 'St Augustine and his Age', Pt 1, 'The Dying World', pp. 201–2.

7 *RMS*, Introduction, p. xiii.

8 'Autobiography', John Couper Powys, quoted in *RMS*, ch. IX, Conclusion, p. 143.

9 G. K. Chesterton, *St. Francis of Assisi* (Hodder & Stoughton, 1923), Ch. II, 'The World St Francis Found', pp. 29–30.

10 W. E. Gladstone, *The State in its Relation to the Church*, quoted in Lesslie Newbigin, *Foolishness to the Greeks* (SPCK, 1990).

11 *ENQ*, 'St Augustine and his Age', Pt 1, 'The Dying World', pp. 205–6.

12 *RWC*, ch. IX, 'The Medieval City: Commune and Gild', p. 204.

13 Ibid., pp. 193–4.

14 Ibid., p. 203.

15 Ibid., pp. 204–5.

16 R. H. Tawney, *Religion and the Rise of Capitalism* (John Murray, 1964).

17 Ibid.

18 William Temple, *Christianity and the Social Order* (Penguin, 1941).

19 Archbishop Laud, quoted in R. H. Tawney, op. cit.

20 John Locke, *Two Treatises of Government* (Everyman edn, J. M. Dent, 1924).

21 Barbara Ward, *Faith and Freedom* (Hamish Hamilton, 1954), ch. 10, 'Work and Wealth', pp. 117–18.

22 Ibid.

23 *ENQ*, 'Civilisation and Morals', pp. 118, 149.

24 *ENQ*, 'Christianity and Sex', p. 263.

25 *RWC*, 'Commune and Gild', p. 206.

26 David Hume, *An Enquiry Concerning Human Understanding* (Oxford, 1966), Part III, Section XII, p. 165.

27 Quoted in Esmond Birnie, 'Utilitarian Economics: A Theory of Immoral Sentiments', *ACE Journal*, 1993.

28 W. S. Jeavons, *The Theory of Political Economy*, quoted in T. Gorringe, *Capital and the Kingdom* (Orbis Books, 1994).

29 R. G. Lipsey, *An Introduction to Positive Economics* (5th edn, Weidenfeld & Nicolson, 1980).

30 Amartya Sen, *On Ethics and Economics*, quoted in T. Gorringe, op. cit.

31 Michael Walsh, *Swords to Ploughshares* (CIIR Publications, 1985).

32 Adam Smith, *An Inquiry into the Nature and Causes of the Wealth of Nations* (Everyman edn, J. M. Dent, 1947).

33 Adam Smith, quoted in Andrew Skinner, 'Adam Smith and Self-Love', *Finance and Ethics Quarterly*, Dec. 1993.

34 Skinner, op. cit.

35   *ENQ*, 'Christianity and Sex', p. 267.

36   *ENQ*, 'St Augustine and his Age', Pt 1, 'The Dying World', pp. 215–16.

37   *RMS*, Introduction, p. xx.

38   *RMS*, ch. VI, 'Religion and Politics', p. 106.

39   *RMS*, ch. II, 'Western Democracy and the New Political Forces', p. 26.

40   *RMS*, ch. VIII, 'The Catholic Doctrine of the State', p. 131.

41   *RMS*, ch. V, 'Communism and the Christian Interpretation of History', p. 77.

42   *RMS*, ch. VIII, 'The Catholic Doctrine of the State', p. 132.

43   Adam Smith, *The Wealth of Nations*.

44   *RMS*, ch. VIII, 'The Catholic Doctrine of the State', p. 133.

45   *RMS*, Introduction, p. xiv.

46   *RMS*, ch IV, 'The Conflict Between Communism and Christianity', p. 64.

47   Quoted in Raymond Williams, *Cobbett* (Oxford University Press, 1983), p. 37.

48   *RWC*, ch XII, 'Medieval Religion and Popular Culture', p. 269.

49   *MR*, Pt III, 'The Vision of Piers Plowman', pp. 172–3.

50   Ibid., pp. 173–4.

51   Ibid., p. 184.

52   *RWC*, ch. XII, 'Medieval Religion and Popular Culture', p. 273.

53   Erasmus, quoted in *RWC*, 'Commune and Gild', p. 207.

6

Can there be a Catholic history today?

FRANCESCA MURPHY

I recently asked a Stoneyhurst-educated philosopher of religion, 'What *is* Catholic history?' He told me that Catholic history brings to the fore facts which secular or Protestant histories ignore. On this view, a Catholic historian might be one who recalls his readers to the popularity, social efficacy and perhaps spirituality of pre-Reformation Christianity in England. An old-fashioned example of this breed is Hilaire Belloc. Belloc marshalled a verbal assault on the Reformation. He hoped to undermine the foundations of Anglicanism by bombarding the material, financial and political causes of its Reformation. Belloc picked off one Reformation 'character' after another, exposing each as denizens of the lower echelons of the new merchant classes, who rose to wealth and political power by despoiling monasteries and churches. Two representative figures of the Bellocian Reformation are the Cromwells – Henry's henchman and Charles I's successor. The depredations of the new middle class gave it a stranglehold on the religion of the land, which enabled it to prevent that return to the Faith which was devoutly desired by the dispossessed many and by some monarchs.

If Catholic history is history by Catholics, or about neglected Catholic topics, then its task is to praise Catholic forms of political and social order, and to bury the post-Reformation settlements. A splendid contemporary instance of this way of writing Catholic history is Eamon Duffy's *The Stripping of the Altars*. Here, rather than encomiums for the social achievements of the fourteenth-century English Church, we have a doxology for her liturgy. Duffy leads the reader to picture the solidity of the pre-Reformation liturgy and Church artefacts – quite literally in the case of the Pax plate, with which Thomas Browne 'smashed' Richard Pond over the head, because Pond did not pay him due precedence, and hand it to him first. Every literate person should hope that they will have the pleasure of reading more such books as *The Stripping of the Altars*, and they should be realistically aware that few have the scholarship or the talent to write them.

I do not think that what Belloc, or even Duffy, has written entirely captures the meaning of Catholic history. The implicit definition of Catholic history behind their works takes it as a sort of deep-sea diving – searching for the lost Atlantis, the sunken nation of Christendom. One may conceive of this Christendom politically, as Belloc does; another may see it aesthetically or liturgically, as Duffy does. But what is being practised could in principle be *any* kind of history. Just as feminist historians remind us of the achievements of countless sparsely recorded women, and ethnic historians recover the contributions of minority groups, so the Catholic historian, working on behalf of that interest group which is the Catholic Church, may counter-attack against the popeless and godless interests, by recording the good achieved and the beauty created by his own Church. Even if the findings of the Catholic side are true, history written by and on behalf of such an interest group is Marxist 'Catholic studies', not Catholic history.

For such history looks for the motor of human behaviour on a material level. It argues that a sea change in religious expression and experience has been purely driven by the desire to melt down images and make off with the gold. This is not Catholic history because it is reductionist. If, like Lord Fisher, one thinks that history is one damned thing after another, then, no matter what *things* one may describe, one is not writing Catholic history. And if one depicts the root causes of religious change as a struggle by one class for political and ecclesiastical control, then one is a Marxist. One may partially define

'Catholic' by the level at which human behaviour is analysed, or as one member of my original audience put it, as a 'quality of interpretation'.

Dawson's 'quality' of interpreting history was symbolic. He tended to interpret historical fields in terms of symbolic events which summed them up. Although he saw himself as a historian of culture, Dawson's interest in symbols was not aesthetic. For Dawson, a culture is a 'moral order', and the morals of a particular culture are channelled and represented by its symbols, such as the forms of its liturgy, its art and its institutions. The liturgy and the art are not 'symbols' when they are enumerated, or factually recorded, however lavish the facts. The liturgy and the art (and so forth) are seen as symbols when their forms are understood as illustrations or representations of a culture's 'moral order'. One recurring symbol in Dawson's books about the making of Europe as Christian is the *coronation* of the once barbarian war leader by bishop or by pope. Dawson writes:

> Take for example the case of the transformation of the barbarian king or war leader by the sacramental rite of consecration as practised throughout Europe in the Middle Ages. This obviously did not convert the feudal monarch into a St Louis or a King Alfred, but it did establish an ideal norm by which rules were judged and which moralised the institution itself. A Christian civilisation is . . . not a perfect civilisation, but it is a civilisation that accepts the Christian way of life as normal and frames its institutions as the organs of a Christian order . . . (*The Historic Reality of Christian Culture*, p. 36)

Such was the coronation of Charlemagne on Christmas Day, 800. Dawson is speaking of the 'transformation' of the heathen war leader into a Christian king. This fellow – or lady, since Dawson wrote in similar terms of the Coronation of Elizabeth II – still has to lead in war, but must at the same time exercise some of the virtues of Christian kingship. The transformation may have been rather more spotted and partial than Dawson often allowed. But the mark of a Catholic history is the description of a lifting up of natural human beings and human culture by and toward Christian spirit. A Catholic historian captures this moment of moral transformation. He is one who can imagine historical events as being to some extent infused with a Christian charism.

The symbol of coronation picks out the moment at which human and once heathen culture is fused with Christian culture: this cultural transition takes place symbolically in the person of the king, and in the changed political role which he must now play. Coronation is a Dawsonian symbol. It does not follow that a Catholic historian is one who believes that Church and State must be welded together. Here is a hypothetical example of what a Catholic history should do. There are many books which describe the technical, engineering discoveries which preceded the creation of the Gothic cathedral – especially the invention of the rib vault. There are other art-historical books which wax poetic about the mystical implications of the way in which light flows through the forms of the slim columns and many windows of the high-vaulted Gothic cathedral. A work of Catholic history would speak of how the engineering discovery of the rib vault was used to make a spiritual principle present in stone and light. A Catholic history would see in the material manifestations of human invention the charism of the Spirit. Catholic historiography is a way of imagining, and can be applied equally to the twentieth century as to the twelfth, and to the creative acts of human beings of every religious hue.

Dawson claimed that England was converted, in the sixth century, not by a new doctrine, but by a new display of power. He was thinking of charismatic individuals, such as St Cuthbert and St Bede and St Ethelreda. The most widely read and widely written variant of Catholic history – from the third-century martyrology to the twentieth-century Catholic Truth Society pamphlet – is the Life of the Saint. When I say that a Catholic historian is one who imagines natural events as being infused with spiritual meaning, I am not thinking of the spiritual as a gaseous substance, steam-powering the direction of history. The spirit appears in history in people. The Catholic historian is writing biographies of the Spirit, showing how the moral energies of particular human beings were inventively deployed within projects which allowed history to move one stage upward. It was only in the late eleventh century that popes and their theologians began to speak about 'Christendom'. In the context of the Crusades, popes called for the defence of the borders of *Christendom*. Before that, the common term describing the wider thing to which Christians belonged had been *Christianitas*, the Christian folk. The term 'Christendom' gradually became prevalent as the meaning became fixed in a particular geographical region, rather than on the dynamic of human action. The genuine object of Catholic history is not the fixed 'place', but the ever-changing, lively and bubbling *Christianitas*, the folk rather than the nation, as Christendom once was. Victor Turner speaks of *communitas* as being the shared sense of liberation, the celebratory experience of passing beyond the boundaries and burdens of daily life which takes place at religious festivals, and at the culmination of pilgrimage. By analogy with that modern usage, one might think of *Christianitas* as the Christian and creative force which sometimes emerges out of human history. Once, *Christianitas* emerged out of the midst of Christendom, as at coronations and Corpus Christi celebrations and when people carted and carved stone. Today, *Christianitas* has perforce to come about as the result of the creativity of individuals and small groups within a secular society. It could be the transforming work of a group of teachers, or of a scientist or of a Christian hat-maker. The Catholic historian is one who can perceive *Christianitas* in any of its infinite material forms – and under the strangest guises – and then capture in words what it is that illuminates and uplifts.

Dawson said that Christian history is distinguished from all others by its missionary character – the sense of having received some message which believers are impelled to travel out to pass on. This sense of mission became, in the nineteenth century, a very human belief in progress. Progress does happen, in that people invent, and imagine and engineer new things. Such people continually shift the bounds of human possibility. It is not the work of the Catholic historian to denigrate these engineering feats. It takes imagination to convey the marvel of the construction of massive bridges, as Paul Johnson does in his *Modern Times*. This is a work of Catholic history, and not because the author went to Stoneyhurst, and not because the subjects belong to the Roman obedience – the bridge and road builders of the last century largely did not. Such human works as building bridges and space ships, and the spirit of adventure in which they were undertaken, witness to the ever-present human urge to transcend apparent limitations. They are as much the natural object of Catholic history as the carving of the smiling angel in Chartres Cathedral.

Thus, as I find it practised by Dawson and others, I understand Catholic history as a quality of imagination. It is the ability to notice when the natural is taking on wings and undergoing a process of spiritualization. This could be called the symbolic imagination, in the sense of an imagination which finds in changing human practices symbols of the hovering Spirit of God. When I wrote this paper, I feared that I should be accused of making the élitist claim that only a few within the broad church of Catholic historians actually made the grade, and thus of having too narrow and intolerant a definition of Catholic history writing. Instead, I found myself charged with propounding a definition of Catholic history which lacked all boundaries. In this Chestertonian position I am pleased to rest. I shall conclude by explaining why.

Christopher Dawson cast his net over the world. Eamon Duffy delves deep into a corner of East Anglia. In this, Duffy follows in the footsteps of David Knowles. Knowles was a master craftsman in the art of Catholic historiography. It is surprising that a conference paper was not dedicated to him. Knowles' three-volume history of English monasticism and his biographies of Thomas à Becket and other medieval English men are narrowly accurate and naturalistic, like the flower carvings in thirteenth-century English church doorways. Knowles was a Benedictine monk for most of his life, and even after his departure from Downside continued to follow the rule of his Order. His this-worldly mentor was Thucydides. His understanding of human character is judicious: many an irony is balanced across his many-sided portraits. He exemplifies the practice of narrative history developed by the Benedictines over the past four centuries, based upon careful examination of original documents. We saw during our conference that the evidential basis of some of Christopher Dawson's theories, such as those pertaining to the proto-puritan work ethic of the Cistercians, can sometimes be rather weak. Knowles was less prone to the liabilities of generalization than was Dawson. He worked within what might be deemed a peculiarly English tradition of Catholic history-writing, dedicated to the exploration of the character of facts, and the fact of characters. However, Christopher Dawson's method was perhaps more *European*, and less empirical. He was looking for the underlying history, in which types of moral intention and human event intertwine. He sometimes tries to make his facts carry more theoretical weight than they can bear upon detailed examination. It is Knowles, and not Dawson, who has had disciples among English Catholic historians. Knowles' method makes sense to the secular historian.

Nonetheless, Dawson attempted to create something to which few contemporary historians could easily put their hand: a conception of human culture as a whole. This is more than just the depiction of the whole of human culture, from its beginnings to the present day. It is the attempt to show human history as a single venture. Modern history-writing tends to avoid the global epic, preferring to dig within one field. In Dawson's own time, secular historians, such as Spengler and Toynbee, attempted the larger canvas. A contemporary Catholic historian attempting a global history has very few such counterparts. For the more genuinely post-Christian our reflection becomes, the more fragmented is its ethical and its historical sense, and the more open to persuasion that the members of different cultures are effectively different species. This leaves open the question of how far the contemporary historical imagination can be *universal*. A modern Catholic historian would have to make a good case for the existence of a universal humanity and thus a universal morality, for such things can no longer simply be assumed. If he follows Dawson's method, he would make the case imaginatively. It is because we need to be reminded how to perceive a universal humanity that I have defined Catholic history in terms of the 'small' human event – *Christianitas* – rather than the institutional and national manifestation – 'Christendom'. A *Catholic* history is, as such, a universal history. We are told that the Enlightenment believed furiously in a universal humanity but conceived of it as an abstraction. We have been been told so often that the Enlightenment is dead that we have forgotten that this is an assertion, requiring argument. It is now given to Christianity to carry forward the Enlightenment project. The future Catholic historian would have to baptize that project, by immersing it in history, and showing, within the myriad historical diversities of ethnic derivation and of cultural ethos, a single human link. In this Heinekenian sense, what my Stoneyhurst friend told me is right: Catholic history discerns evidence of a moral truth which secular historians do not always have the perceptual apparatus to piece together. This is the wider task which, by the breadth and the moral quality of his own vision, Dawson bequeathed to his putative successors.

Can there be a Catholic history today? One may be inclined to say: only if a tradition of Catholic historiography exists, and if, in schools and in colleges and in universities, one historian trains another to imagine the human in this way. It certainly will not assist in the possibility of Catholic historiography if all Catholic academic historians are Marxists, with a somewhat neurotic regard for the Catholic 'nation', or if they are all positivists with a somewhat neurotic disregard for it. A Benedictine may educate his novices, and a professor may train his research students, in traditions of scholarly inquiry. But Dawson had a type of imaginative insight rather than a type of method. And, in the end, imagination exists in individuals, not in colleges. Christopher Dawson was not brought up within a tradition of Catholic inquiry. He worked for most of his life outside of the university. There will be Catholic history if there are individuals acrobatic and adventurous enough to see and to recreate the human and spiritual act of moral and imaginative fusion which Dawson practised.

7

Christian philosophy, Christian history: parallel ideas?

GLENN W. OLSEN

Over a long life, Étienne Gilson (1884–1978) often used, defended, and refined the expression 'Christian philosophy'.[1] The phrase, which he seemed first to have used in 1924 in regard to his study of St Bonaventure, occurs in more than one of the English titles of his books, indeed sometimes even when not in the title of the original French.[2] Almost from the first, it was met with hostility, especially with the complaint that 'Christian philosophy' was a contradiction in terms.[3] More than a decade after his death, Gilson was still being accused of 'extreme confusion', albeit by a less-than-expert critic.[4]

Clearly, Gilson's thought about the nature of Christian philosophy deepened with time, and one can easily be led astray by some of his more summary statements. For instance, his Foreword to the *History of Christian Philosophy in the Middle Ages* says Justin Martyr and Nicholas of Cues mark the beginning and end of the period covered in this book. These are writers not usually included in histories of philosophy, presumably because of the strongly religious orientation of their thought and the difficulty of separating that which is philosophical in them from that which is theological. If the defenders of the purity of reason already have their suspicions raised, Gilson does nothing here to calm them. He immediately gives a definition which may seem to leave unclear how philosophy and theology are to be distinguished: 'We call Christian philosophy the use made of philosophical notions by the Christian writers of those times . . . this book . . . is primarily concerned with the history of philosophical ideas even though, as is generally the case in the middle ages, philosophy is only found in a theological context.' The unconvinced could argue that this definition applies equally well to any systematization of revealed theology as to philosophy, and for that matter describes what today is called philosophical theology. That is, the definition seems to present an amorphous notion. Only the reader careful enough to notice that, if philosophy can be used in a theological context, its own integrity must lie elsewhere will not be misled by such a summary statement.

In general, Gilson seems to have been intent on making two separate but related claims: (1) that philosophy in any period reflects larger cultural preoccupations, and (2) that both historically and intrinsically 'philosophizing under the influence of Christian faith' profoundly enriched philosophical thought, helping human reason to deal more adequately with age-old problems which so-called unaided reason had been unable to penetrate sufficiently.[5] Because the contribution of the present paper lies elsewhere, we cannot explore Gilson's justification of his second claim here, but his *Christian Philosophy* amply illustrates the proposition that historically Christian theology deepened the understanding of such philosophical ideas as being, essence, cause, and participation.

Philosophers took exception to both Gilson's claims, especially the second. Indeed, certain writers made Gilson sound plausible to almost anyone by taking 'Christian philosophy' as only involving the first claim. Thus, David Knowles presented Gilson's position as common-sensical:

> [E]very group or school of thinkers has a social or cultural or confessional background, and . . . this leads it to focus its attention upon certain fields of the great area of thought available for development. A group of Christians, working in a fully Christian society and for purposes that are largely theological, will naturally direct its attention to subjects, such as the existence of God, the

immortality of the soul, human free will, and the like, which come inevitably into the forefront of its interests.[6]

Now in fact the history of philosophy has often been pursued by those who are not common-sensical, so even Gilson's first claim, and Knowles' ever-so-reasonable presentation of it, has been far from undisputedly received. Some words on this are in order, for the question bears on the possible parallelism between Christian philosophy and Christian history.

Secular minds, the kind who against most of the evidence have traditionally presented the history of, say, Greek philosophy in isolation from Greek theology and religion, let alone the Greek stage, not understanding the intimate historical intertwining of all these areas of cultural expression, have bridled at the very idea that a philosophy could be religious, let alone Christian.[7] For their own reasons Protestants, too, having learned from their sixteenth-century masters the denial of natural theology and the analogy of being, commonly have not seen how a body of thought could at once be linked to reason and to revelation without betraying one or the other. Even Catholics, at least initially, also gave much resistance to Gilson's first claim, for, habituated to the two-storey textbook universe of reason and revelation many attributed to Thomas Aquinas, and common in the history of philosophy and theology since at least the time of Christian von Wolff (1679–1754), they had as much difficulty as Protestant Christians understanding how a subject could at once be philosophical and Christian. Philosophy was the realm of unaided reason, and thus by definition could not be Christian. Only after the great debates roused by such books as Henri de Lubac's *Surnaturel,* which of course initially itself aroused opposition and condemnation, some of this leading to refinement of de Lubac's own views, could most Catholic thinkers begin to recover a patristic and medieval way of looking at things in which grace, while formally distinct from nature, was present at the foundation of nature itself.[8]

Gilson, somewhat unnervingly playing to the stands, presented St Thomas as an 'existentialist' to make the point that Aquinas's emphasis was on *esse,* the act of being, rather than on essentialist categories. But no more than any other Thomist did

Gilson propose a confusion of reason, the sum of those things knowable from sense experience with certitude by deduction, and revelation, the sum of those things known by trust in God's revelation. His first claim or observation, rather, was that philosophy is not normally neutral in regard to its historical setting, but imbibes from the culture in which it works itself out things exterior to itself which nevertheless give it shape. If philosophy is practised in a Buddhist culture it takes a different form than if practised in a Christian culture, and in both cases this occurs even if no content from the larger culture is intruded into the philosophical enterprise.

Philosophy inevitably develops differently in a polytheistic environment than in a monotheistic ethos. In the former, because there is no first cause in an Aristotelian sense, no Aristotelian monotheism, the government of the world is, so to speak, by committee, by the gods. Although the gods will be of various degrees of power and influence, and there is likely to be a chief god, by definition no god by him- or herself will control the universe in the manner of the Jewish or Christian God. The direction or drift in things will at the most be the sum of the various gods' negotiations and competitions with one another, for Hera will scheme against Zeus. Such a larger cultural pattern of thought, especially if developed in a world which assumes that the material order has always been, and therefore is not an effect of any god, discourages philosophy from fully under-standing certain subjects intrinsically its own, such as freedom of the will. This observation exactly parallels Stanley Jaki's observation that certain environments, specifically Christianity, have fostered science while others have retarded it.[9] Although there will probably be some sense of and discussion of freedom of the will in a polytheistic culture, this can hardly be at the centre of reflection. If on the other hand philosophy develops in a monotheistic culture, the problem of freedom will be forced by cultural considerations from periphery to centre. If God is creator rather than maker, that is, the source of everything rather than of, at most, simply what order there happens to be, the problem of human freedom becomes acute. If God is the source of all, is there any intelligible sense in which man can be the source of anything? How can a choice be called his? In sum, the larger cultural assumption of monotheism will cause philosophy to reconsider its position, now feeling much more acutely the problem of how humans possibly can be free.

Gilson's point was that, even when philosophy understood as the realm of unaided reason is alert to protecting its boundaries from intrusion, which is rarely the case, inevitably the larger culture shapes its interests, determining which problems will be deemed philosophically central and which peripheral. If a culture has gone through a monotheistic period, furthermore, philosophy will out of habit keep the problem of the individual and of freedom at the centre of consciousness long after the formal props for such concern have disappeared. In a formerly Protestant country, ethics will remain 'Protestantism by other means', that is, have a content that continues to reflect the assumptions of Protestant theology long after Protestantism has lost its place at the centre of the culture. The same is true for formerly Catholic countries, or formerly Marxist countries.[10]

Gilson was interested in the afterlife of 'Christian philosophy', in the ways that philosophy in our own apparently secular times still reflects Christian assumptions, but his use of the term was primarily developed in regard to the period in which philosophy formed in a Christian matrix, namely the Middle Ages.[11] His argument was simply of a historical nature, that, since the rise of Christianity, philosophy in the West has necessarily taken on the shape of Christian preoccupations. This was most true in the period in which Christianity took the form of Christendom, but it is more than residually true to the present.

This paper cannot explore the richness of Gilson's second claim with the space it deserves: he seems more than amply to have justified it, even if we stay with the single work, *Christian Philosophy*. Fortunately, the nature of this second claim, that 'philosophizing under the influence of Christian faith' profoundly enriched philosophical thought, has been partly anticipated in the exposition of his first claim. The question to be addressed in the remainder of this chapter is whether, under the form of either of his claims, there is an idea of 'Christian history' parallel to Gilson's 'Christian philosophy'. A consideration, both preliminary and central to all that follows, must first be addressed.

The person using the term 'Christian history' is likely to meet less resistance than Gilson initially encountered, because the expression 'Christian history' has long been used with various commonly accepted meanings. It has the air of familiarity. Most obviously – and here the parallel with 'Christian philosophy', while real, can deceive – most people are willing to allow labelling this or that historical experience by the name of a shared religion. Jews can have Jewish history, and Moslems Islamic history. If all that is at issue is whether there have been concrete historical phenomena which have taken their shape under Christian influence, this can be granted. 'History', because it includes everything that can be shaped into a narrative, seems less an autonomous body of knowledge than philosophy, and while there may be reluctance to acknowledge Christianity's coloration of any part of philosophy, 'history' seems to encompass so much that we may readily allow various religious currents within it. Indeed – and this is the heart of our preliminary consideration – history seems only to gain a certain definition by ordering 'everything that has happened or claims to have happened' by some set of principles exterior to itself, that is, by introducing some principle of selectivity by which the real can be discriminated from the unreal.

Some illustration is in order. As long as we stick to the Aristotelian definition of history as (to give the later Latin convention) *narratio singularum*, which we can translate as 'the narration of specific things', we can avoid, or not even feel the need for, the definition of 'history in general' or 'universal history'. No pretence need be made that somehow the historical materials are dictating their interpretation (although the historian may feel this to be the case), for clearly each history is the result of a principle of selection which decides to include certain materials and exclude others. Although the decision to write the *History of the Peloponnesian War* depends on that war having taken place (for history, *pace* Simon Schama, is wed to events in a way literature is not), and on there having been a previous history of Athens, Sparta, Persia, etc., the decision to choose this war as the narrative framework of a history clearly lies with Thucydides. So too does the decision to see the war as instructive abut future politics, so instructive that speeches may be crafted (the reader is fairly warned) that represent no reality other than what should have been said on some occasion to make the instructive point. That is, Thucydides' decision to use the war to instruct future generations would have collapsed if the only causal explanation of the war was one over which humans have little or no control, namely as the work of the gods. If the war was nothing more than the result of divine initiatives, no science could be developed on the basis of its study. If an understanding which would be useful for future politics could be produced, it would be because something other than divine causation exists. Thus, Thucydides turned to the study of those causal relations open to human examination, to the study of 'secondary (interworldly or horizontal)', rather than 'primary (divine or vertical)', causation.[12] The gods did not have to be denied, but they had to be ignored in favour of study of those things humans can understand and therefore anticipate, above all politics and human psychology. Beyond observing that interworldly causal relations do exist, Thucydides does not justify constructing a world of men rather than gods, he simply does it, for his principle of selection necessitates such a world. The centring of history on politics and war and human characters in subsequent ancient historical writings is not something solely dictated by the so-called raw facts, although these things had to exist for a dialogue between the historian and the historical record to take place; this centring was one result of what these historians and their audiences considered to be real and worthy of portrayal.[13]

Clearly the fact that there had been a Peloponnesian War made possible an essentially political principle of narrative selection, just as the rise of Rome made possible a narrative built on the course of Empire. Augustine's ability to write a narrative of something not fully observable, his own spiritual development, and his equally novel construction of a narrative around a not fully empirical entity, the City of God, show that politics was not a necessary narrative basis, and that indeed the historian was free to choose his story.[14] Gregory of Tours (538–94) manifests the dangers and possibilities of this freedom, and the degree to which, except for exceptional thinkers like

Augustine, narrative had been hitherto dependent on politics.[15] With the collapse of the Empire in the West, Gregory is not at all sure what his story framework should be, and his *mimesis* tends to be of chaos and disorder. Political history fails him, because politics had failed his times, and it was not yet clear what story other than a political story could be told. He lived in an age when slowly *Heilsgeschichte*, a narrative built around the spread of salvation, was replacing politics as the perspective from which to read history, or rather, was wedding theology and politics. Bede (672/3–735) is the witness to, if not a successful marriage of the two, at least a tolerable concubinage, and in him we find a new historical framework in which primary and secondary causal explanation, revelation and politics, co-exist.[16] History now is universal not simply in the long-established Jewish and Christian sense of God's great deeds in time done ultimately for all, but, as it would be for centuries, a this-worldly narrative, specific in time and space, of the spread of salvation 'beginning from Jerusalem'. History is ultimately the chronicling of the salvation of the human race (though Bede, unlike some of his contemporaries, saw no need to go back to Adam and Eve before taking up the newest stage of the story), but immediately it is the story of how the most recently converted people has joined its history to universal salvation history, a *Historia ecclesiastica* in which a 'church' is at the same time a 'people'.

Karl Löwith correctly argued that there is no universal history without Judaism and Christianity. That is, the notion that all mankind shares in the same history, a linear history moving toward a goal, only appeared historically with the Judaeo-Christian tradition.[17] All histories outside this tradition, even that of Rome, were less than universal, and never – the Stoics came closest to being the exception – saw the whole human story as one story. Löwith also powerfully showed the manner in which, once given birth by Judaism and Christianity, the idea of universal history has persisted to the present, whether in liberal progressive form or in Marxism. The Christian sanction for such an idea may be rejected, but the idea is kept. Perhaps the greatest philosophical figure to embrace a secularized form of the linearity of history (albeit in the shape of a dialectic) was

Hegel, who saw in the one story of mankind the gradual emergence of freedom. Marx a little later, Löwith argues, may be viewed as a secularized Jewish prophet, and Marxism as a form of Judaism. Marx's view of history, beginning with a propertyless, harmonious, benevolent world (Eden), proceeding through class struggle (history), and ending with the heaven of the withering away of the State and of private property, the restoring of Eden, is a form of 'Jewish history' (with heavy Christian overlay).

Such views are not dead. Although in the United States old Christian ideas more commonly take progressive and meliorist forms, only a few years ago, Francis Fukuyama, apparently with a straight face, returned to a Hegelian form of the question whether there is a direction to the history of mankind.[18] Fukuyama developed the double sense of history's end already present in Hegel. If there is a direction in history, an end in the sense of a goal, must it not follow that as we near that goal history in some sense disappears, has an end in the sense of no further development, and we remain permanently in some best state of life? Fukuyama suggested that the logic of modern science and what he, following Hegel, calls the struggle for recognition, the desire of people to leave their mark on history, have led to the collapse of tyranny and the victory of capitalist liberal democracy, the end, in both senses, of the historical process. Here, as with Hegel or Marx, we have the possibility of a conquering of time within time itself, an end of the historical process within history. But Fukuyama retains a doubt. Will man be content in this last state, or will it prove a delusion, banal rather than satisfying, something to be fled for the satisfying terror of history? Will liberty and equality produce a stable, ended, society, or lead inevitably to the quest for re-entry into time? We need not linger over Fukuyama's undigested views. But the questions he poses illustrate rather well a kind of bastardization of Christian patterns of thought, now made the subject of some end of history imminent to the historical process itself.

Christianity, according to Löwith the most self-conscious and honest of the historical traditions on these matters because acknowledging that its views come from revelation and not from history, at least fitfully sees that its principle of historical narrative is not some inevitable framework dictated by the 'facts', but an a priori by which the facts are organized. Only with Christianity's step-children, Hegelianism, Marxism, progressivism, did a certain forgetfulness about where the framework had come from occur, with the resultant delusion that history itself was about freedom, class struggle and its overcoming, or progress. It takes little reflection to see that many of the main components of secular presentation of history to the present, above all the idea of progress, are hardly intelligible without the Christian matrix which formed them.

Our preliminary but central observation, therefore, is that 'Christian history' is a very useful phrase to articulate both the truth that all historical narrative rests on principles of selection brought to the historical record, and the truth that therefore all 'history' will be organized by an adjective, whether 'Christian' or something else. The Enlightenment ideal of a secular, simply this-wordly, history is a lie and a deceit, if its claim is that it is the only true history. Also a deceit is the closely related positivist ideal of self-interpreting facts. Like Marxism in their refusal to stand with the Christians and honestly acknowledge that their principles of interpretation rest on acts of faith, such notions are noticeable for their lack of self-consciousness or self-understanding. In spite of all the recent attacks on the idea of historical objectivity, all the attempts to say 'my history is as good as yours', many of which embrace a relativism as flawed as the naïve objectivism they replace, the Enlightenment heritage is by no means dead.[19] Thus the modern historian, if he is to remain respectable, must, as much as Thucydides, treat divine intervention as something other than it claims to be. By saying, for instance, that since, a priori, miracles cannot occur, and that when they are met in the historical record they may safely be explained as something else, a safe and comfortable, an enlightened and bourgeois, 'history' is made possible.[20] My point is that without a priori starting-points, history has virtually no shape at all, is infinitely malleable or amorphous. One great merit of the idea of 'Christian history' is that it underlines the a priori nature of all historical interpretation, its dependence on something other than a bare historical record. Now we can turn to the claim not simply that Christianity has historically been more honest than its competitors about what it is doing in interpreting history, but that the a priori, the Word, it uses is superior to, more illuminating of, man's situation in history. In a single essay one cannot be exhaustive, and must largely speak by way of examples, making comparison not to theoretical alternatives to Christianity, but to actual alternatives today.

Nothing better illustrates the ways in which Christian theology can deepen the understanding of history than its formation in the individual historian of what I will call a Christian sensibility. Just as in the case of 'Christian philosophy', the claim is not that nothing is understood without viewing the evidence from a Christian perspective – obviously a great deal is – but that a much richer sense of reality is communicated by taking especially Christian anthropology, a Christian reading of what man is, to heart. Above all this avoids all the silliness involved in the idea that history has laws or is a science in any very rigorous sense of that word. A Christian perspective nurtures humility, a sense of mystery, and the gravest doubts about all claimed historical patterns. After all, from a Christian point of view what history is is a drama, the drama of sin and grace.

The chief knowledge that the Christian historian brings to history is of the glory of God. As Paul already said in the first two chapters of Romans, some sense of this glory is open to all humans, that is, it is not specifically Christian. But the Scriptures immensely deepen our natural sense of God's glory by an account of his great deeds. From the scriptural record the believer discovers that the very creation was aimed at man's dominating the world and co-operating with God in co-creation.[21] The Scriptures tell us how God formed a people, that he wishes all to be saved, that he sent his only Son to redeem the race, and that the Paraclete is now present in the Church. Although no clear picture is given of either the course of history after the New Testament period, or of what the end is to which God is leading the race, the New Testament encourages hope as the appropriate human response to this revelation – confidence that God in his good time is accomplishing his will. As Julian of Norwich tells us Jesus told her, 'all will be well, and all will be well, and every kind of thing will be well'.[22]

A sense of the glory of God calls forth in the historian a sense of the mystery of history, of the mystery of God's ways. Even in the Bible, where, for Israel and the earliest stages of Christian history, we have presumably our clearest statement of what God is doing, it is all very mysterious. Constantly human expectations are overturned. The younger brother is preferred. The last shall be first. Jesus says God himself is not simply King, but characterized by lowliness and service. Christ is at once Suffering Servant and Judge, dying Redeemer and Victor over death. Indeed it is the picture of Jesus in the Scriptures which is the heart of mystery. One reason there are so many Jesuses in later portrayal is that he escapes all easy categorization, is always so much more than any one human picture can make him.

Certain things follow from this. Although I have some sympathy with all the attempts, from Orosius in the fifth century past Bossuet in the seventeenth, to write a Christian history in the sense of recounting what God continues to do in time, I am as suspicious of these as was Augustine of Eusebius, the founder of the genre. Even the best flatten the mystery. Some distinctions are in order. The Christian believes that he has certain kinds of insight into God's will, formed by the scriptural account and the reflection of the Church. Thus, the Christian follows Genesis in believing that humans have been made to rule the earth, he follows Exodus in believing that he has been given commandments to obey, and he follows Matthew in believing that he has been called to some form of perfection. In some measure the Christian knows what it is to do God's will, and what it is to violate it. Presumably, therefore, he can say something truly when he says 'Here God's will is done', or 'Here it is not.' Such knowledge, though enough to guide a single life, falls far short of being able to 'read history' from God's side, to tell us what God is doing in the present. We know something of what he wishes done, but hardly anything of how his will works. From creation through the death and resurrection of Christ, the coming of the Spirit at Pentecost, and the earliest Christian mission, the Scriptures themselves give a reading of history, of certain events that are central to history's interpretation. But there is nothing comparable to this once the New Testament account ends. It is not that nothing at all can be said, for, as Eusebius showed, ecclesiastical history can be written. The history of attempts to continue to respond to God's will, the history of ecclesiastical institutions, the history of the spread of the gospel, the history of reflection on the gospel, all these things are possible. We might also say, to jump to the modern period, that Hegel is possible, that is that one may take a theme deriving from Christianity, such as the spread of freedom, and using this as one's principle of selection, write its history. Here the possible theologies of history are endless, and include, for instance, a reading of history according to liberation theology. They are as good as their principles of selection are adequate to capturing the whole Christian message.

Augustine's doubts about Eusebian history were not doubts that one could write ecclesiastical history at all, but doubts that one could with any certitude specify God's will by, for instance, saying that Constantine's reign represented the culmination to which history had been moving. The Christian believes that God is always at work in history, but Augustine did not see that this gives specific information of the kind Eusebius retailed. Augustine believed God is at work in everything, constantly bringing good from evil, but danger lay in the unqualified claim, made about any historical force or party, 'this is the will of God'. Everything in time, every individual as well as the Church itself, is mixed, composed of good and evil. Therefore while some timeless principle, say the first commandment, may express the will of God without reservation, nothing born of time can be anything but mixed. Moreover, because everything is in some sense the will of God, the question, if one is to write a Christian history in the manner initiated by Eusebius, is not whether God is working in all things, but how he is working. Here, beyond such things as chronicling the keeping of the commandments or tracing the spread of the gospel, Augustine thought the Christian has no 'methodology' for discovering God's ways.[23] He himself had felt the call by God in the garden, what Gregory the Great (590–604) was to call the goad of the Spirit, and Calvin in the sixteenth century a sense of vocation. Julian of Norwich, around 1400, thought Jesus spoke to her. Such things could tell one what to do with one's life, might even as at Fatima in the twentieth century give some specific prophecy, but again did not give the kind of information by which a reading of one's times could be attempted with much confidence. One might even, in the spirit of Luther or Herbert Butterfield, go a little further and doubt that even on the relatively simple question of one person keeping one commandment, a historian can 'read hearts', that is, know enough about a single human being to render a certain judgement on motivation.[24] What indeed does it mean to trace the spread of the gospel? The historian can count baptisms given, communions taken, and saints reformed. Yet, important as these things are, the deepest movements of the Spirit seem out of grasp. The theologies of history and Christian histories, therefore, are best read as speculative attempts to guess what history might be about, and attempts to dig below the surface. They, though not unimportant, are always inadequate. We return to the point that 'Christian history', looking at history from the vantage point of Christianity, first should foster a sense of mystery, of drama, rather than Christian histories. In some degree, all the great Christian histories obscure God's nature, make things too clear, too easily take sides, or only see one side.

This said, Christian history – here the parallel with Christian philosophy is exact – understood as the examination of history in the light of Christianity, can give a more adequate and very differently textured account of human events than that normally found in academic history, which is still very much the child of the Enlightenment. A Christian anthropology is very different from an Enlightenment anthropology, and the two result in different histories. I remember Arthur Schlesinger, Jr, a quintessential liberal son of the Enlightenment, to have said somewhere after serving in the Kennedy White House that he, the author of many stout volumes on various aspects of the American presidency, now realized that the history of no presidency could be written. By this I supposed he meant not that nothing could be said, but that now that he had experienced how presidential decisions are made, he under-stood that what the historian considers documents are poor evidence of what took place. It is not just that documents may contain disinformation and obfuscation, but that the heart of decisions taken is likely and intentionally not found there at all. I cannot see that this momentary insight much affected how Schlesinger continued to view history, but it shows that even a non-Christian writer momentarily saw the benefit of writing 'Christian history'. By that I mean that the narratives of the Enlightenment commonly deceive by their suggestion that a historian can confidently chronicle great human events. In contrast, the narratives of Christianity – of Augustine's, not Bossuet's, form of Christianity – profoundly enlighten by suggesting that, since God is the author of history and his purposes are largely hidden, all history is mysterious and only chronicled in hesitation. They communicate what life, seen through a glass darkly rather than by a futurologist in a department of sociology, is really like. They never are confident about reductionist explanations, 'explaining' things as 'really' issues of power, class, or gender. They suspect all the simplifying, non-mysterious, accounts of the Marxists, liberals, social historians, and feminists.[25] These seem hardly human at all, accounts written in great *hubris*, as if one had found the key which unlocks the mystery of life. Certainly, as Anthony Burgess has shown, one does not have to be a practising Christian to see the rightness of the doctrine of original sin, of man's cross-grained nature. There are, even in academia, historians with a sense of human complexity. But the assertion that at the heart of man there is a mystery grounded in the struggle between good and evil is the lantern held before the Christian historian. He or she does not expect life to be something which can be successfully planned, something in which there is much connection between what we want and what we get. This could only be so if we are the authors of history.

The doctrine of original sin points in two ways, articulating both mankind's degradation and grandeur. We are not simply sinners, but sons of God, called to divinization. We can plan, and our plans do not always go astray. They achieve their goals sufficiently to encourage us in keeping to the course. Even according to the rules of the Enlightenment, the study of history well pays our efforts. Much more than this, there are moments in life of transcendence, of surpassing grace. This grandeur in life, the glory of God which runs through things, seems also not present in much historical writing. The favourable implications of our cross-grained nature are as much missed by the sons of the Enlightenment as the unfavourable. That is, just as the tragedy and limitations of human life, its lack of control over the future or failure to understand its own times, commonly is not at the centre of academic history, which in treating even subjects for which there is 'no exit' tends to retain an air of optimism, neither is the sense of genuine goodness in life often communicated. Granted, striking and variegated goodness is less common than mediocrity or active evil. But it is almost as if the secular historian does not know what to do with the goodness – or the strangeness – he comes across. Again, we tend to get a flattened history not attendant to the striking differences between people. I can only guess that egalitarian premises have so influenced modern historians that they tend not to be alert here. Moralizing abounds, Hitler gets condemned, but little attention is given to the forms of heroic goodness which are encountered in everyday life. Christianity, by contrast, with its sense of the unique mission given to each person, makes one suspicious of theories which see humans as interchangeable or equal and predisposes one to sympathy for hierarchical systems, and thus for noticing the great differences between people. I will not belabour the point, but part of the sense of mystery Christian history fosters is an awe before the extraordinary goodness – always so far as we can judge – one sometimes meets in the historical record.

The very categories of 'development' and 'progress', constantly used by the children of the Enlightenment, will be deeply suspect by the Christian historian. Although he will see how such notions trace their lineage back to Christian ideas such as providence, he will also see that they radically flatten such ideas and again pretend that history can be read as a clear story. Thoughtful examination of history in fact raises the gravest doubts about whether there has been general progress. Meditation on a theology of history such as that of Hans Urs von Balthasar should lead to a questioning of the general presentation of history under the category of 'development'.[26] I do not mean that we can or should get rid of all mechanical and organic metaphors of change, but that, if one examines any substantial part of the historical record, such metaphors seem to capture only a small part of what is happening. Taking just the biblical record as an example, the category of the unexpected, of the jump or quantum-leap, but also of the about-face, is at least as important as any developmental category. One can know all there is to be known about the development of Hebrew thought and be unprepared for what the book of Isaiah says. And how much silliness has been written in the eminently justifiable search for patterns of development in the New Testament, say from a low to a high Christology? Not everything should be forced into the mould of development. In this case it would be better to see the New Testament writers as something like the elders of the Apocalypse, who are often placed with the gospel writers on Romanesque tympana, sitting, perhaps chatting, with their cups and instruments in hand, ready to make music, with Christ in the middle.[27] There is high and low from the beginning in this assembly, this Choir of the blessed, points of view as well as development, differing perspectives as far back as we can see. Each Evangelist sees a part of the mystery: four are better than one. The Saviour himself seems hardly bound by the categories of time and space at all, and moves in and out of our world. Categories of development and, especially, of progress, convey very little of the whole. The Christian historian studies with this always before him. Further, he knows that, like his Enlightenment brother, he first sees the surface, the literal sense of Scripture or, so to speak, the human nature of Christ. But he believes this is far less than the whole: the literal sense of Scripture opens on the spiritual sense, the human nature of Christ is wedded to the divine.[28] In sum, although history is more amorphous than philosophy, 'Christian history' stands to the one as 'Christian philosophy' does to the other, both as historical reality and as sobering insight. Gilson thought 'Christian philosophy' made its own case, that any fair-minded person could see how Christianity had historically deepened philosophical perception. 'Christian history' makes the same claim about the understanding of history.

NOTES

1 I thank Donald J. D'Elia and Warren Carroll, the editors of a volume in which a version of the present essay is to appear, for permission also to publish it in its present form. For orientation see Étienne Gilson, *Christian Philosophy: An Introduction*, tr. Armand Maurer (Toronto, 1993). This is a translation of a French work published in 1960, and gives Gilson's mature views. My summary of Gilson is particularly dependent on this book and its very helpful 'Translator's Introduction'.

2 For instance, *The Christian Philosophy of Saint Augustine*, tr. L. E. M. Lynch (New York, 1960; in the original French, simply *Introduction à l'étude de Saint Augustin*, Paris, 1929), and *The Christian Philosophy of St. Thomas Aquinas*, tr. L. K. Shook (New York, 1956; in the fifth edition of the original French, simply *Le Thomisme. Introduction à la philosophie de saint Thomas d'Aquin*, Paris, 1948). The *History of Christian Philosophy in the Middle Ages* (New York, 1955) carried its title from the beginning. For the history of Gilson's phrase, see Maurer's 'Translator's Introduction' in Gilson, *Christian Philosophy*, p. IX.

3 Maurer, 'Translator's Introduction'.

4 Norman Cantor, *Inventing the Middle Ages: The Lives, Works and Ideas of the Great Medievalists of the Twentieth Century* (New York, 1991), p. 328. I have had my say about the inadequacies of this book in 'Inventing the Middle Ages', a short form of which was published in *The Dawson Newsletter* 10 (Spring, 1992): 4–10, and longer forms of which were published in *The Journal of the Rocky Mountain Medieval and Renaissance Association* 14 (1993): 131–49 and in Carlos Barros (ed.), *Historia a Debate: Medieval* (Santiago de Compostela, 1995), pp. 21–30.

5 Maurer, 'Translator's Introduction', p. 1, for the quoted phrase. As Maurer points out, Gilson traces his own thinking on such matters in *The Philosopher and Theology*, tr. Cécile Gilson (New York, 1962).

6 David Knowles (eds D. E. Luscombe and C. N. L. Brooke), *The Evolution of Medieval Thought*, 2nd edn (London, 1988), p. 83. This 2nd edn, as at pp. xi and xiv, works against Gilson's (and Knowles') point of view and confuses issues.

7 Josef Pieper, *Leisure, the Basis of Culture* (New York, 1952) is a powerful, brief, account, dwelling on the origins of Greek philosophy, of the intertwining, of how philosophy emerged from contemplation and was a form of 'thoughtful religion'.

8 Translation by Rosemary Sheed of the revised version, *The Mystery of the Supernatural* (New York, 1967).

9 See for instance *The Road of Science and the Ways to God* (Chicago, 1980).

10 I have developed the idea of 'Protestantism by other means' especially in two articles, 'The Meaning of Christian Culture: An Historical View', in David L. Schindler (ed.), *Catholicism and Secularization in America: Essays on Nature, Grace and Culture* (Notre Dame, Indiana 1990), pp. 98–130, and

'John Rawls and the Flight from Authority: The Quest for Equality as an Exercise in Primitivism', *Interpretation: A Journal of Political Philosophy* 21 (1994): 419–36. I have drawn specific instances of how the larger historical context determines how moral questions are addressed in '1492 in the Judgment of the Nations', in *Actas del II Congreso 'Cultura Europea'* (Pamplona, 1994), pp. 175–81.

11 *The Unity of Philosophical Experience* (New York, 1947).

12 I study this desacralization of the Greek world in 'Cultural Dynamics: Secularization and Sacralization', *Christianity and Western Civilization* (San Francisco, 1995), pp. 97–122.

13 Erich Auerbach, *Mimesis: The Representation of Reality in Western Literature*, tr. Willard Trask (Garden City, New York 1957), is the great study of how changing ideas of what is real and important have influenced 'the representation of reality' in Western culture.

14 I have explored some aspects of Augustine's construction of a narrative around his spiritual development in 'St. Augustine and the Problem of the Medieval Discovery of the Individual', *Word and Spirit: A Monastic Review* 9 (1987): 129–56.

15 I am thinking primarily of the analysis developed by Auerbach in *Mimesis*, ch. 4, and then somewhat revised in his *Literary Language and Its Public in Late Latin Antiquity*, tr. Ralph Manheim (New York, 1965), esp. pp. 103 ff. See Walter Goffart, *The Narrators of Barbarian History (AD 550–800): Jordanes, Gregory of Tours, Bede, and Paul the Deacon* (Princeton, 1988), pp. 114–15, 145–7, 149, 174 ff., 191, and Martin Heinzelmann, *Gregor von Tours (538–94) 'Zehn Bücher Geschichte': Historiographie und Gesellschaftskonzept im 6. Jahrhundert* (Darmstadt, 1994).

16 Glenn W. Olsen, 'Bede as Historian: The Evidence from his Observations on the Life of the First Christian Community at Jerusalem', *Journal of Ecclesiastical History* 33 (1982): 519–30, and 'From Bede to the Anglo-Saxon Presence in the Carolingian Empire', *Angli e Sassoni al di qua e al di là del Mare*, 2 vols (Settimane di studio del Centro italiano di studi sull'alto medioevo, 32; Spoleto, 1986), 1, pp. 305–82.

17 Karl Löwith, *Meaning in History* (Chicago, 1949). Hans Urs von Balthasar has elaborated the nature of salvation history in many books. See for instance *In the Fullness of Faith: On the Centrality of the Distinctively Catholic*, tr. Graham Harrison (San Francisco, 1988), esp. pp. 33–6.

18 Francis Fukuyama, *The End of History and the Last Man* (New York, 1992).

19 Peter Novick, *That Noble Dream: The 'Objectivity Question' and the American Historical Profession* (Cambridge, 1988), is a very good introduction to the quest for objectivity. I have tried to develop defensible ideas of objectivity and relativism in 'Transcendental Truth and Cultural Relativism: An Historian's View', in Paul Williams (ed.), *Historicism and Faith* (Scranton, 1980), pp. 49–61.

20 Two of the sharpest critics of such views have been Hans Urs von Balthasar, who forms a great alternative in the seven volumes of his *The Glory of the Lord: A Theological Aesthetics* (see beginning at vol. 1: *Seeing the Form*, tr. Erasmo Leiva-Merikakis (Edinburgh, 1982), pp. 23 ff.); and Joseph Cardinal Ratzinger, as in *Behold the Pierced One: An Approach to Spiritual Christology*, tr. Graham Harrison (San Francisco, 1986), at pp. 30, 42–6, and *'In the Beginning . . .' A Catholic Understanding of the Story of Creation and the Fall*, tr. Boniface Ramsey (Huntington, Indiana 1990), at pp. 13–29. See also Georges Chantraine, 'Exegesis and Contemplation in the Work of Hans Urs von Balthasar', in David L. Schindler (ed.), *Hans Urs von Balthasar: His Life and Work* (San Francisco, 1991), pp. 133–47.

21 I have studied the influence of this idea in 'From Bede to the Anglo-Saxon Presence' (see n. 16 above), and in 'Twelfth-Century Humanism Reconsidered: The Case of St. Bernard', *Studi Medievali*, 3a Serie, 31 (1990): 27–53.

22 *Showings* (Long Text), ch. 27 (Thirteenth Revelation), tr. Edmund Colledge and James Walsh (New York, 1978), p. 225.

23 Paula Fredriksen, 'Tyconius and Augustine on the Apocalypse', in Richard K. Emmerson and Bernard McGinn (eds), *The Apocalypse in the Middle Ages* (Ithaca, 1992), pp. 20–37, is very good on Augustine's 'radical agnosticism' (p. 34).

24 Herbert Butterfield, *Christianity and History* (New York, 1950).

25 See my essay, 'Marriage, Feminism, Theology and the New Social History: Dyan Elliott's *Spiritual Marriage*', *Communio: International Catholic Review* 22 (1995): 343–56. I reviewed the same book in *Speculum* 70 (1995): 363–4.

26 This is found through all his writings, but see Hans Urs von Balthasar, *A Theology of History* (New York, 1963), esp. pp. 134–40. I am in substantial agreement with the analysis and critique of the earliest Christian thinking about progress by Wolfram Kinzig, *Novitas Christiana: Die Idee des Fortschritts in der Alten Kirche bis Eusebius* (Göttingen, 1994). See also Paul Freedman, 'The Return of the Grotesque in Medieval Historiography', *Historia a Debate: Medieval*, ed. Barros, pp. 9–19.

27 Peter K. Klein, 'Introduction: The Apocalypse in Medieval Art', in Emmerson and McGinn (eds), *Apocalypse*, pp. 159–99, at 160–4, 184, traces the development of portrayal of the twenty-four elders. See also in the same volume, Dale Kinney, 'The Apocalypse in Early Christian Monumental Decoration', pp. 200–16 at 201, 203–5, 207, 210–13.

28 Hans Urs von Balthasar, *Word and Revelation*, tr. A. V. Littledale (New York, 1964), pp. 22 ff. I have written on the senses of Scripture in 'Allegory, Typology and Symbol: The *sensus spiritalis*, Part 1: Definitions and Earliest History', *Communio* 4 (1977): 161–79, 'Part II: Early Church through Origen', ibid.: 257–84.

Historical imagination and the renewal of culture

MICHAEL O'BRIEN

On summer nights I like to take my children up the hill behind our house. We live far out in the country and no lights from other houses can be seen. The sky is like black glass reflecting nothing, but dazzling with billions of stars and planets. At the crest of the hill we lie in the grass. It takes a little time but we eventually grow quiet and still. The children lie on my chest or snuggle under my arm and look up. We gaze up, up into the infinite pool which bears the stars into being. Above us, on especially clear nights, with the aid of a low-power telescope we can locate a tiny smudge of light which is the closest galaxy. It is spinning, spinning, but it is so far away that one could look for a whole lifetime and not see it alter. There are other galaxies out there, I tell my children, that whirl into each other like discs blending in space without colliding. They pass through each other, those billions of worlds, at thousands of miles per second, yet they do not appear to move at all. The children can just barely believe it, but they do believe it because I am their father and they trust me.

'The universe is deep,' I tell them. 'You can look into it forever.'

And so they look with new eyes. The interior eye adjusts and they see what it is so difficult for us adults to see: existence is not one-dimensional, or two-dimensional or three or five. Creation is not a flat theatre backdrop to our lives. It is deep. You can look into it forever.

A few weeks ago I was visiting at the home of a family which lives on a farm down the road from where we live. They had recently moved there from the city, and it was their first experience of living in the countryside. The father of the family and I were engaged in a heated theological debate, when the door flew open and his twelve-year-old son burst in, I should say floated in. The boy's eyes were full of tears and his mouth was open wide, unable to speak for a few moments. We stared at him. His face was full of wonder and his arms raised in a gesture that bore a remarkable resemblance to the ancient *orans* position of prayer, a gesture that is a timeless one, a mute reaching for transcendence.

'Oh papa,' he whispered, 'I have seen the most beautiful thing. I have seen a *deer*.'

It is impossible to convey the sense of awe with which he breathed this word. We stared at him, wondering what he meant. A deer? We have all seen deer. Then my neighbour and I looked at each other and understood that perhaps after all we had not ever really seen a deer. At least not in the way this child had just seen one. And later there came the revelation to both of us that we, with our prodigious intellects and our fiercely defended positions, often talk about things we have not really seen, or known, or loved well. We have pictures in our mind which form concepts and ideologies. We are clever, articulate impressionists, but we have not gazed into the liquid galaxies of a wild creature's eyes as it gazed back equally uncomprehending upon us. We have not stroked the red velvet hide. We have not touched the bone antlers and felt them toss. We have not seen it leap as it bolted for the sanctuary of the trees.

There are times in the summer when my children go out in the dusk, dancing around on tiptoes, leaping like Nijinsky, chasing fireflies. If they succeed in capturing a few, they bring them home in jars, and drift off to sleep gazing at the phosphorescent light, startlingly bright, a fabulous bestiary, unexplainable and totally captivating – a covey of fireflies winking off, then on, then off, then on, contrapuntally in the dark of the children's bedrooms. Who is the captor, who the captive?

Six times I have attended the birth of my children. Each time as they emerge from the womb there comes from some unknown source within me and my wife an upwelling, rather a fountaining of wonder, reverence, tears, laughter, exultation. A new being has shown its hidden face and begun to assert its identity. O marvel of marvels, this child is ours and yet not ours. He is from our flesh, and yet he is so much more than us. Who is he? Where did he come from? This miraculous being, never before seen, never to be repeated. An epiphany of the infinitely creative mind of God.

In his book, *Painting and Reality*, the Thomist Étienne Gilson says that each work of art is a new created being. This is precisely so. Although it is not conscious, organic being, it has presence. It has identity. It occupies space. It is unrepeatable. It pushes back the darkness by simply being there. And according to its fidelity to reality (implicitly or explicitly) it expands the realm of light by the authority of its *word*.

It is a commonplace that written into creation are words. What do they say? Where do they come from? Nature contains metaphors of a higher order which animates creation, and originates beyond it. We swim in a tropical sea of such signs, some easily read, others posing difficult questions. But in all situations, Nature reminds us of the primal lesson that existence is inexpressibly beautiful and undeniably dangerous. We are not in charge here. We are subject to a sometimes bewildering complex of laws. Only a fool or a madman will assert that nature is an expression of his own mind. Cro-Magnon man crouching in the caves of Lascaux knew this well, though he would not have been able to articulate it. When he smeared charcoal and pigment on the stone walls, depicting the heaving gallop of deer and bison, he was performing a task that has rarely been surpassed for sheer style, purity, authenticity and perception. This is immanent experience and transcendent experience meeting in the drama of the hunt, of one creature wrestling for the life he would extract from the death of another. This is more than a news item about food gathering. This is more than a tale about hunger filled. This portrait speaks to us across thousands of years with an immediacy that communicates the rush of adrenalin, the terror, exultation, feasting, gratitude, power and longing. Depicted here is the search for permanence and completion, and also a witness to the insufficiency that greets us again each morning. This is a probing of the sensitive, mysterious roots of life itself. And the little stick men chasing the galloping herds across the wall are a singular message about where prehistoric man placed himself in the hierarchy of being. That he could paint his marvellous quarry, that he could thus obtain a mastery over the dangerous miracle, must have been a great joy and a puzzle to him. That he portrayed his quarry as beautiful is another message. The tale is only superficially about an encounter with raw animal power. The artist's deeper tale is about the discovery of the power within him – man the maker, man the artist! This was not prehistoric man watching primitive television. This was religion.

I do not have much sympathy for the ideas of men such as Carl Jung and Joseph Campbell, although many of my fellow artists do. They have written a great deal about the role of symbol and myth. In this regard, I think they are on to a true insight when they speak of the centrality of those faculties in the human psyche. But the insight is limited: Campbell, for example, has written that 'all religions are merely misunderstood mythologies' – please note the word *all*. G. K. Chesterton once pointed out, in his 1903–4 controversy with Robert Blatchford, that the modern mythologists' position really adds up to this: Since a truth has impressed itself deeply in the consciousness of many peoples of varying times, religions and cultures, then it simply cannot be true. The new mythologist, he said, has failed to examine the most important consideration of all: that people of various times and places may have been informed at an intuitive level of actual events which would one day take place in history; that in their inner longings there was a glimmer of light, a presentiment, a yearning forward through the medium of art toward the fullness of Truth that would one day be made flesh in the Incarnation. Perhaps it is the mythologists who need to be 'demythologized'.

When I was a youth my family lived for several years in the high Canadian Arctic, hundreds of miles above the tree line, in a small Inuit (Eskimo) village. I recall the material impoverishment of the Inuit people during those years. So many of them lived in igloos and cardboard shacks during the nine months of winter, and in caribou-skin tents during the very brief summer.

Their possessions were few, but often beautifully made. Stone lamps for burning seal oil were ingeniously designed and flawlessly symmetrical. Carvings of animals, birds, human and mythological subjects were of unsuspected eloquence and elegance, a haunting new language for the heart and eye. I can still remember one black shining carving that must have weighed six or eight pounds in the hand, a tumbling convolution of heart-stopping perfection that depicted a terrible and beautiful thing. The toothless old woman who carved it grinned at me as we sat beside her fire in a tent on the shore of the Arctic Ocean. She sat on an empty packing crate scavenged from the Hudson Bay Company outpost, surrounded by stone shavings, her scrapers and knives, and the smell of decaying smoked fish, while willow twigs snapped and burned under a boiling tea kettle. She called her carving, 'Man Wrestling with Polar Bear'. In the north men do not wrestle with bears. In such encounters men always lose. This image was a solid metaphor of the interior wrestling which is our abiding condition and calling: courage overcoming fear. Weakness overcoming impossible odds. It was pondering existential questions in the only language available to her, and it was for that reason inherently religious.

Later I lived for many years in the interior forests of British Columbia in the Rocky Mountains. I can still remember the face of a little Indian girl crouched by a mud puddle, arranging bits of broken glass, bottle caps, trash and detritus from the forest, creating a miniature garden of Eden. Her face was so beautiful, so totally absorbed, so happy. Dressed in rags, she was busy about a holy task, that of restoring a damaged creation to some vision of order and beauty.

I recall another man we knew for a few years. A dangerous man. He was a criminal who had spent most of his life in prisons. He became a friend of our family. His alcoholism was the release valve of a deep rage and sense of worthlessness. When he drank he was violent – relentlessly, mercilessly vicious. There were reasons for all this: he had been abandoned as a child. His mother had frozen to death. He had starved. When he eventually found his own father he stabbed him. He tried to stab me once. And yet when he did not drink he was like a lamb.

Sober, he had a rather sweet temperament, and he was always sincerely sorry whenever he disrupted our home. He begged our forgiveness. We always gave it and started over again. The point of this story is that he was one of the most gifted artists I have ever met. He was never a happy man; he lived in a twilight of perpetual anguish. Except when he was painting or carving. Then for a few brief hours he was full of . . . of joy. I recall a bowl he made once in the shape of a highly stylized raven. It was so very much a work of genius that it belonged in a museum. I told him that. When I asked about it some time later he shrugged, and said he had sold it to a tourist for ten dollars. He bought a bottle of wine with the money and drank it.

I would not tell such stories if they were not part of a larger pattern that proceeds apace in the culture of the West. I do not exaggerate when I say that I know many, many writers, painters and poets of outstanding talent who simply sink beneath the waves of our culture and never bear the fruit they are called to bear. That mediocrity and falsehood are everywhere exalted; that fortunes are wasted on junk, while things of irreplaceable beauty and truth fail to be born, or are created at superhuman cost only to be marginalized; that the spiritual sources which are the timeless origins of creativity have been largely blocked and displaced by commercial pseudo-culture – these are all factors which present not a few problems for the gifted person. His own dismay is his chief enemy. Lack of response from his society is his second. That there are exceptions to this pattern, sometimes glorious exceptions, the result of privilege, place and cold hard cash, is no argument against the death of the imagination. They are exceptions which prove the rule.

Chesterton once wrote about Cobbett's history of the English Reformation that the Protestant Cobbett was a singularly honest man. Cobbett did his research well, and came up with the politically incorrect conclusion that some enormous 'unmentionable crime' had occurred in England. I think the same phrase could be applied to the current state of Western culture: we have suffered some colossal but unmentionable tragedy that does not seem for the moment to offer much promise of changing for the better. Indeed it is so all-pervasive that in many places it has invaded the cultural life of the Church.

In his seven-volume work on theological aesthetics, *The Glory of the Lord*, Hans Urs von Balthasar gives the following warning:

> No longer loved or fostered by religion, beauty is lifted from its face as a mask, and its absence exposes features on that face which threaten to become incomprehensible to man. We no longer dare to believe in beauty and we make of it a mere appearance in order the more easily to dispose of it . . .
>
> Our situation today shows that beauty demands for itself at least as much courage and decision as do truth and goodness, and she will not allow herself to be separated and banned from her two sisters without taking them along with herself in a mysterious act of vengeance. We can be sure that whoever sneers at her name as if she were an ornament of the bourgeois past, can no longer pray and soon will no longer be able to love.[1]

In *Painting and Reality*, Gilson laments that 'churches have largely become so many temples dedicated to the exhibition of industrialized ugliness, and to veneration of painted *non-being*'.

In her book on aesthetics, *Feeling and Form*, the American philosopher Susanne Langer confirms Gilson's analysis of most contemporary church art, and adds that such works 'corrupt the religious consciousness that is developed in their image, and even while they illustrate the teachings of the Church, they degrade those teachings . . . Bad music, bad statues and pictures are irreligious, because everything corrupt is irreligious'.

And so, what are the solutions? A return to classical iconography? That may be part of a restoration but it certainly will not be all of it. Perhaps a return to some principles which the artisans of the Gothic era understood? Perhaps we will want to return to some other period that we have idealized? Yes, there are things to be learned there, but they are not the whole story.

Arthur Koestler, in his book *The Act of Creation*, says that we are now living in a period of 'oversaturation' and that there are two alternative responses we can make to this: 'emphasis' and 'implicitness'. He is saying by this that we can increase the voltage and pour on the stimuli in an attempt to grab the attention of the jaded modern imagination. Or we can move in the direction of an economy of understatement, and through subtlety restore the appetites of modern man to simplicity. Although there is a truth here, I believe his either/or remedy is somewhat simplistic. We do indeed need to avoid the tempta- tion to increase the dose of a bad drug. We do indeed need to grow in simplicity. However, there are other possibilities. Because art has an inherent restorative power, and furthermore because it always has an authoritative voice in the soul, we must trust that over time works of truth and beauty created from authentic spiritual sources will help to bring about a cultural reconfiguration and a reorientation of man. The question we need to ask is not so much what sort of surgery should be applied to a sick body, but what are the first principles of health.

Let us go back to some earlier periods in the history of the imagination to see if there are some things to be learned there.

I believe that the sacrifice of Isaac was the seminal moment, and image, which represents and inaugurates the rise of the West. It was a radical break with the perceptions of the Old Age. When God led Abraham up the mountains of Moriah, he was building upon a well-established cultural pattern. Countless men were going up to the high places all around him, and were carrying out their intentions to sacrifice their children. But God led Abraham by another way, through the narrow corridors of his thinking, his presumptions about the nature of reality. There was something monumental and irrational in Abraham's act of obedience. This was not a typical pagan, greedy for cultic power, for more sons or for bigger flocks. This was an old man who by his act of obedience would lose everything. He obeyed. An angel stayed his hand, and a new world began. From then on, step by step, God detached him from his thinking and led him and recreated him, mind and soul. And thus, by losing everything he gained everything. God promised it. Abraham believed it. Upon that hinges everything which followed in subsequent history.

The Old Testament injunction against graven images was God's long process of doing the same thing with a whole people that he had done in a short time with Abraham. Few if any were as pure as Abraham. It took about 2,000 years to accomplish it, and then only roughly, with a predominance of failure. Idolatry was a very potent addiction. And like all addicts ancient man thought he could not have life without the very thing that was killing him.

Idolatry tends in the direction of the diabolical because it never really comes to terms with original sin. It acknowledges man's weakness in the face of creation, but it comes up with a solution that is worse than the problem. The idolater does not understand that man is so damaged at a fundamental level that power cannot heal him. Magic will not liberate him from his condition. It provides only the *illusion* of mastery over the unseen forces, the demons and the terrors, fertility and death. Ritual sex and human sacrifices are potent emotional experiences (I speak vicariously). They are stolen moments of *power over*, a temporary relief from *submission to*. They are, we know by hindsight, a mimicry of divinity, but pagan man did not know that. He experienced it as power-sharing, negotiating with the gods. To placate a god by burning your children on its altars was a potent drug. We who have lived with 2,000 years of Christianity have difficulty understanding just how potent. God's adamantine position on the matter, his 'harshness' in dealing with this universal obsession, is alien to us. We must reread the books of Genesis, Kings and Chronicles. It is not an edifying record.

When God instructed Moses to raise up the bronze serpent on a staff, promising that all who looked upon it would be healed of serpent bites, he used the best thing at his disposal in an emergency situation, a thing which this half-converted people could easily understand. He tried to teach them that the image itself could not heal them, but by gazing upon it they could focus on its word, its message. The staff represented victory over the serpent, and their *faith* in the unseen victor would permit the grace to triumph in their own flesh as well as in their souls. And yet, a few hundred years later we see the God-fearing King Hezekiah destroying Moses' bronze serpent because it had degenerated into a cult object. The people of Israel were worshipping it and sacrificing to it. Falling into deep forgetfulness, they were once again mistaking the message for the Origin of the word. The degree to which they were possessed by the tenacious spirit of idolatry is indicated by numerous passages in the Old Testament, but one of the more chilling ones tells of a king of Israel, a descendent of David's, who had returned to the practice of human sacrifice. The Old Testament injunction against images had to be as radical as it was because ancient man was in many ways a different kind of man than we are. That late Western man, post-Christian man, man without God, *homo sine Deo*, is rapidly descending back into the world of the demonic, complete with human sacrifice on an unprecedented scale, is the subject for another essay.

Jesus Christ was born into a people just barely weaned of their idolatry. From a human womb God came forth into his creation. 'An earthly tree, a heavenly fruit', as a medieval carol describes it. At last, God revealed an image of himself, but so much more than an image – a *person* with a heart, a mind, a soul, and a face. To our shock and disbelief it is a human face. It is our own face restored to the original image and likeness of God.

The Old Testament begins with the words, 'In the beginning . . .'. In the first chapter of John's Gospel are the words of a new genesis.

> In the beginning was the Word,
> and the Word was with God,
> and the Word was God . . .
>
> And the Word became flesh
> and dwelt among us.

Here we should note not only the content but the style. The text tells us that Jesus is man and he is God. But it does so in a form that is *beautiful*.

Because the Lord had given himself a human face, the old injunction against images could now be reconsidered. Yet it was some time before the new covenant took hold and began to expand into the world of culture. Jewish Christians were now eating pork and abandoning circumcision. Paul in Athens had claimed for Christ the altar 'to the unknown God'. Greek Christians were bringing the philosophical mind to bear upon the Christian mysteries. Roman converts were hiding in the catacombs and looking at the little funerary carvings of shepherds, seeing in them the image of the Good Shepherd. Natural theology began to flower into the theology of revelation. Doves, anchors, fish, and hieratic gospel scenes were at first scratched crudely in the marble and mortar, then with more precision. Hints of visual realism evolved in this early graffiti, yet Christianity was still the religion of the Spirit and the written word. In this regard I think often of an inscription on a marble plaque in the catacomb of San Callistus, the tomb of a thirteen-year-old girl martyred by the pagan Romans because of her refusal to submit to idolatry and sexual seduction – the words of the inscription leap like fire across the centuries: 'Sleep, little dove, without bitterness, and rest in the Holy Spirit.' Who cannot be moved by these words? Who can fail to sense a deep affinity with our little sister, our mother in the spirit? We will see her face to face one day, this small overcomer of lions.

Most important, Christianity is the religion of the Eucharist, in which word, image, spirit, flesh, God and man, become one. It is the Eucharist which recreated the world, and yet for the first two centuries the full implications were compressed, like buried seed, waiting for Spring. When the Edict of Milan liberated the Church from the underground an amazing thing happened: within a few years churches arose all over the civilized world. As that compressed energy was released the seed burst and flowered and bore fruit with an astonishing luxuriance. The forms were dominated by the imperial Christ who was painted on the domes of the apses. The architectural dome represented the dome of the sky, above which is the waters of the universe, above which is Paradise. This was no longer the little Roman shepherd boy, but a strong Eastern man, dark, bearded, his imperial face set upon a wrestler's neck, his arms circling around the dome to encompass all peoples, to teach and to rule the entire cosmos. He is the *Pantocrator*, the Lord reigning over a hierarchical universe, enthroned as its head – one with the Father-Creator and the Holy Spirit.

This strong emphasis on the transcendent Christ was not without its dangers. The possible alliance of the imperial powers of the State with the imperial Christ, for example. Or the possibility of losing the full significance of the humanity of Christ. Yet this was mitigated by the growth of small-scale icon-ography borrowed from the funerary encaustic painting of Rome and North Africa, bringing the Lord and his saints into practically every home. Believers sometimes wore icons on cords around their necks, blessed them and blessed others with them. Miracles and exorcisms occurred through the use of icons. The Holy Spirit was obviously anointing the practice. An unofficial theology of sacramentals developed. And yet there was the danger of a subconscious lapse into the psychology of idolatry. There were abuses. From the third through the seventh century the Fathers of the Church corrected, instructed, encouraged – notably Saint Basil the Great, Saint John Chrysostom, Saint Gregory of Nyssa – but the spirituality and theology was still largely undefined; it badly needed clarification.

Saint John of Damascus (*c.* 675–749), writing in his *Concerning the Holy Icons*, made the major contribution to this end, pointing out that the Old Testament Jewish people honoured the tabernacle which bore an image or *eikon* of heavenly things, the Cherubim which overshadowed the mercy seat of the temple, and indeed the temple itself. These were hand-made, 'built by the art of men'. Holy Scriptures spoke against those who worship sculpted images and also those who sacrifice to demons (*daimonia*). 'The Gentiles sacrificed, and the Judeans sacrificed', John said, 'but the Gentiles to demons and Judeans to God', Although he was insistent that for man to give form to the Deity (*Theion*) is 'the height of madness and impiety', he reminded the faithful that God has now become man, not only in the *form* of man as he appeared to Abraham, but truly *in essence* man. Thus, to honour an image of Christ or the disciples of Christ was to honour the Lord himself.

> Many times, doubtless, when we do not have in mind the Passion of our Lord, upon seeing the icon of Christ's Crucifixion, we recall His saving suffering and fall down and worship, not the material, but that which is represented . . .
>
> It is the same in the case of the Mother of the Lord. For the honour which is given to her is referred to Him Who was made of her incarnate. Similarly also, the brave acts of holy (*hagoi*) men stir us up to become brave and zealous, to imitate their virtues, and to glorify God. For the honour that is given to the best of fellow-servants is a proof of goodwill toward our common Lord, and the honour which is given to the icon passes over to the *prototype*. Now this is an unwritten tradition (*agraphos paradosis*), as is also the

worshipping towards the East and the veneration of the Cross, and very many other things similar to these.

That the Apostles handed down much that was unwritten, the Apostle of the Gentiles says in these words, 'Therefore, brethren, stand fast, and hold the traditions which you have been taught, whether by spoken word or by a letter of ours' (2 Thessalonians 2:15).[2]

Saint John of Damascus made the clear distinction between idolatrous worship and profound veneration (*proskynousi*) or honouring (*timosi*). Nevertheless, this teaching did not prevent the horrifying iconoclastic controversy which disrupted the development of iconography in Byzantium for more than a century (726–843). This definitive crisis over the undefined doctrine was replete with riots, murders, martyrdoms and the destruction of countless icons. The iconoclast heresy was rooted in a sort of early puritanism, perhaps a longing on the part of many Christians to return to the rigid certainties of the Old Testament – perhaps, too, an early manifestation of the Protestant dogma of *sola scriptura*. The Iconoclast Council of 754 decreed: 'The guilty art of icon painting is a blasphemy. Christianity has overthrown paganism root and branch, not only the pagan sacrifices but the pagan images . . . From a sacrilegious lust for gain, the ignorant artist represents what ought not to be represented, and seeks, with his soiled hands, to give shape to what ought only to be believed in the heart.'

The situation demanded a definitive teaching from the Church, and this was provided by the Seventh Ecumenical Council at Nicaea in 787, although the controversy continued to rage for many years after. The Council Fathers declared:

The more a person contemplates the icons, the more he will be reminded of what they represent, the more he will be inclined to venerate them by kissing them, prostrating himself, without, however, evincing towards them the true adoration which belongs to God alone, yet they are to be offered incense and lights, as are the holy Cross and the holy Gospels.

In the Monastery of Saint Catherine at Mount Sinai there survives a unique collection of Byzantine icons and manuscripts.

A foundation of the emperor Justinian, the monastery managed to ride out the iconoclastic storm because of its isolation and other unknown factors. There are three very early icons there which are possibly Roman in origin and are believed to be from the sixth century: one of Christ, one of the Apostle Peter and one of the Holy Virgin. Although they are rendered with elements of stylization characteristic of classical Byzantine art, there is a warmth, a naturalism and a humanity in them which is absolutely gripping, especially in the face of Christ. It radiates presence. This is the Christ of the gospels, the man-God who teaches with authority. This man-size image is probably the oldest painted icon of the Lord in existence. It exemplifies an integration of the human and the divine which I think has not been equalled since then. The mainstream of later Byzantine art tends increasingly to the highly stylized, stunningly beautiful symbol-sacramentals (the Orthodox Churches would maintain that the spirituality is closer to sacrament). It is overwhelmingly focused on the transcendent, theologically and artistically, forming a tradition which continues uninterrupted to this day, with the exception of pockets of late Western European iconography influenced by the Renaissance and the Baroque. In the remnants of the early icons at Sinai, however, there is a witness to what might have been, and perhaps what still may be.

Saint John of Damascus once wrote that when Adam fell, man lost the likeness of God but he did not lose the image of God. Only with Christ's redemption does it become possible for us to be restored to the original unity of image and likeness. The theology of the Latin West, no less than that of the East, was also concerned with the *Imago Dei*. Whenever the awareness of man's complete identity declined there were aberrations in the sphere of human activity, and culture expressed it like a barometer. For this reason we should keep in mind the *Imago Dei* as we consider further developments in art history, for the struggle to sustain that awareness is the hidden dynamic of the historical imagination.

For the sake of brevity we must now make some dizzying leaps across several centuries, centuries which include the rise of monasticism, medieval manuscript illumination, and chant. But we cannot fail to note in passing Saint Benedict's Rule, which transformed the face of post-Roman Europe, and which included for good reason a reminder to artists in the community that they remember always that their art must be subordinated to their monastic calling. I think also of Spanish-Byzantine iconography, in particular the commentary on the Apocalypse by an eighth-century monk, Saint Beatus of Liébana. A tenth-century artist named Maius, a monk of the Monastery of San Miguel, illuminated it with the flamboyant colours and absolutely unique iconography of medieval Spain. Manuscripts of Beatus' Apocalypse are in the collections of the Bibliothèque Nationale, Paris, the Biblioteca Nacional, Madrid, and the Pierpont Morgan Library, New York.

The imagery of the Morgan Beatus is dazzling. Purple dragons coil around the acid-yellow cities of man. Emerald seraphs spin the azure disc of the cosmos. Indigo scorpions sting their victims. Archangels plunge stiff from the heavens, swords outstretched, lit by neon. Gardens explode with ripe fruit, axes fall, heads roll off the martyrs' bodies like harvests in an orchard. Blood spurts, entrails spill. Rivers of ink spew from snake mouths. Trumpets blow. The messenger to the church at Sardis scowls in warning: 'You have the reputation for being alive; yet you are dead. Awake! Awake and strengthen the things that remain.' More trumpets blow. Blood! Fire! Flood! Two monks bear witness against the Antichrist. Hot gold light bursts from their lips. The Antichrist kills them as his servants dismantle Jerusalem, stone by stone. Hovering over all, the fierce face of Christ on his throne, waiting for the Last Day – the Great Judge – far more terrifying than the beast who gorges on the ruby flesh of saints.

There is an interesting little colophon inscribed at the end of the Morgan manuscript:

> Let the voice of the faithful resound and re-echo! Let Maius, small indeed, but eager, rejoice, sing, re-echo and cry out!
>
> Remember me, servants of Christ, you who dwell in the monastery of the supreme messenger, the Archangel Michael.
>
> I write this in awe of the exalted patron, and at the command of Abbot Victor, out of love for the book of the vision of John the disciple.

> As part of its adornment I have painted a series of pictures for the wonderful words of its stories, so that the wise may fear the coming of the future judgement of the world's end.
>
> Glory to the Father and to His only Son, to the Holy Spirit and the Trinity from age to age until the end of time.

There is a pun in the colophon. The reference to 'small indeed', was no flourish of scribal humility, especially when measured against the artist's name, *Maius*, literally 'major'. It was a subtle joke, and we who live a thousand years later can laugh and ponder the illusory nature of time.

There is so much that is to be learned from this period that I fear to do it injustice, to become bogged down in a complex of several important trails. We might discuss the Irish, for example, a subject which pulls me with a certain vertigo. We might dwell on Romanesque architecture. We might recall that the crucifix through which the Lord spoke to Saint Francis, instructing him to 'go and rebuild my Church which is falling into ruins', was a Byzantine icon. And we really cannot bypass the influence of Saint Thomas Aquinas, whose writings so greatly affected his times and subsequent ages. Let me at least refer to two of Aquinas's important insights: 'a work of art is a good in itself', and 'all beauty is a reflection back to he who is perfect Beauty' – words which also leap like fire across the ages. When medieval man, much less wealthy than we are, created his churches and cathedrals, he did not merely make them sturdy and functional. They were not practical to heat or to maintain. But they were beautiful. Above all they were awesomely, instructively, mystically beautiful. Rooted in the earth, they soared heavenward.

In *Religion and the Rise of Western Culture*, Christopher Dawson says that medieval political philosophy was dominated by the ideal of unity.

> Mankind was one great society, and above all the regenerated human race, that portion of mankind which was incorporated in the Church was united by its membership of Christ, its Head, by its allegiance to the divine law and by its dedication to one transcendent end. This unity formed a complex hierarchical organism, a body with many members, each having a vital function to fulfil, each with its own office and ministry for the service of the whole.

The doctrine of society involves the principle of hierarchical subordination at every stage, but unlike the Aristotelian theory it does not involve total subordination or the institution of slavery. For every individual member of the whole is an end in himself, and his particular *officium* or *ministerium* is not merely a compulsory social task but a way of service to God through which he shares in the common life of the whole body.[3]

Dawson points out that

the feudal system rested in the last resort on the foundation of serfdom and on the power and privilege that were won and maintained by the sword, so that the feudal state could never entirely escape from the condition of anarchy and disunity out of which it had arisen. The medieval city, on the other hand, was essentially a unity – a visible and tangible unity, sharply defined by the circle of its walls and towers and centred in its cathedral, the visible embodiment of the faith and spiritual purpose of the community.

The cathedral of Chartres, for example, was built not only by engineers but by all kinds of men. Serfs and kings laboured side by side, laying stone upon stone. It was expected that no one would put his hand to the task unless he was in the state of grace, and confessors were always on the site to ensure that this could be so. It is our best evidence that medieval man was imbued with the sense that matter itself is good, very good, and that it can be transfigured, that a stone is not just a stone. That a rose is not a rose is not a rose, with apologies to Gertrude Stein.

On the west portal of the cathedral of Chartres there is a carving of Christ and Adam. In this image Christ faces outward, manly, solemn, strong, and behind him stands the naked Adam, tremulous but trusting, gazing over the shoulder of his Saviour at the Beatific Vision. Christ is mediating. Christ stands *with* man and covers his nakedness before the face of the Father. This is not a prefigurement of the later Protestant doctrine of 'imputed righteousness', in which Christ *hides* man's sin from God. It is in fact a purely Catholic understanding: Christ is here *restoring* Adam, in all his guilt and glory, to the original unity which he had before the Fall – to his dignity as a son of the

Father. Interestingly, the art of the times was rarely signed. Sculptures of surpassing genius were not infrequently inscribed with the words, 'Non nobis Domine, non nobis, sed nomini Tuo da gloriam!' – 'Not to us, O Lord, not to us, but to Thy name be the glory.' This is no indication that medieval man believed himself to be a nonentity. On the contrary, it is an indication that he found his ultimate meaning, his identity, within the living organism of Christ's body, that in losing himself he was finding himself. Here was a humble Christian humanism, like that of the Roman iconographers of Sinai, who were also anonymous. Contrast this to the modern age of depersonalization in which almost every artist, including the Christian artist, takes pains over his public reputation and leaves nothing unsigned.

Dante is the figure who rises above the whole period as the exemplar of the Christian vision. He was late-medieval man, and perhaps also a precursor of what would be best in the Renaissance era, which was only just beginning during the final years of his life. Steeped in the learning of the Middle Ages, he had read the *Summa Theologiae* of Aquinas and the encyclopaedic works of the times, and most of what was then known of the Latin Classical and post-Classical writers. He was a poet-prophet, a man of both heaven and earth, who could speak of the greatest delight of his soul, his love for Beatrice, and find in her, and through her, a passage to the Beatific Vision. Dante's *Divina Commedia* begins with the poet losing his way in a gloomy wood, and is consummated on the heights of the mystical pageant when he sees the face of his beloved Beatrice. Representing divine philosophy illuminated by revelation, she leads him up through nine moving heavens of intellectual preparation into the true Paradise where the blessedness of eternal life consists in the sight of God. There her place is taken by Saint Bernard, a type of loving contemplation, who commends the poet to the Blessed Virgin, at whose intercession he obtains a foretaste of the Beatific Vision, the 'Exalted Light', the 'Living Light' of the Holy Trinity, reigning at the uttermost heights of the hierarchy of existence. Matter is neither to be annihilated nor escaped, but rather embraced as the path to the ultimate vision in which all powers of loving and knowing are fulfilled and consumed in a union with the Divine Essence who is Love. Love is the origin and the end. Love is the impelling force of the ascent. The citizens of the *inferno* and the *purgatorio* have each in their way failed in some aspect of love. Love is the transfiguration of the immanent world and the path of real transcendence. Love is the unifying principle of creation. In *Paradiso* Dante writes:

> Within its depths I saw ingathered,
> bound by love in one volume,
> the scattered leaves of all the universe.

Matter is good, very good. But it is not an end in itself. This crucial distinction blurs and fades and is in danger of being lost during the period which comes after Dante. The imbalance in the humanism of the Renaissance is well illustrated, to my mind, by the painter Sandro Botticelli. Unquestionably a master, gifted with a fertile imagination and great charm, he was, like many of his contemporaries, intrigued by the possibilities of return to the culture of the classical age. Thus, his Madonnas and works such as his *The Birth of Venus* are practically indistinguishable from each other, except for the degree of clothing worn by the central figures. But this nudity was not the classical pursuit of perfection as a means to a higher end. The *Venus* of Milo was not about sex; it was a search for harmony, the Greek concern for the divine order – *kosmos* triumphing over chaos. The new humanism of the Renaissance was more concerned with man's passions and powers than with his place in the 'great chain of being'. If man is the measure of all things then why not explore his nature, his senses, his politics, his psychology as if they were ends in themselves? Even religious themes must be subsumed in the service of this quest. Technical mastery, therefore, and the breaking of new ground, became a primary concern. Even the giant, Leonardo, anguished over a chronic sense of the insufficiency of his creative powers. Leonardo once wrote, I believe it is in his notebooks, that his greatest suffering in life was the gap between the images he conceived in his imagination and his ability to execute them in paint.

The preoccupation with mastery of technique, to the detriment of the word it was supposed to convey, is one of the primary characteristics of the Renaissance. However, we should not judge that period rashly. Let me illustrate this with a story. This is my first encounter with Europe. Being a Canadian I come from a country that is culturally very young. We ooh and aah over crumbling buildings that are about a hundred years old. Europe's massive accumulation of cultural artefacts is over-powering to a visitor from the New World. This is not to say that we do not have culture on the other side of the Atlantic. We have some, though it is being swept under by the tidal wave of commercial culture, ersatz culture. We are also surrounded by a great deal of natural beauty. Our land is still largely savage and dangerous. It is beautiful, but it is raw beauty, much of it unmediated by the human hand. Perhaps Europeans view these things somewhat differently, but my North American friends who return from culture-forays into the Old World usually speak of what they have seen in tones of reverence, and a curious mixture of pain and exultation. For example, a friend of mine recently described his first encounter with Michelangelo's *David*. I am sure that everyone has seen photographs of this colossus. It is the most famous rendering of the tale of a lad who slew a giant against all the odds, and through the transmutations of art became another kind of giant.

I had never liked this statue of David for a number of reasons: its nudity seemed an aggressive assertion in the old dialogue between the rights of art and prudence; its undeniable brilliance (and possible arrogance) seemed an embodiment of what was unbalanced in the spirit of the Renaissance. It seemed to be potentially more an invasion of the imagination, rather than an incarnation of the true story of that little shepherd, a tale which is really about the divine Spirit transfiguring human weakness. No, this carving seemed to be more about man's sense of his own power. This was no primitive stick man. I considered it a work that was far from being a baptism of the imagination. Yes, it was a masterpiece, but above all a triumph of *technique*. Moreover it had become in the ensuing centuries an overdone cliché. My friend confessed to me that he too had gone to Italy knowing that he would be taken on a tour of Florence, that he would see this work, and, of course, that he would be suitably impressed. But he felt the same sort of aversion to it as I did.

During the tour he became separated from the group, and searching blindly through the corridors of the Galleria dell'Accademia, he came upon the statue from the wrong direction. Suddenly there it was. His first glimpse of it was from the reverse. Most of us have viewed it from the front, and from this direction we see a powerful body firmly planted on the earth, posed, balanced, muscular, set in its essential form, like the triumph of the will. But my friend saw it first from an entirely different vantage point. Viewed from behind, the figure appears to be glancing back over his shoulder. The image of the noble torso is here dominated by David's facial expression. The eyes, the mouth, the brows, the sinews of the face, are taut with an emotion which is so quintessentially human: a split second of uncertainty and a groping for faith, the moment when courage overcomes terror – not as animal instinct but as a spiritual decision. From the front it appears as an embodiment of confident resolve; from the rear it is about doubt. That was the artist's intention and that is its *word*. It is concerned above all with the struggle of the human spirit.

Michelangelo's *David* is not about sex, it is about character. Although it raises some unanswered questions about prudence, it is in the same spiritual line as Andrea Del Castagno's painting of David, Masaccio's *Expulsion from Paradise*, and Donatello's champion *Saint George*, all of which are ultimately concerned with the dignity of man. All of which are far from the spirit of Donatello's *David*, which is a sensual bacchus or satyr dressed (or rather undressed) in biblical costumes. In that difference can be seen the central problem of the Renaissance.

How did my friend recognize the word in Michelangelo's *David*? How did I recognize it and thrill to the burst of new perception when he related his experience? We recognized it because this truth was already a living thing within us. The artist had exteriorized our own experience and given it a shape, a form, a name, an identity. We were able to step outside of ourselves and to look within. Art had liberated the perception, incarnated the invisible reality.

In Shakespeare's *The Winter's Tale*, Leontes says of a statue:

> I am overwhelmed: does not this stone rebuke me
> For being more stone than it?

In *A Midsummer Night's Dream* there is another passage which always moves me. Toward the end of the play Theseus says:

> More strange than true: I never may believe
> These antique fables, nor these fairy toys.
> Lovers and madmen have such seething brains,
> Such shaping fantasies, that apprehend
> More than cool reason ever comprehends.
> The lunatic, the lover and the poet
> Are of imagination all compact:
> One sees more devils than vast hell can hold,
> That is, the madman: the lover, all as frantic,
> Sees Helen's beauty in a brow of Egypt:
> The poet's eye in a fine frenzy rolling,
> Doth glance from heaven to earth, from earth to heaven;
> And as imagination bodies forth
> The forms of things unknown, the poet's pen
> Turns them to shapes, and gives to airy nothing
> A local habitation and a name.

Here we have Shakespeare the artist commenting through his dramatic persona on the nature of art itself. One might disagree with his comment if it were taken only in isolation, if we did not know his delightful sense of irony, and if we did not have the body of his plays, which is the fuller context, which bears witness over and over again to his belief that drama gives to invisible *realities* a local habitation and a name.

For all the new awareness of our humanity which the Renaissance gave us, it galvanized forces which had been fermenting for centuries. It reinforced and accelerated the damage done by the divorce of the Church of the East and the West, the schism of four centuries before (AD 1054). What began as a difference in theological emphasis had begun to show fracture lines long before the official break, and eventually opened a chasm, not only in the world of theology and ecclesial culture, but in the very structure of man's perception of the nature of reality. Until then a universal theology that was simply

Catholic had more or less sustained the integration – the working relationship if you will – between the human and the divine, between transcendence and immanence, between intellect and imagination, between beauty and truth, between law and spirit, between the hierarchical cosmos and (for all its flaws) the sociopolitical order.

That integration had never been perfect, and indeed any thumbnail summation of those centuries of transformation must pass too lightly over the many qualifications and exceptions. But the pattern was established: the intoxications offered to man in the discovery of his identity on a new frontier would prove irresistible. From the Renaissance onward man became more and more concerned with himself, with his self-definition, and as a result he was to become increasingly a one-dimensional being. This was a consequence he could not have foreseen, because at the beginning of the 'rebirth' he was saturated in the sensations of liberation. His brave new world could not yet appear to him as a kind of spiritual 'flatland', for it was a time of beginnings, adventures, an explosion of possibilities. We who live at the culmination of a very brilliant and cruel century are the inheritors of the flaws in that vision.

In a 1946 article in the journal *Lumen Vitae* Dawson writes:

> But if the combined influence of Renaissance and Reformation made for a wider diffusion of literary culture and the intellectualising of religious education, it also tended to increase the practical and utilitarian elements of culture. Both the Byzantine East and the medieval West had shared the same ideal of contemplation and spiritual vision as the supreme end and justification of all human culture: an ideal which finds classical expression in St Thomas and Dante. But from the fifteenth century onwards culture and education became increasingly concerned with the claims of the active life . . . this in turn led to the cultivation of the economic virtues of thrift and industry and to the acquisition of 'useful knowledge' as the main end of education. There can be no doubt that secular utilitarianism was the direct product and heir of the religious utilitarianism that developed on the soil of Protestant and specifically Puritan culture.[4]

We cannot deny what was great in the Renaissance, nor can we ignore the fact that the post-Renaissance world needed a spiritual revival. But neither can we escape the suffering these periods have imposed on us. Humanism split off from the Catholic sense of the *Imago Dei* has not given us progress in any deep abiding sense. It has given us the development of technique. It has given us the triumph of subjectivism. It has given us despiritualization, and despiritualization eventually has given us dehumanization, and dehumanization is now showing every sign of working out its terrible logic: in the end, unless there is a return to our true identity, the world will degenerate into the purely diabolic, which means the annihilation of man.

Art has always asked the question: What is man? *Who* is he? Where is he going? These questions did not cease to be asked after the Renaissance. Neither did they fade from the picture after that second great blow, the Reformation. Yet from that point on the split widened and began to work out in *praxis* the consequences of its theory.

In *The Dividing of Christendom*, Dawson writes that the Baroque period which followed the Reformation has been viewed more or less pejoratively, but was in fact a positive development.

> Looked at from the Northern and Protestant angle, the baroque culture appears as a secularized version of medieval Catholicism; from its own standpoint, however, it represents rather the desecularization of the Renaissance and the reassertion of the power of religion and the authority of the Church over social life. All the resources of art, architecture, painting, sculpture, literature and music were enlisted in the service of Catholicism, and if to the Northerner the result appears theatrical and meretricious, this was due to no lack of spirituality. It was a passionate, ecstatic, mystical spirituality that has little in common with the sober pietism of the Protestant North, but it was intensely vital, as we can see from the lives and writings of the Spanish saints and mystics of the sixteenth century who initiated that great movement of Baroque mysticism which swept Catholic Europe in the first half of the seventeenth century.[5]

Dawson reminds us of the many giants who arose during that period: in the north, Saint Francis de Sales, mystic, humanist and reformer; in the south, Saint Ignatius of Loyola and Saint Philip Neri; the ascetic ecstasy of painters such as El Greco, Ribera and Zurbaran; the new church music exemplified by Palestrina. Shakespeare himself, says Dawson, although he transcends his time, can only be fully understood as 'a Baroque genius', along with Cervantes, Galileo, and Bernini. He argues that contrary to the largely negative view of the Baroque period held by nineteenth-century art historians, we should understand it as a fairly successful attempt to restore the old integration. It created a new cultural unity based on a religious foundation. It diffused itself even in Northern Europe through the influence of the royal courts, which had become (with the exception of the Netherlands) the great patrons of art and culture.

It should be no surprise that as the movement evolved the resurgence of religious sensibility gradually gave way to pomp and pageantry and the embellishment of the State. Fabulous interior decoration was indeed a pursuit of the lost ecstasy; however, I think it began to fail as it gradually mutated from a metaphor of paradise into the metaphor of human domination and anthropocentric sensuality – no longer the transfiguration of the senses but a glorification of sensual experience as an end in itself. Some of it is exquisitely beautiful; some of it is obviously a desperate attempt to escape the cold winds of the anti-incarnational trends of the Reformation. I think of Rubens in this regard. Although he painted some liturgical pieces, including a theatrical tableau of the crucifixion of Christ and an operatic landslide of souls falling into hell, he was very much a man of his times, searching for the lost synthesis, yet achieving only a conglomerate of interests. I try not to think overmuch about his heaps of cavorting, very overweight, naked ladies. Why all that pink flesh? Why all the desperation to return to the bacchanal in the forest glade? Twentieth-century man, who has suffered from over-exposure to flesh and under-exposure to a sense of mystery, may marvel at the painterly technique but he can barely resist a condescending smile. Poor Rubens, we think, forgetting that we suffer a worse malady.

To return for a moment to the giants – the ones who in fact achieved a synthesis out of the collapse of the old vision – one thinks immediately of the Protestant Rembrandt, the tremendous humanity of the father figure in his *Return of the Prodigal Son*, or the immense dignity and pathos of his etchings of the passion of Christ. One cannot help but think of him as the spiritual companion of the Catholic El Greco. The dark brooding shadows of Rembrandt's northern Europe were not so different from the electric skies of Toledo, geographies of the soul which seemed back-lit by photographic silver, as if every wintry Spanish landscape is a metaphor of a more vast spiritual landscape, as if nature itself, north and south, must writhe in anguish over the despoilation of man, as if all discreet coverings must now be torn not only off his flesh but off his soul as well. This stream of post-Reformation religious painting radiates hope and dread wrestling at close quarters, as if words and anti-words threaten at any moment to burst from the plane of the canvas to overwhelm us with their most difficult questions. No longer the serene, ordered, baptized humanism of the iconography of Giotto, Cimabue and Duccio, those Italo-Byzantine, early Renaissance men. This was the new man of the West, his humanism striving mightily to retain the old Christian sense of God's victory over the chaos of the human condition. This is the best inheritance of the Post-Renaissance age, a new iconography of man – man at war with himself and God; man losing the war, but in the losing finding himself again. This is incontestably sacred art. But it is no longer liturgical art.

Geniuses such as Rembrandt and El Greco were no longer the rule. They were phenomena, standing like lonely outposts, one might even say prophets, above a geography of lavish ornamentation, reaction, counter-reaction and the increasing subjectivization of practically everything except science. When the world will not listen to its prophets it must find other guides. Scientism and the Enlightenment were the inevitable results. From then on the mainstream of art would more and more be anthropocentric, generating the cult of the secular genius extracting masterpieces from his divine self. Few would know how to sing *Non nobis Domine.* Everyone would sign their works. Everywhere a sliding into decorative effects or alternately, feeding on the stimuli of war and politics. *Liberté, Egalité,* the guillotine. Napoleon, empire, the age of revolutions. Art must now serve the revolutionary new man, the masses. Delacroix, Géricault, Goya, each of these admirable painters produced a mix of sociological romance and existential angst. Much truth, much protest against a violated world, and much melodrama.

In the field of religious art the effects of Protestant Puritanism and Catholic Jansenism were being felt. Each in its seemingly disparate way had over-reacted, overemphasized, each denied the 'whole truth about man', adding strain to the fundamental split in consciousness, throwing a pall of mistrust over everything sensual. The senses have proved themselves highly treacherous and well-nigh unconvertible, they said, therefore let us deny the senses or escape them. This viewpoint rejected the Catholic vision of the restoration of all things in Christ, and replaced it with a mimicry of Catholic transcendence. Like all heresies it left residual poisons in the system. Thus, Christian art entered its most shameful period. It attempted to escape the gnawing sense of absence, the numbness, the cold, by a plunge into emotional sentiment. Maudlin art arose from both Catholic and Protestant sources, the saccharine oleograph and the biblical etching replete with operatic effects and languishing gestures – these too, like their secular counterparts, were longings for a golden age that never really existed. It created a pseudo-religious culture that was a tragically stunted facsimile of deep religious experience.

And then followed the nineteenth-century Romantic movement. Here too are to be found many flashes of light, much that dazzles and delights. The starved emotions of Western man yearned alternately for a return to Nature, to the heroism of the Middle Ages, to the sensations of religious experience, or combinations of all of these. But the movement was really about feeling, bursts of mood and drama to feed the hungry imagination. It was also a subconscious attempt to return to mystery, imagination, wonder and (unbeknown to many of its devotees) to a restored moral order. Rossetti's *Girlhood of Mary Virgin* and Holman Hunt's *The Finding of Christ in the Temple* are touching works, but they are of a piece with other Pre-Raphaelite painting, which was absorbed in sensuous poetic imagination and dream. Drawing heavily on literary sources, lovely pastiches were created, richly coloured, evocative. Renditions of the Arthurian legend and religious themes were usually indistinguishable in style. They approximated many of the book illustrations which enlivened adventure novels for the young. It was great stuff but it lacked the exigencies of biblical faith; it owed little allegiance to the authority of the God of Mount Horeb and Tabor, nor to his Church. It was a movement anchored tentatively in reality, for the Romantics admitted that Nature can still teach us things. Aesthetic experience in itself, they said, is not only emotionally rewarding, it is instructive.

There were moments of real greatness: Wordsworth's *Lines written a few miles above Tintern Abbey*, Tennyson's *Ulysses* and Matthew Arnold's *Dover Beach*. Keats summed up the unifying methods in *Ode on a Grecian Urn*.[6]

> 'Beauty is truth, truth beauty,' – that is all
> Ye know on earth, and all ye need to know.

We need to know a great deal more than that, but the Romantics did not really understand this. They thought they had stumbled upon a primary illumination, when it was really a half-truth. But they did not seem to be aware that a beautiful half-truth can be far more misleading than an ugly lie. It was better than what had just preceded them, of course, and so they concluded that this must be progress. They were in reaction to what Blake called, in his poem on Milton, those 'dark Satanic mills' of the industrial revolution. Their sentiments were often deeply religious, yet they did not seem to know, as Dante knew, that to play with the things of God without humility, as if these gifts were possessions or mere myths, to exercise spiritual power without submission to God's laws, was really a very old and dangerous error, one by which so many individuals and civilizations have fallen. Blake's mysticism, for example, was derived from cabalistic, alchemical and Swedenborgian sources, and he was ever impatient with the codified ethics of organized religion. The nature mystics, for their part, were preoccupied with spirituality in a way that was essentially a pursuit of divinity *in nature*. Consciously or subconsciously, they were pantheists. The flight from materialism was laudable, but it failed to produce a definition of man that encompassed the full meaning of his identity. Thus, it could not hope to provide the needed resistance to the dehumanizing trends of the times, trends which grew into colossal forces, and which eventually unleashed the crimes of the twentieth century.

In his *Annotations to Sir Joshua Reynolds's Discourses*, Blake makes a valid point:

> Degrade first the arts if you'd mankind degrade.
> Hire idiots to paint with cold light and hot shade.

Blake saw many things rightly, even to the point of prophetic clarity. But many things he judged wrongly, among them Christ's Church. Despite his heroic effort to respiritualize his times with hot light and hotter verse, and for all his longing to build Jerusalem 'in England's green and pleasant land', Blake's religion was a prodigy of subjectivism. His visions had no counterpoise in the imperatives of divine law and Church law. A century and a half after his death, at the end of the twentieth century, the triumph of subjectivism has become well-nigh universal. The dark Satanic mills have been succeeded by brightly lit Satanic laboratories.

The Impressionist movement in art followed the Romantic period. Who cannot love the Impressionists? Who can fail to admire them? Who among us does not have his favourite painting or two, or twenty? Reacting against the massive urbanization of the nineteenth century, the slums, drabness and dehumanizing toil, and following the lure of the hint of transcendence that is indeed written into nature, they played with colour, movement and harmony, all of which they accomplished by the fracturing and reassembly of light. But this fracturing process necessarily involved a blurring of distinctions – of identity. The reassembly did not often produce a resurrected being, but rather a sense of all existence dissolving into the ultimate identity of cosmic light. Man is largely absent from their paintings, and even the works of man, cityscapes, bridges, the backyards of homes, are treated as extensions of nature, as if they too are prismatic beams of that single, unifying principle of light. The effects are startling, moving, and they are, I think, a valiant attempt to find fugitive beauty in the midst of the industrial revolution. They are fundamentally spiritual, but they are a spirituality in the line of monism.

The post-Renaissance developments in art have given us a very great gift, and that is the understanding that the subjects of art are practically limitless. Nevertheless, the artist's ability to explore the new frontiers are still, as always, dependent upon his capacity for truth, and equally important, his capacity for love. Art, which is acknowledged widely as an act of love, will *be* an act of love to the degree that it is also an act of truth. It is a form of communication that can only occur when there is faith in the possibility of *communion* between human beings, and moreover faith that there is something to communicate which gives life. I think the Impressionists succeeded to a degree. They restored man to consciousness of the beauty of nature. They reverenced its truth and loved its light. Although they did not expand our understanding of the ultimate meaning of light – which is a reflection of Uncreated Light – they contributed momentously to the expansion of the eye's grasp. Their purpose was not to teach – Art usually fails when it attempts to be didactic. Their purpose was to impart the reality, not to talk *about* it. They brought a joyful, contemplative sense back into the gallery and (after the development of inexpensive printed reproductions) into the home. They also showed us that there is still a kind of natural theology at work in the consciousness of secular man, that fertile ground is there, waiting for revelations, perhaps still open to signs of a much more vast and beautiful kingdom than even nature itself can offer.

Though solitary figures like the Catholic Cézanne and Protestant van Gogh were religious men, they, like most of their contemporaries, were the inheritors of that rendering-down process which robbed post-Renaissance, post-Reformation, post-Enlightenment man of his sense of the hierarchical cosmos, a creation that contains light but is not Light itself. What the Impressionists achieved is glorious but symptomatic.

The Cubists followed swiftly upon the heels of the Impressionists. They too believed they were pushing back the frontiers of the possible. Pablo Picasso stated, 'art is a form of magic designed as a mediator between this strange hostile world and us, a way of seizing power by giving form to our terrors as well as our desires' (F. Gilot, *Life With Picasso*). In 1945 he said that painting was 'an instrument of war for attack and defence against the enemy'. He did not mean only the political chaos which his generation had just suffered through. No, it is the authority of Natural Law, the hierarchical world, the voice of conscience, and the institution which proclaims the right formation of conscience, which are the anarchist's 'enemy'. The artist-as-protean-being can create his own conscience. He is lord *over* life. Picasso thought that by dissecting the structure of reality he could reassemble its constituent parts – abstracted, purified, mastered. When personhood has been negated, identity disappears. Why not dissect the corpse? The results, though certainly impressive, were at the same time cold. He could not bring anything back to life. Possibilities for wider expression were evidenced in works such as *Guernica*, Picasso's protest against the Fascist bombing of the city of Guernica during the Spanish Civil War. It is interesting to note, however, the one-sidedness of art when it becomes the servant of a political ideology. In Picasso's work there is no parallel outrage against the Communists' wilful destruction of hundreds of Spanish churches and countless cultural works, nor their murder of more than 6800 clergy and hundreds of thousands of Catholic laity, not to mention the many millions murdered by the Soviet empire. The rage of *Guernica*, that brave new icon of the humanist's cry for 'justice', falls far short of universal compassion.

Various art movements have emerged since the first decades of the twentieth century. The common theme which unites them, beneath their differing styles and ideological feuds, is an immanentized cosmos. The transcendent God is dead. Perhaps man too is dead? Burdened with the colossal weight of this question and the 'silence' of God which greets it, the culture of negation has arisen. Manifestations range from the poignant, the silly, the cynical, the simply empty canvas, to eruptions of the diabolical. For example, in February of 1990 some 500 works of art and several artists were brought from the former East Germany to Paris by the French Ministry of Culture. In one typical work a live woman was covered in cattle blood and her male counterpart enacted a mock castration with a chainsaw. Nudity and butchery were everywhere, and though the exhibit was hair-raising and nauseating, it was not the most extreme art event that has occurred in recent years. It is important to note that preoccupation with absurdity, violence and death is not peculiar to artists oppressed by their governments. It is endemic to all post-war Western societies. With the fall or decline of overt tyrannies we must not assume that man will now right himself and produce works of art restored to a sense of beauty, truth and virtue. The opposite may occur, if the East German exhibit is an accurate barometer. The locus of the revolution may be shifting from the exterior political sphere and plunging into the interior, riding on the vehicle of public culture. In that way it may penetrate to the soul of man in a way that violent regimes never can, for they alienate their citizens, rendering them perpetually on guard. The most effective revolution is the one that appears a liberation.

In the West, most public galleries devote literally acres of exhibition space to abstraction and absurdity, to the demolition of the image of man. At the same time they squeeze contemporary realism into obscure side galleries, when it is not altogether in storage. This is most revealing: hierarchy cannot be avoided in human affairs. As the revolution becomes the establishment it imposes a new hierarchy of values on the people. Yet in order to maintain the illusion of freedom, the new cultural élite must pay lip service to pluralism. Everyone is equal. Everyone must have his share of the public forum, including the devil, because in 'Flatland' no single truth is better than another. In practice, however, it is found that some of us are more equal than others.

I have frequently heard from otherwise sensible people that the last remaining tyranny left on the planet is the Roman Catholic Church. The English painter Francis Bacon, who I think epitomizes the spirit of the post-war generation of painters, has produced a series of portraits reinterpreting Velásquez's paintings of a pope. Bacon paints the pope encased in glass, a schizoid screeching face with the top of his skull blown off. Bacon says, 'Man now realizes that he is an accident, that he is a completely futile being' (J. Russell, *Francis Bacon*).

The blatantly anti-Catholic blasphemy-artist Andres Serrano, the photo-pornographer Robert Mapplethorpe and the horror-sculptor Mark Prent are his heirs. Whether or not such artists are aware of it, the underlying impulse is the need to demolish any claims that spiritual authority might have on the conscience and the imagination. It is an assault on the hierarchical cosmos, and ultimately against the principle of fatherhood, the source of which is God the Father. This is not Goya protesting the horrors of war; this is rather the consciousness which creates the horror, and celebrates it, and would enshrine it as the highest artform.

Lines from the *Purgatorio* come to mind:

> O human race, born to fly upward,
> Why, at a little wind, do you so fall?

Unless there is a return to the search for the *Imago Dei*, man will continue to fall down two main false trails: on one hand an increasing sterility, rage, absurdity and nihilism; and on the other hand a return to cultic paganism. This is more than a theoretical possibility. It is a growing phenomenon.

A few years ago I was asked to be a judge at a juried exhibition of Christian art. Only a minority of the pieces submitted could be called in any reasonable sense Christian, for a great deal of it represented young artists submitting to peer pressure, the need to show that they were *au courant* with the latest-breaking developments in art history. Many of them were the victims of a certain *cold rationalist gnosticism*. Another well-represented genre was a predictable exercise in heroic revolution – a lukewarm Catholic version – which is to say these paintings were didactic vehicles of deformed theology which I call, tongue in cheek, *neotheo-gnosticism*. Then there were the cultists, the new *hot pagan gnostics*. I recall one Catholic artist in particular, a nice young woman who had obtained a masters degree in theology, was highly gifted as a painter, possessed a gentle nature, was intelligent and intensely sincere. With considerable pride she showed me one of her recent paintings. It was a work of artistic merit, technically speaking, quite visually pleasing. It was a self-portrait, she said. Titled, *Icon*, it depicted a pile of snakes writhing in the womb of the central figure.

Somewhat horrified I asked her why she had done this. Judaeo-Chrisitanity, she explained, had unjustly maligned the serpent. And in order to rehabilitate this symbol it was necessary to take the serpent into her womb, to gestate it, and eventually to bear it into the world as a sacred feminine icon. I pointed out that the meanings of symbols are not merely the capricious choices of a limited culture. We cannot rearrange them like so much furniture in the living room of the psyche. To tamper with these fundamental *types* is spiritually and psychologically dangerous because they are keystones in the very structure of the mind, and reinforce our understanding of the shape of reality. They are a language about good and evil: furthermore they can be points of contact with these two realities. To face evil without the equipment Christianity has given us is dangerously naïve. But my arguments were useless. She had heard a better tale from a famous theologian. When I refused to hang the picture in the exhibit, this gentle person became unexpectedly fierce, and displayed all the moral outrage of the unjustly condemned. I would guess that she considered me a Catholic version of a KGB bulldozer.

It brings to mind a passage of von Balthasar's in *The Glory of the Lord*:

> In a world without beauty – even if people cannot dispense with the word and constantly have it on the tip of their tongues in order to abuse it – in a world which is perhaps not wholly without beauty, but which can no longer see it or reckon with it: in such a world the good also loses its attractiveness, the self-evidence of why it must be carried out. Man stands before the good and asks why it must be done and not rather its alternative, evil. For this, too, is a possibility, and even the more exciting one: Why not investigate Satan's depths?[7]

Several years ago I attended the World's Fair in Vancouver. The theme of the Fair was Transportation and Communication. I wandered through the pavilions for a day with my children, a mind-blowing over-saturation in the technological society. However, I noted that there was a marked lack of art in the entire exhibit, a departure for world fairs. The little in evidence was consistently political art or industrial art. At the main plaza of the site rose its centrepiece, a solid gold coin, man-size, worth hundreds of thousands of dollars. It was an overgrown model of the Canadian one dollar coin, on which is emblazoned a northern water-bird called the loon. This cheap brass coin is generally referred to in my country, with a certain irony, as 'the loonie'. It is our golden calf.

As I was heading toward the exit at the end of the day, children in tow, I was feeling quite despondent. The whole affair seemed really like some great temple erected in honour of our current deities. I was lamenting to my oldest son the absence of real art when he grabbed my sleeve and tugged, pointing back to a pavilion which we had somehow missed in all that maze of industry and commerce.

'Dad, Dad,' he urged, 'Cheer up! There's some art!'

And sure enough, rising above that mini-city of sterilized architecture, affixed to the wall of a giant box-shaped building, was a very beautiful sculpture. Twenty or thirty feet high, it depicted a man dressed in flowing robes with his arms raised to the heavens. Intrigued, I thought it must be a priestly figure, and assumed we were seeing the back side of the Christian pavilion. We retraced our steps to the entrance and found to our utter surprise that it was the Soviet pavilion. The sculpture was titled *Cosmos*. You must remember that this was 1986 and there were no signs anywhere that the Soviet empire was soon to fall. But it struck me that even after seventy years of a relentless effort to crush and pervert religion, the tyrant-State could not eradicate intuitions that live at the very roots of the soul, in the catacombs of the imagination, and may at any moment emerge in disguised forms.

I once had a conversation with an exiled Russian painter, an enlightening encounter for me. This was in the early 1980s and he had just come with his wife and little daughter from Moscow, the beneficiaries of that brief thaw which permitted thousands of Jewish people to emigrate from the Soviet Union. He had been a professor at the Moscow Art Institute, a privileged citizen-artist with a salary and a dacha. He had lived a kind of double life during his last years there, and had exhibited at the famous free exhibit held in a Moscow park, a show of dissident art which KGB bulldozers had flattened. Dismissed from the Institute, hounded by the KGB, half of his friends dead or missing, he seemed to me a dark, driven soul. I made the presumptuous comment (naïve, spoiled Western fellow that I am) that now he must be very happy to have become a free artist in the West. He gave me a look of pity and growled, 'In Moscow we were suffering. We were dying and starving, but we loved each other. We looked at each other's work and we understood it.'

'He hates your country,' his wife said.

'He does?' I replied amazed.

'Yes, I hate your country,' he said. 'There they kill us, but here they kill the heart. You are already dead! You are a dead people!'

A violent complex emotion was released in these harsh words, a reaction that we ignore at our own risk. He gave voice to what is felt by most expatriate artists in my acquaintance: they feel that the people of the West have by and large become unable to understand what is being said to them. We listen without hearing, look without seeing. It is not that the *émigré* artist produces imagery too esoteric for comprehension or limited by provincial experience. On the contrary, his suffering has allowed him to break through to universal truths, the perennial object and language of art.

For several years I have entered my paintings in a national exhibit of religious art in Toronto. Always, and I underline the word *always*, the very best work in those shows is produced by refugee artists from Russia, Ukraine, Poland, Hungary, Romania, the Czech Republic and so on. Their work radiates authenticity. It has integrity of content and mastery of form. There are, of course, untalented ex-Soviet artists and some very fine Western ones, but the general pattern is sharply defined. The work of the exiles is consistently superior, technically and spiritually, to North American work, which on the whole is mediocre, and at its best is usually clever posturing. I dread to think what these Eastern people think of us. Our only excuse may be to recall that the culture of negation which took seventy years to germinate and ripen its deadly fruit under the pressure of brutal dictators has been no less relentless in the West, and in fact by evolving smoothly and efficiently in the democracies, may in the long run prove the most effective form of violation. There has been little public violence to alert us to our peril. No jackboots, no incarceration in gulags or state mental institutions, no falling into the pit of official non-personhood. Yet, a large number of artists disappear from the cultural life of the West, dying not from grotesque assaults but from a slow, discrete suffocation.

The modern artist suffers in all aspects of his being. Of the two obstacles facing him, the exterior and the interior, it is difficult to say which is the more formidable, but I am inclined to think it is the interior. Practically all artists now suffer from what T. S. Eliot called, in an essay on the Metaphysical Poets, 'the dissociation of sensibility'. Unification of thought and feeling becomes more difficult to the degree that the artist is an atomized individual, adrift in time, grabbing at sense and sentiment as if to anchor himself in a weightless cosmos. In his famous essay, 'Tradition and the Individual Talent', Eliot suggests that the remedy is to be found where it has always been found, by obtaining 'by great labour' a sense of tradition. The historical sense, he says, is a perception 'not only of the pastness of the past, but of its presence . . . This historical sense, which is a sense of the timeless as well as the temporal and of the timeless and the temporal together, is what makes a writer traditional.' Eliot makes the distinction between a vital sense of tradition and *traditionalism*, which fixates on certain periods of artistic 'success' and will not budge from them.

> What is to be insisted upon is that the poet must develop or procure the consciousness of the past and that he should continue to develop this consciousness throughout his career.
>
> What happens is a continual surrender of himself, as he is at the moment, to something which is more valuable. The progress of an artist is a continual self-sacrifice, a continual extinction of personality.[8]

These are strong words. I do not think Eliot means by *extinction of personality* some form of self-annihilation or a succumbing to the dehumanizing forces of modern civilization. I believe he means by this a turning away from all that feeds the *false* self – egocentricity, the cult of artist-as-personality. He is pointing toward the tradition of the icon-painter and the Gothic sculptor, who believed they were finding themselves as they lost themselves, content to be at play in the fields of the Lord, in an ordered, creative universe suffused with grace.

Grace is our word. The unification of feeling and form, intellect and imagination, spirit and talent, past and present, *Logos* and man-made words, can only be rediscovered to the degree that we surrender to grace. 'Everything is grace', said Bernanos, echoing the saints. Grace is everywhere. Sanctifying grace. Actual grace. Extraordinary grace. Grace in torrents. But we have forgotten how to ask for it.

Is it too late for us? No, it is not. Numerous works of art are being born from us, all around us. I think especially of Henryk Górecki's magnificent *Symphony No. 3*, his cycle of sorrowful songs memorializing the suffering of man, with its meditations on the *shoah*, the Holocaust. It is reported that when this work was first played on public radio, people listening to it on their car radios while driving the hallucinogenic, utterly dehumanizing New York State throughway, pulled over to the curb, and wept. They could not explain their reaction. Why did they weep? What faculty, long suffocated, was liberated through the medium of this work of art?

I think also of Rachmaninov's *Vespers*. Of the religious plays of the American actor-dramatist Leonardo Defilippis, especially his *Maximilian: Saint of Auschwitz* and *Saint Francis: Troubadour of God's Peace*. Of the films of the Russian Christian Andrei Tarkovsky, especially his *Andrei Roublev*. Of the Italian film *The Tree of Wooden Clogs*, by Ermanno Olmi, which to everyone's amazement won the Grand Prize at Cannes in 1978. I think of the fiction of William Golding, especially his novel about original sin, *Lord of the Flies*, which is also a stark analysis of the thinness of civilization's veneer; his exploration of prophecy and apocalyptic themes in *Darkness Visible*; and *The Spire*, which is about the building of a medieval cathedral, which is really about the tension between man's longing to transcend through creating and his abiding impulse to self-divinization. I think of Georges Rouault's heroic effort to baptize abstraction, his incandescent paintings of gospel scenes and his crucified Christ from the solemn Miserere series. I think of Cézanne's table tops, full of fruit, that proclaim the miraculousness of the ordinary, imparting to us the realization that nothing, simply nothing, is ordinary.

I think of Solzhenitsyn's hero Oleg Kostoglatov in *Cancer Ward*, who in the final lines of the novel, a free man at last, liberated from the gulag, and from internal exile, and healed of his cancer, lies down in a train carriage and is suddenly seized with anguish. He buries his face in his coat (which is his only home), leaving us with the incontrovertible sense that the greatest cancer is unseen, and is within the soul, waiting to be faced. Implicit in Oleg's willingness to feel again is the promise of resurrection, waiting for us, there, within, if we would only believe. Elsewhere in *Cancer Ward* Solzhenitsyn quotes Pushkin: 'In our vile times . . . man was, whatever his element, either tyrant or traitor or prisoner!' I think it can be said that we are all prisoners, but the Christian is a prisoner in Christ and with Christ, and thus he is the only free man on the planet.

I think of a painting by Constance Stokes, *The Baptism*, which hangs in the National Gallery of Victoria, in Melbourne. In this work Christ and John the Baptist stand in the Australian desert, its landscape and sky defined by gashes of cobalt, cerulean blue, burnt orange and sienna, expressing an epiphany of stillness and presence that is rarely equalled in these times.

I think of the extraordinary novels of the Jewish American writer Mark Helprin, especially *A Soldier of the Great War*, in which his central character, Alessandro Giuliani, a thoroughly modern young man, is shattered and recreated and emerges an old wise man in search of epiphanies on mountain tops. It is an epic narrative in the old style, a relief from the cloying psychological obsession of so much modern fiction. It is a sign that the unification of sensibility is still possible. It is reflective, rich in poetic imagery, a marvel of 'implicitness', yet without that sense of being a disguised tract or closet theology. It is a story about God.

I think of the Canadian Catholic painter William Kurelek, who painted a mural of Christ titled *Toronto, Toronto*, echoing the Lord's lament over Jerusalem. A marvel of 'explicitness', it depicts the saviour of the world standing on the steps of Toronto's city hall with his arms spread wide, beseeching the crowds of busy shoppers and the hurtling traffic to stop, to listen. Only a single child in the hundreds of passers-by is able to notice.

'Wisdom! Be Attentive!' resounds the proclamation of the Byzantine Divine Liturgy, just before the Word of God is spoken. We are hardly able to notice. We are too busy. We seldom hear. We can barely see. We have no time. We do not attend the Great Liturgy of being in which we are always and everywhere immersed.

John Paul II has frequently warned the people of the West that materialism is far from dead, and may in the long run bring about a far more comprehensive destruction of the human community by turning man into a consumer without conscience. For materialism, which is the bed of modern humanism, seeks to erase 'the whole truth about man' one way or another. And beyond humanism lies the ominous realm of the anti-human, the anti-word and the final anti-word – the destruction of everything, the ultimate denial of our powerlessness. To have power *over* life, and to have it on the level of totality offered by nuclear warfare, may prove irresistible – cataclysm as the final artform.

The antidote is humility. We must begin where the path always begins, by becoming empty in order to be filled. To be silent. To be still. To wait. To listen. To feel in our bones that we are creatures. To raise our hands, childlike, in the *orans* position, asking for grace.

To *rejoice* in our powerlessness, to find again our simplicity and thereby to discover our true greatness. To know that we are damaged but not destroyed. To learn that within us is a repository for truth and for love, and a potential for forms of creativity that are practically infinite. These are gifts, but they are not our possessions. They are not our power *over* creation but an act of love made *with* creation and in honour of he who lives beyond and within creation. He who is perfect beauty, perfect truth, perfect love.

Not until we see a movement of gifted people turning away from materialism, willing to be empty, willing to be poor, willing to be filled with something other than their ambitions and fabricated self-images, will we see a true renaissance, a second spring. I believe that a rebaptism of the imagination is already happening. It is small, fragile, but quite capable of overturning the culture of death. I believe that as it gathers momentum we will find again, to paraphrase Shakespeare, our home and our own true name.

A new iconography is waiting for us; it will be built upon all that the historical imagination has given, but reinvigorated by a new consciousness. Our perceptions, more accurately our *soul*, will be restored to divine order when we find again our proper place in the hierarchy of creation. In submission to natural and supernatural law, to the absolutes, in obedience and prayer, by opening our interior life and the intellectual life to the full authority of the Holy Spirit, we will germinate a little seed. And from it entire forests can spring, and may yet cover the earth.

> In the beginning was the Word,
> and the Word was with God,
> and the Word was God . . .
>
> And the Word became flesh
> and dwelt among us.

And that has made all the difference.

NOTES

1   Hans Urs von Balthasar, *The Glory of the Lord*, vol. 1 (Ignatius Press, San Francisco, 1982), pp. 18–19.

2   Saint John of Damascus, 'Concerning the Holy Icons', in Constantine Cavarnos, *Orthodox Iconography* (Institute for Byzantine and Modern Greek Studies, Belmont, Massachusetts, 1977), pp. 49–54.

3   Christopher Dawson, *Religion and the Rise of Western Culture* (Doubleday, Garden City, N.Y., 1958), pp. 171–2. (Gifford Lectures, 1948–9.)

4   'Education and the Crisis of Christian Culture', *Lumen Vitae*, vol. 1, no. 2, April–June 1946, Brussels, pp. 210–12; adapted and developed in Dawson's *Understanding Europe*, Part II, Chapter XIII, 1952.

5   Christopher Dawson, *The Dividing of Christendom* (Sheed & Ward, New York, 1965), p. 197.

6   For the purpose of defining their common ethos, I have here deliberately linked the Victorian poets, Tennyson and Arnold, with the Romantics.

7   Hans Urs von Balthasar, *The Glory of the Lord*, vol. 1, p. 19.

8   T. S. Eliot in 'Tradition and the Individual Talent', *Selected Essays* (Harcourt Brace & Co., 1932).

Conclusion:
Eternity in time

STRATFORD CALDECOTT

Surrounded by what Christopher Dawson (in *Understanding Europe*) called an 'extroverted hedonistic mass culture', which is 'at once a drug and an intoxicant and a poison',[1] we stand embroiled in the death-throes of the civilization of the Enlightenment – or is it the birth-pangs of a 'culture of death'?[2]

Our world, the world of most of the readers of this volume, came to birth in the death-throes of a previous civilization, which has been called Christendom. It still bears the fragments of that shell upon its back, but they are falling fast. Perhaps, as Stanley Jaki and others have argued, it could have come about in no other way, for only the belief in an all-wise Creator, in his historical Incarnation, and in the free, creative and intellectual powers of a man made in his image, could have provided the necessary conditions for the development of modern science and the associated Age of Exploration. If so, Christians in some sense bear a special responsibility for modernity – and for the crisis of planetary survival into which modernity has seemingly plunged us.

As Christopher Dawson saw so well, every human culture flourishes on the basis of a religious faith that requires self-transcendence. Our emerging 'culture of death' tries to ape this process by a continual ferment of technological and speculative innovation, but all that results is an expanding flux of activity on the material level, and on the psychological level an addiction to change and novelty. In the culture of death, there is no transcending the material level, for nothing that *cannot be measured* is regarded as objectively real. Human life has no 'real' value apart from the going market rate, and if we animals have any purpose on earth it is merely to maximize our pleasure whilst ensuring the survival of our offspring. The dignity of a free person is reduced to this: we are here to be entertained, and we can determine our destiny only by choosing *how* we are to be entertained – by satellite, cable or video. Not really much of a choice.

This is I admit, a caricature. The lineaments of the pseudo-culture I have sketched are only faintly visible beneath the more complex realities of a civilization presently in ferment. But I contend that the *dynamic* towards this caricature exists. It has been set loose by a loss of faith in the one Principle that can hold together all the varied forces of nature and of the human imagination. We have to discover and understand the reasons for that loss of faith before we can venture on its recovery. And it seems that the loss was both inevitable and avoidable.

THE PAST

Postmodernism, with its attendant nihilism, reveals latent flaws in the rationalism of the Enlightenment. The Enlightenment itself exposes flaws in the Reformation and Renaissance that preceded it. They in turn reveal flaws that lay hidden beneath the surface of the magnificent but fragile Gothic synthesis – a weakness that was exploited by Nominalism. That fragility can be traced back (I believe) to the fact that the Gothic civilization had developed in partial isolation from the Byzantine or Greek tradition. Periodic injections of Classical culture mediated by Islam, and even of the strong current of monastic spirituality that flowed from the Eastern deserts through Cassian and Benedict, could not substitute for a calm synthesis of the Greek, Roman and Semitic principles within Christendom that *should have been* the heritage of Christianity and the making of Europe. Instead, Latin Churchmen developed the dualistic rationalism that led to Deism, Positivism and an increasingly exploitative attitude to the natural world.

Yet we must go back further than the Eastern Schism to understand the contemporary crisis, for the sundering of Catholicism from Orthodoxy itself has deep roots. The failure of Christianity to hold together the two halves of the Classical world it had inherited, and which were represented by Rome and Constantinople, can be understood better by introducing a third symbolic city into the picture: Jerusalem. If Jerusalem had not fallen in AD 70, if instead – by whatever unimaginable chain of events – it had been effectively converted to Christianity, perhaps the great synthesis might have been achieved. But the Jewish people as a whole did not receive Christ as the Messiah, and Jerusalem did in fact fall.[3] The scientific historian would have to describe this as a coincidence, but one who is freer to speculate may wish to place more weight on providence and prophecy. Between the earthly and the heavenly city – which were united in the Body of Christ that is the true temple – a deadly separation had opened up. As a Benedictine Abbot (the late Denis Huerre) has put it, 'The gaping wound in the side of the Christian "body" is the absence of Israel, the Jewish Catholic Church.'[4] Quoting Louis Bouyer, he adds: 'it is we who have failed with regard to the Jews, beginning with that total indifference to the Church of the Jewish Catholics as it was being whittled away to nothing'.

The drama as a whole may have turned on the free decisions of just a few individuals – perhaps of only one. If Peter, James and John had remained awake to pray with Jesus, if Judas had repented of his treachery sooner (and who knows whether the latter might have been dependent on the former), one wonders whether the death of Christ on the Cross would still have been necessary. But as soon as Jesus had been rejected by one of the Twelve he had chosen, the Cross became – if it was not already – inevitable. The Jewish nation did not convert, Jerusalem fell, and Christianity turned to the Gentiles. Its centre of gravity shifted West, following Peter and Paul to Rome. It inherited the weaknesses as well as the strengths of the Empire, including the cultural fault-line that ran through the Balkans to North Africa.

If Jerusalem had become the centre of the new faith, it might have drawn all nations and peoples to itself. Instead, the vengeful ghost of a monotheism not fully integrated with Christianity was able to emerge from the deserts of the south to become the scourge and terror of Europe.

The fatal gap between the earthly and the heavenly Zion was never more obvious than in the failure of the Crusaders to distinguish the two. Attempting to recapture the Holy City and hold it by brutal force of arms, they succeeded only in definitively splitting Christendom and laying the foundations of secular modernity.[5]

All through the subsequent fragmentation of Europe, the collapse of the economic and social framework of feudalism, the rise of the merchant classes and the nation state, 'philosophic reason' continued to profit at the expense of the contemplative intellect. The Protestant Reformation destroyed the dream of a united Christendom even in the West, and the humanists of the Renaissance forged a new unifying culture that was able to span the Catholic-Protestant divide only by opening the way to a new paganism and secularization of knowledge. Hilaire Belloc once wrote that if it had not been for the Reformation, the energies of the Renaissance would have fuelled a new golden age. Thanks to the Reformation we know now, more clearly than we did before, that the kingdom of God cannot be imposed through force or fear. That discovery of the human personality and the value of subjectivity was, however, entangled with certain negative consequences that have to be taken into account. An increasing emphasis on choice and action meant a corresponding neglect of contemplation; the cult of human interiority led, paradoxically, to the creation of an exteriorized and technological civilization. The basic problem was the inversion of the normal relation between *head* and *heart*. If the 'heart' as the seat of human affection is not subordinated to the spiritual intelligence of the 'head', what then governs man is a mere sentimental impulse, employing technical reason as the instrument of its power. Man is then a slave of a different sort, a slave incapable of liberation, unless he again becomes capable of humility.

THE FUTURE

The reader may prefer another way of 'reading' the history of European civilization. Inevitably, though, our understanding of the past cannot be separated from our vision of the future, and the way we act will help to shape that future. We live at the end of a century of unprecedented change. A Catholic trying to make some sense of the times will look at the past and see Christ at the centre, the key to its mystery, the 'secret hidden from all ages'. The details of our interpretation will differ. If we look to the future, we see the same great Figure, for all times are one in him, the Alpha and Omega.

The Pope's Apostolic Letter *Tertio Millennio Adveniente* ('As the Third Millennium Draws Near', 1994), contains a highly developed theology of history, and it seems appropriate to end this volume with some account of it. The Pope is concerned above all with the overcoming of the present crisis of civilization by the development of a 'civilization of love' (n. 52). The Second Vatican Council and the postconciliar popes are credited by this document with preparing a 'new springtime of Christian life which will be revealed by the Great Jubilee, *if Christians are docile to the action of the Holy Spirit*' (n. 18, my emphasis). The new springtime is to be achieved by the reunion of Christians and the reintegration of humanity around the figure of Christ, who is the 'Redeemer of humanity and the Lord of History' (n. 19), the One who 'fully reveals man to himself and makes his supreme calling clear' (n. 4, citing the Council's *Gaudium et Spes*, n. 22). Of course, there is no guarantee of this. Truth should impose itself 'by virtue of its own truth, as it wins over the mind with both gentleness and power' (n. 35), but the figure of Christ has been obscured many times by 'past errors and instances of infidelity, inconsistency and slowness to act' (n. 34), by the 'use of violence in the service of truth', and by other sins which have prevented the Church from 'fully mirroring the face of her crucified Lord, the supreme witness of patient love and of humble meekness' (n. 35). Have we learnt from this, or will we repeat our mistakes yet again?

Preparing for the year 2000 has become, the Pope himself says, 'a hermeneutical key to my Pontificate' (n. 23), and it is surprising, in a way, that this document which lays out his entire strategy, making sense of all his encyclicals, pilgrimages and other initiatives – including those we may still expect in the remaining years of our century – should have received so little attention in the world's press. In another way, it is not so surprising. Even faithful Catholics with time on their hands have a hard job keeping up with the latest documents from Rome. This document, however, together with the encyclical on ecumenism (*Ut Unum Sint*, 1995) and the accompanying Apostolic Letter *Orientale Lumen* (Light from the East, 1995), lay the foundations for dramatic developments in the Church and the world that will affect all of us.

The document on the millennium opens with St Paul on the mystery of the Incarnation and the sending of the Holy Spirit: 'When the fullness of time had come, God sent forth his Son, born of woman', and 'God has sent the Spirit of his Son into our hearts, crying "Abba! Father!"' (Galatians 4:4, 6). In Part I, the Pope expands upon this passage with a brilliant summary of salvation history, placing next to passages by Paul the Prologue of John's Gospel, commenting:

> The fact that in the fullness of time the eternal Word took on the condition of a creature gives a unique *cosmic value* to the event which took place in Bethlehem two thousand years ago. *Thanks to the Word, the world of creatures appears as a 'cosmos'*, an ordered universe. And it is the same Word who, *by taking flesh, renews the cosmic order of creation.* (n. 3)

Part II begins with the entry of eternity into time, the 'fulfilment' of time by the Incarnation. It is in God that man finds self-realization, that human time reaches its fullness and transcends its limit. In Christianity, the Pope writes, time – and therefore history – has a 'fundamental importance', because 'In Jesus Christ, the Word made flesh, time becomes a dimension of God, who is himself eternal' (n. 10). From this arises the 'duty to sanctify time' through the liturgy, and against this background the Pope explains the 'custom of Jubilees' which point to the definitive 'day of salvation' in which all of God's promises to his people are fulfilled.

In Part III, the Pope moves on to explain how, since the Second Vatican Council, the Church has in fact been preparing for the Great Jubilee of Christ's birth – the Council having been called not in response to a particular heresy, like previous councils, but in response to modernity itself, and the need for it to be assimilated, converted and transformed. Through great synods, local jubilees, papal journeys and encyclicals, the work of the Council has been continued and extended.

In Part IV, the next period of preparation is divided into two phases, the first of which (now over) focuses on the *precondition* for reconciliation with God, namely the need for repentance and conversion from past mistakes. Here the Pope breathes new life into the ecumenical movement, for he is committed to the hope that we will celebrate the Jubilee 'if not completely united, *at least much closer to overcoming the divisions of the second millennium'* (n. 34). This is where his encyclical *Ut Unum Sint* ('That They May All Be One', 1995) fits into the grand plan. Not only does he call for the recognition by the Church of more non-clerical and even non-Catholic martyrs to Christianity (ibid., n. 84, and *Tertio*, n. 37), but by acknowledging the sins of Catholics (not excluding popes) as contributing to the division of Christendom, he removes what was a major obstacle in the path of real reconciliation between the Churches. In *Ut Unum Sint* (n. 95) he even asks humbly for the help of non-Catholics in discerning new ways in which the Bishop of Rome might exercise his ministry as a 'service of love recognized by all concerned'.

The second phase of preparation (1997 to 1999) has a Trinitarian structure. Here the Pope's earlier theological encyclicals come into their own. For 1997 is focused on Christ, the Son of God (*Redemptor Hominis*, published in 1979), 1998 on the Holy Spirit who makes the Son known and creates the Church (*Dominum et Vivificantem*, 1986), and 1999 on the Father to whom the Son returns and whose keynote is mercy (*Dives in Misericordia*, 1980). This Trinitarian structure repays careful attention. Each of the three years is also linked to one of the three great virtues, faith, hope and charity; and to one of the three sacraments, baptism, confirmation and penance – in each case with an ecumenical and a Marian aspect. In 1997 we might expect, for example, further instruction on the reading of Scripture, for the Pope tells us that to recognize who Christ truly is, Christians 'should turn with renewed interest to the Bible' (n. 40). In 1998 one might expect the culmination of recent attempts to resolve the dispute between Catholics and Orthodox over the theology of the Holy Spirit and the insertion of the *filioque* clause in the Nicene Creed. In 1999, under the sign of the Father and of Charity, what comes into focus is the 'Church's preferential option for the poor', the cancellation or reduction of international debt, the challenge of secularism, and the dialogue between religions. Historic meetings with Jewish and Muslim leaders are anticipated in places such as Bethlehem, Jerusalem and Mount Sinai.

The Jubilee itself will be celebrated simultaneously in the Holy Land, in Rome and in the local Churches (n. 55). At its heart will be the Eucharist, which is itself the living presence of the Saviour who took flesh in Mary's womb approximately 2000 years ago. An International Eucharistic Congress will take place in Rome, and a 'meeting of all Christians' at a location yet to be decided (no doubt in the Holy Land, if this can be arranged).

In the Conclusion of the document (Part V), the Pope situates the themes of his remaining encyclicals by relating them to the question of the *new evangelization*, describing the history of the Church's missionary endeavours to Asia, America, Africa and Australasia, and finally to the 'new Areopagus' of contemporary civilization and culture. He affirms with the Council that both past and future belong to Christ. In him 'can be found the key, the focal point and the goal of all human history' (*Gaudium et Spes*, n. 10). And finally, as in all his Letters, he turns to Mary, 'the unassuming Young Woman of Nazareth', entrusting to her intercession this new 'Advent' of preparation for the year 2000. 'She, the Mother of Fairest Love, will be for Christians on the way to the Great Jubilee of the Third Millennium the Star which safely guids their steps to the Lord' (n. 59).

If this hope for the Great Jubilee is to be even partially realized, the implications for world civilization will be immense. The entire modern world, with its continual technological revolution, its expanding global market and its war on innocence, is founded on the division of Christendom. What a transformation would become possible if Christianity were to overcome its divisions, learn from its mistakes, and convert the modern world to a supernatural faith! It is certainly a mistake to assume, as we so often do, that things will go on much as they have in the past. Whether the Christian hope proves true or false, things cannot be the same. The pace of change is accelerating; the experience of time itself is almost tangibly different from one decade to the next.

THE PRESENT

In his book, *Religion and the Modern State*, Christopher Dawson wrote of the long history of tension between the Church and the World, and of 'the Catholic solution' to the question of history that found its 'classical expression' in the work of St Augustine, particularly in the *City of God*.

> History was no longer a mere unintelligible chaos of disconnected events. It had found in the Incarnation a centre which gave it significance and order. Viewed from this centre the history of humanity became an organic unity. Eternity had entered into time and henceforward the singular and the temporal had acquired an eternal significance. The closed circle of time had been broken and a ladder had been let down from heaven to earth by which mankind can escape from the 'sorrowful wheel' which had cast its shadow over Greek and Indian thought, and go forward in newness of life to a new world. (p. 80)

The Catholic interpretation of history, he writes, 'differs from any other in its combination of universalism with a sense of the uniqueness and irreversibility of the historic process. Its rejection of millenniarism frees it from the short views and the narrow fanaticisms of the sectarian tradition.' For despite the importance it may attribute to anniversaries and jubilees, it does not commit itself to announcing a firm date for the end of history, or apply the categories of the Apocalypse too literally to any particular moment of historical time. On the other hand, it also 'avoids the false universalism of the rationalist historians who insist on the fundamental identity of human nature in all circumstances', and thus 'preserves the prophetic and apocalyptic sense of mystery and divine judgment. Behind the rational sequence of political and economic cause and effect, hidden spiritual forces are at work which confer on events a wholly new significance' (pp. 80–1).

'The house of the world seems closed and guarded; its masters have no rivals left to fear. But suddenly the wind of the Spirit blows and everything is changed', Dawson goes on. 'No one has ever been able to foresee the age to come. The Augustan age could not have foreseen the triumph of Christianity, nor the Byzantine age the coming of Islam. Even in our own generation, the best political observer of twenty years ago never guessed the possibility of the destruction of parliamentarianism in Central Europe by the advent of Fascism' – nor, we might now add, the sudden downfall of Communist tyranny in 1989. 'But while all this is a scandal and reproach to historical rationalism, it offers no difficulties to the Catholic who lives in the presence of mysteries and who knows that "the way of man is not himself"' (pp. 82–3).

In an essay called 'Is Humanism a Religion?', written in the 1920s, G. K. Chesterton wrote in characteristic fashion as follows:

> The fact is this: that the modern world, with its modern movements, is living on its Catholic capital. It is using, and using up, the truths that remain to it out of the old treasury of Christendom; including, of course, many truths known to pagan antiquity but crystallized in Christendom. But it is *not* really starting new enthusiasms of its own. The novelty is a matter of names and labels, like modern advertisement; in almost every other way the novelty is merely negative. *It is not starting fresh things that it can really carry on far into the future* [my emphasis].[6]

Many would still agree with him, despite the advent since Chesterton's time of such things as nuclear energy and e-mail. Are these 'new things' the possible basis for a civilization? Or are they merely dangerous ways of empowering a technological élite with energy and information they seem to be incapable of turning to any civilized use? If our moral capital has been exhausted, no process of technological ferment can liberate the human spirit – except perhaps in some Gnostic sense by freeing our minds from bodily contact and human presence. Divorced from the 'permanent things', such material progress can only foster the petty enslavements of consumerism, and the superficiality of an education for which the achievements and even the language of tradition have become meaningless.

In another essay entitled 'The Return to Religion', Chesterton writes of the signs – visible even in his own time – that materialism cannot sustain itself and is crumbling fast.

> The agnostics will be gratified to learn that it is entirely due to their own energy and enterprise, to their own activity in pursuing their own antics, that the world has at last tired of their antics and told them so. We have done very little against them; *non nobis, Domine*; the glory of their final overthrow is all their own. We have done far less than we should have done, to explain all that balance of subtlety and sanity which is meant by a Christian civilization. Our thanks are due to those who have so generously helped us by giving us a glimpse of what might be meant by a Pagan civilization. And what is lost in that society is not so much religion as reason; the ordinary common daylight of intellectual instinct that has guided the children of men.[7]

He may not have realized quite how much worse things could get; but the principle remains the same. 'We did not ourselves think that the mere denial of our dogmas could end in such dehumanized and demented anarchy', as Chesterton writes, but end it does. At this very moment the tide is turning in another direction, the sap is rising in the stem. The seeds of new life buried in the earth by the Incarnation of Christ cannot be destroyed, but merely await the conditions under which growth will be possible.[8]

The Second Vatican Council may have helped to create those conditions. On one interpretation, the Council permitted the Catholic Church to take what was left of value in the Reformation and Enlightenment into herself – to assimilate and gradually (though not without struggle and discomfort) to transform it. The Council, together with the conciliar and post-conciliar popes, has also prepared the way for a reconciliation with the separated Eastern Churches. By overcoming the exaggerated dualism of nature and grace that had predominated in Catholic intellectual circles for two centuries, the Council fathers also created the possibility of overcoming those other dualisms of head and heart, reason and intuition, East and West. We may well ask how many obstacles – other than the recalcitrant human will – still stand in the way of a genuinely Christian humanist renaissance, and of a renewed 'Sophianic' Catholicism.

I will bring these threads together by quoting another author from the same European Catholic tradition as Dawson and Chesterton, one who has perhaps done more than anyone since St Augustine to explore the theological dimensions of world history, and whose influence on Pope John Paul II is well known: Hans Urs von Balthasar. In a collection of sermons entitled *You Crown the Year with Your Goodness*, he seems to me to sum up the authentic Christian attitude to history, and evoke the spirit in which we are to prepare ourselves for the surprises God has in store for us, as the drama of divine and human freedom continues to unfold in the years, and in the millennium, to come.

> Let us add that world history after Christ can never be the same. In the year nil, at the beginning of our calendar, the absolute change of direction occurred. A certain naïveté, once possible, has been lost forever. Jesus said, 'He who does not gather with me scatters' (Lk 11:23). The modern technological world may have tremendous problems that seem utterly remote from the Gospel, but ultimately it comes down to the attitude adopted by Jesus in his living and dying: the attitude of perfect, selfless love, service to the very last and the fruitfulness that comes from it. This is the innermost meaning and core of all mankind's questions, including those of politics, economics and other fields. And the attitude shown by Jesus is the attitude of God himself to the world. Thus anyone who follows Jesus is walking in God's footsteps, in the footsteps of absolute truth and goodness. Many people may do this without knowing Jesus, but since he has come to us, his fragrance has spread invisibly through world history, and many a one follows this fragrance without knowing it. 'God is able from these stones to raise up children to Abraham,' says John the Baptist.
>
> We are in the season of Advent, and it sends a shiver of fear through us, warning us of the approach of something that is final and ultimate; it is as inevitable as that an expectant mother must give birth, as certain as that a voice in the wilderness presupposes someone crying out. So we must look and listen; we must pay attention; we must turn and attend to this voice. Turn and repent of your sins, says the Baptist again and again. What does this

mean? It means we must search for that turning point in our innermost self, the place where we turn from the 'I' to the 'thou' and to God, from sterile living for ourselves to fruitful living for others by following God, Emmanuel: God-with-us and God-for-us. Then, together with the Virgin who is with Child, we too can bring a real, tangible child into the world, a child who will be fruitful in the world and in world history; and not just any child, but the same child that Mary bore: 'For whoever does the will of my Father in heaven is my brother, and sister and mother' (Mt 12:50).[9]

NOTES

1 *Understanding Europe* (London and New York: Sheed & Ward, 1952), p. 251.

2 The phrase, of course, belongs to Pope John Paul II. See especially his 1995 encyclical, *Evangelium Vitae.*

3 I should emphasize that I have no sympathy for any attempt to *blame the Jews* for the death of Christ and subsequent disasters. The drama of the Incarnation and Passion was to a great extent enacted, necessarily, within Judaism: Jesus and his disciples were themselves Jewish. Besides, there are mysteries within mysteries. Jesus did not, *at his first Coming*, fulfil all the prophecies of the Messiah.

4 *Letters to My Brothers and Sisters: Living by the Rule of St Benedict* (Collegeville: Liturgical Press, 1994), p. 34.

5 The sack of Constantinople by the Fourth Crusade in 1204 (with its acts of sacrilege echoed six hundred years later by the revolutionaries in the Cathedral of Notre Dame, marking the inauguration of the rationalist 'religion') is regarded by many as a more definitive breach than the official schism of 1054, for all its mutual excommunications.

6 Published in a collection entitled *The Thing* by Sheed & Ward in 1929.

7 *The Well and the Shallows* (London: Sheed & Ward, 1935).

8 During the conference for which most of the present papers were written, considerable interest was expressed in the phenomenon of the so-called 'New Age' movement, which reflects the breakdown of materialism in another way than the simple return to Christianity – even a transformed Christianity. The whole question of alternative spiritualities is a vast and important one, and I hope to devote a future conference of the Centre for Faith & Culture to this topic.

9 Hans Urs von Balthasar, *You Crown the Year with Your Goodness* (San Francisco: Ignatius Press, 1989), pp. 255–6. See also *A Theology of History* and the fourth volume of his series *Theo-Drama*, both also published by Ignatius Press.

Notes on contributors

STRATFORD CALDECOTT is the Director of the Centre for Faith & Culture, Westminster College, Oxford.

FERNANDO CERVANTES is lecturer in Hispanic and Latin American Studies at the University of Bristol, and the author of several works on the cultural and intellectual history of Spain and Spanish America.

JOHN MORRILL is Reader in Early Modern History at the University of Cambridge and Fellow and Vice Master of Selwyn College. He has written and published sixteen books mainly on Renaissance and Reformation periods. He was ordained to the permanent married diaconate of the Catholic Church in June 1996.

FRANCESCA MURPHY is lecturer in Systematic Theology at the University of Aberdeen and is the author of *Christ the Form of Beauty* (T&T Clark).

AIDAN NICHOLS OP is a well-known English Dominican writer, author of *The Panther and the Hind* (T&T Clark) and other books of theology and Church history. He lives in Cambridge.

MICHAEL O'BRIEN is a painter and novelist, author of *Father Elijah* and *Strangers and Sojourners* (Ignatius Press).

GLENN W. OLSEN, Professor of History at the University of Utah, is a specialist in medieval intellectual and ecclesiastical history, and has published widely also on contemporary issues.

DERMOT QUINN is Professor of History at Seton Hall University in South Orange, New Jersey, and a frequent contributor to *The Chesterton Review*.

CHRISTINA SCOTT is the younger daughter of Christopher Dawson and lives in London. In 1993 she was awarded an honorary doctorate at St. Mary's College, Notre Dame, USA for her contribution as her father's biographer and literary executor.

RUSSELL SPARKES works as an ethical fund manager for the Methodist Church, and is the author of *The Ethical Investor*. He is a Research Associate in Economics of the Centre for Faith & Culture.

NOTE: *Aidan Nichols, Dermot Quinn, Russell Sparkes and Francesca Murphy are also advisers of the Centre for Faith & Culture.*

Index of names

Abraham, 158, 162
Ackroyd, P., 48
Acton, John E., 15, 32, 70, 76
Adalbert, St, 61
Adams, Henry, 64
Anscombe, Elizabeth, 44, 49
Aquinas, St Thomas, 81, 83, 95,
    96, 101, 102, 105, 133, 166,
    168, 173
Aristotle, 101, 134, 136
Arnold, Matthew, 64, 178
Auerbach, Erich, 149
Augustine, St, 12, 13, 14, 57, 61,
    71, 75, 80f., 97, 100, 101,
    137f., 142, 143, 145, 149,
    201, 204
Ausonius, 100

Bacon, Sir Francis, 109
Bacon, Francis, 182
Balthasar, Hans Urs von, 37, 73,
    88, 89, 90, 91, 92, 146, 150,
    157, 184, 191, 204, 205
Barker, Ernest, 32, 70
Barraclough, Geoffrey, 67
Basil, St (The Great), 59, 113,
    162
Beales, A. C. F., 49
Beatus of Liébana, St, 165

Bede, The Venerable, 7, 126,
    138
Bell, George, 18
Belloc, Hilaire, 16, 41, 93, 115,
    123, 124, 196
Benedict, St, 59, 165
Benedict Biscop, St, 59
Bentham, Jeremy, 109, 111
Bernanos, George, 19, 188
Bernard, St, 80, 168
Bernini, Gian Lorenzo, 175
Beveridge, William, Lord, 110
Birnie, Esmond, 121
Blake, William, 178, 179
Blamires, David, 31, 46
Blatchford, Robert, 154
Blondel, Maurice, 38
Bloy, Léon, 38
Bonaventure, St, 131
Boniface of Crediton, St, 60
Bossey, J., 45
Bossuet, Jacques, 73f., 142, 145
Botticelli, Sandro, 169
Bourne, Francis, 42
Bouyer, Louis, 38, 195
Bremond d'Ars, Yvonne de, 38
Brereton, William, 8
Brownlow, William Robert, 41
Bryant, Arthur, Sir, 95

Tolkien, J. R. R., 40
Trethowan, Illtyd, 37, 47
Tristram, E. W., 26
Turner, Victor, 127

Vance, J. G., 45
Van Gogh, Vincent, 180
Velásquez, Diego de Silva y, 182
Voltaire, 107, 108

Wall, Bernard, 22, 38, 47
Walsh, Michael, 111, 121
Ward, Barbara, 42, 43, 107, 110, 121
Ward, Josephine, 28
Ward, Maisie, 28, 46; *see also* Sheed, Maisie
Ward, Wilfrid, 28

Watkin, E. I., 17, 26, 37, 45, 46, 47, 48, 76
Waugh, Evelyn, 40, 42
Wells, H. G., 14, 94
White, Antonia, 30, 46
White, Hayden, 85f., 91
Wilberforce, William, 117
Wilfrid, St, 59
Williams, Charles, 40
Williams, Raymond, 122
Wiseman, Nicholas, 43
Wolff, Christian von, 133
Woolf, Virginia, 40
Wordsworth, William, 178
Wust, Peter, 36

Yorke, M., 48

Zurbaran, Francisco, 174